IMPROVING SOCIAL INTERVENTION

JOHN CARRINGTON SPENCER (1915–1978)

IMPROVING SOCIAL INTERVENTION

CHANGING SOCIAL POLICY AND SOCIAL WORK
PRACTICE THROUGH RESEARCH

A Volume in Memory of
JOHN CARRINGTON SPENCER (1915–1978)

Edited by
JOHN GANDY, ALEX ROBERTSON and
SUSAN SINCLAIR

CROOM HELM
London & Canberra
ST. MARTIN'S PRESS
New York

© 1983 J. Gandy, A. Robertson and S. Sinclair
Croom Helm Ltd, Provident House, Burrell Row,
Beckenham, Kent BR3 1AT
Croom Helm Australia, P.O. Box 391, Manuka,
ACT 2603, Australia

British Library Cataloguing in Publication Data

Improving social intervention.
   1. Social science research
   I. Gandy, John   II. Robertson, Alex
   III. Sinclair, Susan
   361.6'1'072   HM51

   ISBN 0–7099–2251–5

All rights reserved. For information write:
St. Martin's Press, Inc., 175 Fifth Avenue, New York, N.Y. 10010
First published in the United States of America in 1983

Library of Congress Cataloging in Publication Data
Main entry under title:

Improving social intervention.

   1. Social policy––Research––Addresses, essays, lectures. 2. Social service––Research––Addresses, essays,
lectures. 3. Spencer, John Carrington––Addresses,
essays, lectures. I. Gandy, John. II. Robertson, Alex.
III. Sinclair, Susan. IV. Spencer, John Carrington.
HV37.146   1983   361.6'1'072   83–8713
ISBN 0–312–41070–0 (U.S.)

Printed and bound in Great Britain

CONTENTS

FOREWORD

JOHN SPENCER: AN APPRECIATION

Susan Sinclair

        John   Spencer died on June 25 1978 after a year
of illness which he faced with   great   courage,   and
this   book is published to commemorate his life. Its
authors are all colleagues who   have   either   worked
closely with him or who share his interests in
social   policy   research,   but   they   make   their
contributions on behalf of a great many more friends
and   colleagues in Britain and Canada and throughout
the world.
        John Carrington Spencer was born   in   1915.   He
was educated at St. Paul's School, London, where his
father was one of the housemasters delightfully
portrayed by Compton Mackenzie in <u>Sinister Street</u>.
He   studied   Philosophy,   Politics   and Economics at
Balliol College, Oxford and Social Sciences   at   the
London   School   of   Economics. His first post, after
leaving L.S.E., was with the Probation Service of
the Surrey County Council to which he returned after
the   war.   His War service was with the Royal Indian
Artillery in India and Burma. He attained   the   rank
of Major and was twice mentioned in despatches.
        From 1946 to 1953 he was successively assistant
lecturer and   lecturer in Social Sciences at L.S.E.
He was awarded a Ph.D. for a thesis on the effect of
military service on crime, which was published in
1954   as   <u>Crime and the Services</u>. In 1953 he left
L.S.E. to become Director   of the Bristol Social
Project. This was an experiment in action research
which was set up in response to proposals made by a
group   of   leading Bristol citizens who were anxious
that   "a   study   should   be   made of a developing
community in Bristol in   an   attempt to establish
means of tackling those stresses and   strains   which
arise   in   the   form of delinquency and other
disturbances." The project was funded   by   the
Carnegie United Kingdom Trust and sponsored by the

An Appreciation

University of Bristol. It focussed mainly on the symptoms of social disorganisation - crime, juvenile delinquency, child deprivation - in selected areas of Bristol, examined against the background of the social structure of the neighbourhoods and the group and family life in these areas. Another of the aims of the project was to effect social change through collaboration between layman, professional social worker and social scientist, and this called for a combination of research and community organisation which was to become a continuing feature of John Spencer's work. The report on the project was published in 1964 as <u>Stress</u> <u>and</u> <u>Release</u> <u>in</u> <u>an</u> <u>Urban</u> <u>Estate</u> with Norman Dennis and Joy Tuxford, members of the project team, as co-authors.

In 1958 John Spencer was appointed for a year as Simon Research Fellow in the University of Manchester. Here he carried out the research into white collar crime which was the subject of his contribution to the volume of essays presented to Herman Mannheim by his former students, published in 1965 as <u>Criminology</u> <u>in</u> <u>Transition</u>.

After his year in Manchester, John Spencer went to Canada where he spent eight years which were clearly among the most enjoyable and productive of his working life. He was first appointed to an associate professorship in the University of Toronto's Faculty of Social Work and, from 1963, held professorships jointly in the School of Social Work and in the University's Centre of Criminology. In this new setting he was able to develop ideas which had their origins in his earlier research. His Canadian colleagues were receptive to his ideas which they found stimulating and often directly relevant to their own work. They particularly welcomed his commitment to an interdisciplinary approach to teaching and research, in both social work and criminology, which moved them to adopt new patterns of teaching in the University of Toronto and other institutions throughout Ontario. His colleagues also welcomed his further attempts to cross professional boundaries by involving practitioners in the social work and penal services with academics, primarily to achieve more effective teaching but also with the longer term aim of influencing the making of social policy. To this end he drew directly on his experience in the Bristol Social Project by seeking to interest practitioners in the design stage of research projects and by encouraging them to contribute to problem formulation and analysis.

John Spencer's work in Canada was not confined to the University of Toronto, although that was the focal point of all his activities. He was one of the few Canadian academics in the 1960s who was interested in the role of the voluntary organisations in the provision of social services, and that interest brought him into close contact, as consultant and research adviser, with many voluntary organisations concerned with criminal justice and family welfare. He was a member of the National Scientific Committee of the Canadian Mental Welfare Association; he carried out research for the Canadian Welfare Council and for the Welfare Councils of Ontario and Metropolitan Toronto; he was a member of the Marriage and Family Life Association of the Anglican Church of Canada and, during his last year in Canada while on leave of absence from the University of Toronto, he served the then recently established Vanier Institute of the Family as Director of Research.

John Spencer's strong links with Canada and his warm and fruitful relationships with individual colleagues were not broken when, after much heart-searching, he decided to accept an appointment at the University of Edinburgh. He made fairly frequent return visits to Toronto, accepting invitations to give occasional lectures and, in 1976, spending a semester as Visiting Professor at the University's School of Social Work. Nor was the traffic one way; he was visited in turn by several of his Canadian colleagues eager to resume a fruitful working relationship with him, and these reunions were always occasions for celebration.

In 1967, John Spencer was appointed to the newly established chair of Social Administration at the University of Edinburgh, a post he held until his death. This was at the time of rapid expansion of University education in Britain and of wide ranging developments in social work training and, when he arrived at Edinburgh, it was to a department already planning for change. He presided over the establishment of undergraduate degree courses in social policy and an extensive programme of postgraduate research and, with the benefit of his Canadian experience, the expansion and reorganisation of one of the largest and longest-established schools of social work in Britain. These changes took place against the background of fundamental changes in the structure of the personal social services and the Scottish

juvenile justice system and, as in Canada, John
Spencer became involved with many public bodies and
voluntary organisations in the field of welfare and
penal policy and he drew on that involvement to the
advantage of his work within the University. He
served on a Scottish Development Department
committee on Social Provision in Public Housing
Schemes; he was chairman of the Army Welfare
Committee of Enquiry appointed by the Ministry of
Defence; he was a member of the Scottish Advisory
Committee on Social Work; he served on the Thomson
Committee on Criminal Procedure in Scotland and, at
a local level, he was deeply involved with the
Craigmillar Festival Society. He was the first
chairman of the Children's Panel Advisory Committee
of Lothian Region and his last book, Face to Face
with Families, written in collaboration with Nigel
Bruce, dealt in a sympathetically critical way with
the Children's Hearing System in Scotland.

John Spencer's continuing commitment to
research and his belief in the importance of the
contribution of research to the policy process was
widely acknowledged by colleagues in other British
Universities and his advice was frequently sought on
the setting up of new departments, appointments to
chairs and at the planning stage of research
projects. His notable contribution, however,
particularly in his own department at Edinburgh, was
in making available his scholarship, experience and
wisdom to other people to help them to examine their
own work and take appropriate action. He did not
enjoy the tasks of University administration, but he
was a committed and imaginative teacher and his
introductory lectures to the traditionally large
Edinburgh first year class were characterised by
humanity and humour as well as serious academic
content. His senior students and colleagues
especially appreciated his gift for infusing new
ideas into an academic (or any) discussion – ideas
often drawn from his prodigiously wide reading and
offered in a manner that helped to generate new
ideas in others. His colleagues also found that his
very democratic handling of the department during a
time of rapid change and substantial expansion made
it a congenial and exciting place in which to work.

It is difficult to draw a distinction between
John Spencer as an academic, social researcher,
committee chairman, consultant to government
department or voluntary organisation and John as a
private person. He had a warm family life and his
wife and son and daughter are known and appreciated

An Appreciation

by his colleagues and many of his former students. He was a man of rare spirit who was both loved and valued by those who knew him. He had a gentleness that was reassuring to others and a delightful sense of humour, but neither the gentleness, nor the shafts of humour, concealed the uncommon degree of perceptiveness and insight which gave him great understanding of the human situations he observed and experienced. His early death has been felt as a personal loss by a wide range of people in University departments, voluntary organisations, government departments and all the other communities of which he was a member. We have gained by knowing him.

Part I

RESEARCH AND POLICY-MAKING

(a) Policy-making and the Political Context of Research

1

COMPARATIVE SOCIAL POLICY AND THE POLITICS OF COMPARISON

Roy Parker

Social researchers are apt to deplore the apparent lack of influence which their work has upon the formulation of policy or upon its practical application. They infer that research plays little or no part in the politics of social policy. This conclusion rests upon two assumptions. First, that only the kinds of studies which they undertake count as research and, secondly, that the influence of research is measured by the extent of its direct application. However, if research is defined more broadly to include modest reviews or the gathering of information and if the indirect political uses to which it may be put are also taken into account, then a different and more complicated picture emerges. This can be illustrated in several ways but I shall do so by reference to international and intra-national comparisons.

I. THE INVESTIGATION OF FOREIGN EXPERIENCE

There is a good deal of evidence that governments investigate the systems and procedures of other countries, particularly when new developments in social policy are under consideration. They do this in a variety of ways, some of which would not generally be classified as social research. Take, for instance, some British committees of enquiry.

The Royal Commission on Capital Punishment (Gowers, 1953) was specifically required to look at the position in other countries. A questionnaire was sent to the governments of all the members of the Commonwealth; to eight European nations as well as to the USA and seven of its states. Some of that evidence was used to support and justify the case

for the abolition of capital punishment. The Robbins
Committee on Higher Education (1963) chose to
include a chapter in its report on international
comparisons showing, by and large, British
backwardness. It concluded that action along the
lines it recommended was necessary in order "to
avert the danger of a serious relative decline in
the country's standing". The Finer Committee on
One-Parent Families (1974) had a special study of
the relevant income maintenance systems in other
countries prepared by the International Social
Security Association, although in their report the
Committee gave little prominence to the results. "We
found", they wrote, "that we needed to use the
experience of these countries with a good deal of
caution". More recently the Royal Commission on the
National Health Service (Merrison, 1979) also looked
at foreign experience, although they went about it
differently. No special studies were commissioned;
instead, the members and the staff made journeys to
Canada, Denmark, Eire, Holland, Sweden, the USA,
West Germany and Yugoslavia, amounting in all to 90
separate meetings. It is difficult to be sure what
influence this had upon the outcome of their
deliberations: more, one suspects, than appears in
the report because a good deal of the evidence which
they received invoked international comparisons.
That being so, the collection of
'first-hand' information in the course of their
visits would have allowed the commissioners to
assess more critically the claims and counter-claims
being made about what was done abroad.

What other purposes are served by such
committees of enquiry gathering information from
abroad? It may enable some members of the enquiry
team to modify the views of other members. It may
improve the committee's reputation for thoroughness
and open-mindedness and thereby foster the
credibility of their advice in general. At the very
least the inclusion of comparative material will
protect commissioners from the charge that they
failed to take account of 'valuable lessons from
abroad'.

Yet some major committees of enquiry pay little
or no attention to evidence from other countries.
For instance, the Seebohm Committee (1968) decided
early in its life not to make visits overseas, even
though similar enquiries about the organisation of
the personal social services had been instituted in
nearby countries like Holland and Denmark. One
reason for the decisions may have been the pressure

upon the Committee at the outset to report quickly (Hall, 1976); but, unlike the debates about the British health services, those concerning the personal social services had not been conducted in terms of international comparisons – and showed no signs of doing so whilst the committee sat. Almost nobody was advocating reforms along lines similar to what was being done in other countries and, in any case, the unification of services, to which the Committee was asked to direct its attention, had not been achieved elsewhere. Nevertheless, it is noteworthy that the Seebohm Report itself, and the reorganisation which followed, did become important reference points in the discussion of policy in other countries like Canada and the United States.

Governments may set about investigating foreign experience in more direct ways rather than leaving it to committees of enquiry. Specific research may be commissioned for the purpose; for example, the United States Department of Justice funded a Glasgow University enquiry into the Scottish children's hearings system (Martin and Murray, 1981). Or studies may be undertaken internally, especially where there is an international division which possesses the relevant experience. Consider, for instance, the United States social security administration research report on mandating private pensions in Europe (Horlick and Skolnik, 1978) in the preface to which it is pointed out that:

> Like other countries, the United States has looked for ways to cope with long-range financing problems of retirement benefits and an aging population. Some of the solutions that have been proposed have existed in Europe for some time ... the European experience in the social security field is older than ours, and in studying it we can see which of their solutions might be imitated and which avoided.

This enquiry was not open-ended. It started with proposals which had been before Congress and sought to discover how other countries had fared using schemes similar to those in mind. The same kind of example could be provided by most other countries.

In Britain direct initiatives have been taken by particular departments of state to examine foreign arrangements. For instance, the economic advisor's office of the Department of Health and

Social Security has made on-the-spot enquiries in Canada and the United States into their schemes of private health insurance, no doubt as part of the review of the possible scope for the introduction of something similar in Britain. Likewise, a visit to the USA was arranged by the Department of Education and Science in order to assess the feasibility of inaugurating student loans for higher education. Advisory and consultative bodies, like the Central Policy Review Staff, also utilise comparative material in the analysis of some of the issues which they are required to investigate. For instance, members of the CPRS visited other countries like Canada and France to see how they approached the prevention and treatment of alcoholism.

Such government sponsored enquiries are by no means new. In the nineteenth century, for example, Poor Law inspectors were despatched to other countries to prepare general reports on their arrangements for dealing with pauperism, or to conduct special studies such as that into the operation of schools for poor children at Mettray and Dusseltal. Some comparative material lay closer at hand. In response to mounting pressure for the extension of boarding-out for Poor Law children in England and Wales, an inspector was sent to make a thorough examination of the system in Scotland where it had been widely employed for many years (Aldgate, 1977). By indicating the dangers as well as the benefits, his report left many questions unresolved, thereby lending support to those who counselled caution.

During the latter part of the nineteenth century, the office of special inquiries and reports in the Education Department devoted a good deal of its activities to monitoring educational progress and performance abroad: in the year 1896 alone, special reports were published on aspects of educational policy in Belgium, France, Denmark and Germany as well as a detailed analysis of the controversy in Manitoba which had arisen from the attempts of the Catholic minority to have separate schools reinstated after the repeal of the denominational system in 1890 (Education Department, 1897). Similar reports on developments in education in other countries were produced by the United States National Bureau of Education. Its publications for 1891 contained special accounts of secondary education in New Zealand, secondary and technical training in Britain as well as a history and review of the condition of public kindergartens and _ecoles gardiennes_ in several European countries (Education Department, 1897). No doubt the National Bureau in the USA was so actively concerned with foreign examples partly because the evidence they provided offered an additional means through which Federal influence might be brought to bear upon the respective states, at which level responsibility for education was vested.

The collection and analysis of information about other countries is not, of course, the exclusive preserve of governments. Pressure groups or promotional bodies may cite foreign examples and employ comparative statistics in order to justify what they propose. Or the need for a greater priority to be accorded to certain areas of social policy may be urged by reference to comparisons which cast domestic performance in a particularly poor light: what Sweden, France, Germany or Holland do, it will be claimed, 'puts us to shame'. On the other hand, opponents of a proposal may find it valuable to show that a similar scheme has failed elsewhere. For example, the supposed shortcomings of British socialised medicine have been used to advantage by the opponents of an American national health scheme for many years.

Clearly, therefore, a good deal of information is collected by governments and by others about social policies abroad. Yet relatively little of it appears to be used as a blue-print for making modifications or for shaping new measures at home. Why, after what are sometimes extensive reviews, should the practices of other nations so rarely be adopted - at least as they stand? Do the kinds of enquiries which have been illustrated really serve no purpose, or do they fulfil ends which are more indirect and less obvious?

II. THE POLITICS OF INTERNATIONAL COMPARISONS

Answers to such questions may be found by considering the _politics_ of comparison; that is, by endeavouring to see how international comparisons are used in the political processes which surround the evolution of domestic policies.

The investigation of foreign schemes may be initiated by those who already have something similar in mind. The evidence from abroad is then intended to make their case more convincing, either by showing that what they propose can work, or by demonstrating that the general direction they want to take is in line with that being followed in other countries with which valid comparisons can be drawn. The aim, therefore, is not to adopt someone else's system but to accumulate ideological or practical endorsements for a course which has already been chosen. When this is the objective it becomes of the utmost importance which other countries are selected for examination: there needs to be a plausible resemblance in their levels of economic development and a sufficient similarity in the prevailing ideology to avoid the tables being turned by the comparisons being denounced as inappropriate. In any case, it is hardly likely that a conservative administation will choose to advertise the achievements of a socialist state or vice versa; although their revealed shortcomings are another matter.

It is interesting in this respect to see how the social policies or administrative arrangements of disapproved regimes are excluded from comparative analysis. Indeed, certain policies may be played down or ruled out altogether at home because they are associated with, or are seen to be symbolic of, that regime. Take, for instance, the way in which the development of health centres in Britain was retarded under conservative governments partly because of their assumed similarity to the Soviet polyclinics: health centres smacked of socialism (Hall et al., 1975). Likewise, once the Third Reich had adopted eugenist policies as part of its Aryan ideology it became increasingly diffiucult for these kinds of policies - towards the sterilisation of the mentally subnormal for example - to be advocated in Britain, although they had earlier attracted support from various strands of the political spectrum (Searle, 1976).

War, in particular, accentuates the distinctions which are made between approved and disapproved regimes. The upheaval of war creates the opportunity for making new popular comparisons. Certain sharp contrasts - as between allies - come to be more widely known and then regarded as unacceptable; a reaction which it becomes difficult for governments to ignore. There is the example of the way in which the introduction of family allowances in Britain in 1945 was influenced by the different levels of service pay and dependants' allowances which prevailed amongst the forces of the allied powers. The more generous treatment received by American troops could not be disregarded by a British government intent upon preserving wartime morale in its own forces. Once British servicemen had become accustomed to the more favourable pay and dependants' benefits which were provided as a result, it became politically difficult to reduce or withdraw them upon demobilisation. Family allowances offered a way of managing that difficulty at comparatively low cost and without making concessions to the claims for wage increases by those returning to civilian occupations (Hall et al., 1975).

Disapproved regimes are not the only ones to be disregarded when comparisons come to be made. There are others which are simply discounted, especially in the third world, on the grounds either that 'we have nothing to learn from them' or because dissimilarities are automatically assumed to make comparison a pointless exercise. As a result the possible relevance of experiments in, say, the provision of simpler medicine or community education are never seriously considered. Even when schemes from abroad are extensively reviewed there may also be no intention of applying foreign experience if the main aim is simply to monitor the performance of actual or potential rivals - often in the commercial or military fields.

Yet other studies of overseas experience may be undertaken without any immediate intention of imitation because their purpose is to look at the way in which a particular social problem has evolved and to assess whether a similar prospect lies ahead in the home country. The aim is to see 'what might confront us in ten years' time'. Investigations of these kinds are therefore preparatory and precautionary. Urban riots in the United States provided Canada with an opportunity to assess how seriously they might be threatened in their cities and to decide what steps were needed in order to minimise that risk (Hellyer, 1969). Where trends appear to indicate that one country is indeed following a path already travelled by another, and that the problems to which that trend gives rise are serious, then the experience of the problem itself, as well as the state's response to it, are likely to be monitored with considerable care.

Thus, there are many reasons why governments or interest groups in one country should wish to be informed about the social policies and practices of other countries without there being any intention of utilising that knowledge as a guideline for their own plans.

Nonetheless, it would be misleading to conclude

that the collection and examination of material from abroad is never any more than a political ploy or a precautionary measure. It may be of considerable importance for an administration to determine whether schemes similar to those which they contemplate have actually worked out as intended in other countries where they have been adopted. It makes good sense, however briefly, to look to the nearest approximation of what is proposed, if only in order to avoid the obvious pitfalls. Added to which, the study of foreign welfare schemes may be both cheaper and less controversial than setting up experiments at home.

In other instances it may be genuinely believed that what has been fashioned abroad can be copied, at least in part or in principle. In the process of finding out about it in more detail, however, it may often become disappointingly obvious that this cannot be done. Social policies are introduced, modified or abandoned in specific political settings; they are the products of particular conflicts of interest and of particular distributions of power. Once the fine details of foreign schemes begin to be understood the unlikelihood of their successful introduction into different political, economic and social environments tends to become readily apparent. Federal states are different from unitary states; states with large and well organised trade unions are not the same as those with small or disorganised ones; states with a predominantly young population stand in marked contrast to those with a high proportion of older people; and so the list could be continued. The point is obvious but it needs to be reiterated because, at least to some of the interested parties, the significance of these differences is liable to be glossed over in their enthusiasm for schemes which they have been shown elsewhere and by what they have been told about them.

One other reason why more tangible results are often expected from the investigations of arrangements abroad than are ever realised may lie in the received accounts of how social policies have developed. A good example is the popular belief that, after careful examination, the British insurance scheme of 1911 was modelled upon the German precedent. Certainly Braithwaite, a young and promising civil servant, was sent to Germany in 1910 to report on that country's scheme of national insurance. In his account of the matter, however, he wrote:

> English legislation was later on said to
> be derived from LG's intensive study of
> the German system! What is true is that he
> himself went to Germany for a holiday and
> saw and was told something about it; that
> some Labour Members went there; that the
> Poor Law Report contains a short summary
> of it, and that a memorandum had been
> prepared at the Treasury; that I was given
> five or six days in Germany and reported
> on it, and that Dawson later got out an
> official paper to show the scales of
> contribution and benefit in Germany
> (Bunbury, 1957).

The British system of national insurance was
undoubtedly constructed with reference to Germany
but much of that actually served the purposes of
political management. There was, as Hennock has
pointed out, a complicated mixture of at least
"three attitudes which together made up the stance
of the British policy-makers towards what they found
in Germany: revulsion, imitation and rivalry"
(Mommsen, 1981). What was at stake was winning
acceptance for the principle of insurance, the
existing application of which in Germany had to be
put to advantage without invoking the hostility
which tended to be aroused towards arrangements
which were thought to smack of unacceptable
German-style regimentation and compulsion. By
presenting the British proposal as superior and
appealing to sentiments of rivalry and nationalism
it was possible to minimise this danger. Neither the
reasons for the British legislation nor its detailed
design actually bore much resemblance to what has
often been described as its German counterpart.

Thus, in the first place, comparative studies
may be undertaken to serve political purposes
without there being any intention of imitation.
Secondly, where practical lessons are genuinely
sought for the assistance which they may render in
shaping domestic social policy the very process of
investigation is likely to re-emphasise the
dissimilarities between the political, economic and
social environments which make the prospect for
transplantation extremely dubious. Thirdly, the part
played by international comparisons in the
development of social policies has tended to be
presented as a matter of straightforward emulation

or imitation. Less attention has been paid to the politics of comparison. All of these factors help to explain why the influence which comparative research has upon domestic policies is often misinterpreted.

III. INTRA-NATIONAL COMPARISONS

As well as a politics of international comparison there is, of course, a politics of comparison within countries. I shall explore this additional dimension with the help of two questions. First, what kinds of comparisons are made within countries in order to exert or counteract political pressure? Secondly, what is the relationship between internal and external comparisons?

The most common comparisons that are employed for political purposes in the United Kingdom are probably those between local authorities – especially between those of similar size and jurisdiction. If it can be shown that a particular county performs significantly worse in some respects than all its neighbours - and that this is either 'unfair', 'unjustified' or 'unacceptable' - then a new source of influence may be available. It may be mobilised in different ways: by appealing to civic pride; by obliging central government to intervene; or by vitalising a new or flagging local lobby. On the other hand, of course, what central government, discontented rate-payers, an opposition party or local amenity groups regard as good or bad performance may vary considerably. What is clear, however, is that too marked a divergence from the norm established by other local authorities lends itself to political exploitation - albeit in various directions.

Of course, as with international comparisons, a common technique for neutralising the effect of adverse comparison is to show good cause why the variation should exist or why it cannot be avoided. This may be done by demonstrating that there are significantly greater needs than elsewhere; by drawing attention to a crippling legacy or by claiming the unreliability of the statstics being used. Nonetheless, the availability of comparative statistics is important, providing as they do useful resources for those in search of a telling political argument. Certainly, there is a sharp appreciation of the political potential contained in comparative statistics. Local authorities may be reluctant to submit returns upon which central government, intent upon closer control, may then be able to base its case for encroaching upon their cherished autonomy. Which local comparative statistics are published, when, and with what purpose in mind are sensitive issues. For instance, obtaining comparative statistics may be a first and deliberate step in establishing a norm, which is used later on in a political fashion. In the mid-1960s the publication of the health and welfare development plans (Ministry of Health, 1963) seems to have served this amongst other purposes. For example, in matters like the provision of residential accommodation for the elderly the Ministry of Health was able to conclude that "local authorities appear to be achieving appropriate provision with something in the range of 18 to 22 places for every 1,000 persons aged 65 or over". The point was put somewhat carefully in the preface to the report where it was explained that the purpose of the plans was

> neither to lay down a standard pattern nor to state principles and objectives dogmatically. Rather it is, by showing the picture as a whole, to stimulate discussion, study and experiment, and make it possible for local authorities to consider and revise their own intentions in light of what others are doing and proposing [my italics].

In the 1950s and the 1960s the annual publication of statistics for children in the care of local authorities enabled a policy of boarding-out to be encouraged by central government through repeated reference to the high rates being achieved in some areas. Indeed, the 'boarding-out league table' almost became the criterion by which performance, vision and professional achievement in child care were judged.

Some conclusions might be drawn, therefore, about the requirements that local comparisons within countries have to meet if they are to provide live political ammunition. First, like has to be compared with like as far as possible. This is more easily achieved within a country than between countries. Indeed, the Department of Health and Social Security's cluster analysis of local authorities (Imber, 1977) has established, in a way, those comparisons which are most legitimate.

Secondly, just as there are some international comparisons which it is unwise for those seeking

influence to use, so within countries. I suspect
that in Scotland, let us say, a reference to the
value of English experience or example may set a
proposal back. Local, regional and national pride
are lively political facts which those who employ
the weapons of comparison ignore at their peril. It
is not by accident that the adjective 'invidious' is
so often met in the company of the noun
'comparison'.

A third characteristic of the comparisons which
seem to have political force at the local level is
that they are indeed local. Comparisons with
traditional rivals and close neighbours are likely
to be the ones which generate most interest and
which have the most immediate impact; probably
because they refer to places known to a lot of
people at first hand and which are covered by the
same local news media.

Fourthly, when it comes to local comparisons,
political safety is often sought within the ranks of
the broad majority. In the case of British local
authorities there are also external pressures which
discourage them from stepping too far out of line –
pressures which the political parties, the local
authority associations and central government have
an interest in maintaining. Innovators and
front-runners may be useful to encourage the others;
but the direction has to be one meeting with the
approval of superordinate authorities. If in the
present British climate of public expenditure
constraint, a local authority continues to spend
more than its neighbours, it stands in danger of
sanctions being imposed in order to bring it into an
acceptable proximity with the 'norm'.

Finally, local comparisons, and the review of
particular local experiments are more likely to have
a direct influence on what is done elsewhere than in
the international context. Senior staff move between
areas and bring with them ideas and convictions
which were forged in other parts of the country.
Similarly, the existence of the party system
provides important ideological and practical
channels through which the policies of a few
localities may be spread to many more. Quite simply,
given a common framework of law and of
administrative machinery more imitation is
practically feasible.

These few conclusions may apply with much less
force where the internal comparisons in question are
those between different provinces, republics or
states of a federal nation. In Canada, for example,

some of the differences in matters of welfare
practice and policy that exist between the Maritimes
and the Prairie provinces, or between Ontario and
Quebec, may be as great as some of those between
independent states. Even in countries like the
Soviet Union, with the outward appearance of
considerable centralisation and unified national
policy, notable differences are found in the
provisions available in different republics. In
federal states where the separate jurisdictions also
embody different cultural traditions - in language
or religion, for example - or where there are wide
disparities in economic prosperity and (sometimes in
consequence) an active separatist movement, the
politics of comparison may more closely resemble
those discussed in connection with independent
nations rather than those which exist at the local
level.

So far international and intra-national
comparisons have been considered separately: but
what connections exist between them? What
considerations affect the choice of one or the other
when comparisons come to be made?

If there is great disparity between the
performances or circumstances of internal
jurisdictions or administrations an international
comparison may be introduced by those who wish to
play down or obscure such variations. Conversely,
under the same circumstances an internal comparison
might be pressed by those who see advantage in
drawing public attention to evidence of the
territorial inequalities suffered by people with
equal status as citizens. In yet other instances the
two kinds of comparison might be used in tandem:
'there are admittedly adverse comparisons to be
drawn between our country and others (for instance
in rates of infant mortality) but the differences
are as great, if not greater, in different regions
of our own country'. Whether, and if so how, a
foreign or a domestic comparison is stressed is
likely to be influenced by the relative magnitudes
of the differences in question, as well as by the
interests being mobilised or addressed.

In the politics of social policy the ability to
control the definition of social problems is of
considerable importance. Thus, whether - and by whom
- a problem is portrayed as local or national may be
crucial to its political fortunes; indeed, it may
affect whether it is regarded as a problem at all.
The classification of a problem as local partly
depends upon comparing it with what occurs in other

local areas and, in doing so, showing that it is not typical.

Another way of re-defining something as more or less of a pressing problem is to change the context; this may be done, for example, by applying an international frame of reference to what was previously seen only in its national or regional setting. Two things tend to happen as a result. First, local variations disappear in the process of national aggregation that usually follows. Secondly, and perhaps as a consequence, the problem itself assumes a different significance. Take, for instance, the fact that there are now about one hundred thousand children in care in England and Wales; numbers have been rising in recent years so that grounds exist for disquiet about the effectiveness of public policies, especially in the field of prevention. Yet in Canada approximately the same number of children is in care although drawn from a much smaller population (Hepworth, 1980). Given that having fewer children in care is normally regarded as a desirable objective (although it could be interpreted differently) a comparison with the Canadian rates might be used in Britain to show that, relatively speaking, there was not so much cause for concern as might at first have been thought. Indeed, the comparison might even be used to suggest something of a success for preventive policies or for British local government more generally.

A further illustration of the relationship between the choice of comparison and the processes of problem definition may be found, as has already been pointed out, in the need to judge, for purposes of planning and political tactics, how a problem or issue is likely to develop. One way of obtaining answers - depending, of course, upon the issue - is by looking at what has happened in other countries which are considered to be a decade or two ahead on a course that will almost certainly have to be followed as well. However, looking ten or twenty years ahead with the help of established experience in other countries may be too distant to have much political value. The temptation may be to seek comparisons closer to home in time - and perhaps in space. It is noteworthy, for instance, that the recent Canadian Senate report on retirement policy (Croll, 1979) mainly included comparative material drawn from amongst the provinces or from the United States. This is understandable given that the problem is seen as one of providing adequate

16

pensions for a growing pensioner population; but it
is less justifiable if the problem is also seen to
include the supply of health and welfare services to
many more physically dependent people amongst the
most elderly. But that part of the problem, which
Britain is now confronting, is not imminent in
Canada. In these circumstances the comparisons or
examples are drawn from those provisions or
countries which seem to be facing the same
contemporary issues, not from those which have
already passed through and beyond that phase.

The choice of comparisons is also liable to be
influenced by their symbolic significance. External
points of reference may be preferred to internal
ones for just such a reason: Quebec looking towards
France might be an example. The potentially powerful
symbolism of certain comparisons should not be
overlooked in explaining which comparisons are
chosen and which are rejected.

IV. RESEARCH AND SOCIAL POLICY POLITICS

I began by posing a question about the
relationship between 'comparative research' and the
shaping of domestic policies. In endeavouring to
answer it I have concentrated upon the indirect ways
in which research - often of an unsophisticated kind
- is used in the political arena. Has this suggested
any general lessons about the role of academic
research in social policy? I believe so and would
hazard six observations: there are probably more.

First, and most obviously, the fact that a
close interest is expressed in research findings (or
in the commissioning of research) entails no
necessary connection with their adoption as
guidelines for change. That being so, social
researchers should not be surprised when their
hard-won evidence and thoughtful recommendations
appear to be shelved. Furthermore, because they are
shelved in terms of any practical application it
should not be assumed that the research has not been
used - albeit in ways unforeseen by its authors.

Secondly, a great deal of work goes on both
within and outside governments in order to provide
'intelligence': special reports are prepared;
summaries are made by personal assistants; enquiries
are instituted and positions reviewed. Much of this
would not usually be classed as research, although
it fulfils many of the political purposes which
conventional research can also fulfil. To understand

17

the political impact that academic research might
make, therefore, it is necessary to appreciate the
nature and extent of the wider information systems
into which it is often incorporated by politicians,
professionals and administrators. In that setting
the long, untimely report of the academic
researcher, together with its proposals for radical
change, may run a poor second to the short, timely
intelligence report in which the likely options are
laid out and recommendations made with a keen eye
for their political feasibility.

Thirdly, since most conventional social policy
research - whether evaluative or analytical - is
unable to carry out work in a full range of areas
its results stand to be dismissed as
unrepresentative when they are brought into play
politically. It is a similar vulnerability to which
comparisons are prone when they cannot be shown to
be innocent of the charge that like is not being
compared with like. Much research, therefore,
whether comparative or not, is politically fragile.
At one time sampling techniques looked as if they
might overcome this weakness but in many areas of
social policy they are difficult to apply. Moreover,
the movement away from a positivist approach in
social research and the more widespread use of
qualitative methods may also make research results
more difficult to defend when they come to be
employed politically. In consequence, academic
research may be regarded as more of a liability than
an asset, even when its findings confirm preferred
options.

Fourthly, and partly in contrast, some research
may have a significant political impact because of
what it reveals about impending problems;
information upon which a defence can be prepared or
a pre-emptive move made. Studies which extrapolate
convincingly from present circumstances to show what
is in store if nothing is done may prove to be very
effective in raising the priority of an issue -
without necessarily influencing what is actually
done about it. The forecasting of costs in relation
to highly predictable demographic trends
(particularly if the time span is short) is likely
to have that kind of effect - especially upon
policy-makers. They realise that matters can no
longer be allowed to drift and agree that decisions
have to be taken. Given that in most areas of social
policy at any one time deliberate policy decisions
are <u>not</u> made, this has important implications for
priorities and thereby for the withdrawal of other

issues from the political limelight. If the analysis of trends is regarded as a form of comparison over time, then, again, the relevance of my examples to a wider appreciation of the interactions of research and policy is confirmed.

My fifth point is that once research is broadly defined in the way that I have suggested, governments are seen more clearly to have an extensive command over intelligence of various kinds – a command which is increasing with developments in micro-technology and, in Britain, with the trend towards the publication of fewer statistics or research reports. If, furthermore, bodies like the Social Science Research Councils increasingly accommodate government-directed priorities in their expenditure on research, the slide towards a state monopoly of intelligence is further accelerated. Since, as I have tried to show, research results which are deployed with tactical skill can increase political manoeuverability – and thereby power – the need for alternative centres and sources of research becomes increasingly urgent.

Finally, it would be wrong to end without re-emphasising that I have been at pains to discuss the political uses of research and that that does not necessarily correspond with anything that might be said about the academic contribution of research; but it does point to two things:

(1) that if academic research is intended to have a political impact it usually has to be designed or reported on differently from that which is intended to make an academic contribution, and

(2) that the investigation of the politics of research could itself make an important contribution to our understanding of the political economy of social policy, not least (returning to my main example) were the emphasis shifted somewhat from the study of comparative social policy towards the study of the politics of the comparisons which are made.

REFERENCES

Aldgate, J. (1977) The Identification of Factors Influencing Children's Length of Stay in Care.

Unpublished Ph.D. Thesis, University of Edinburgh.

Bunbury, H. N. (1957) (ed.) Lloyd George's Ambulance Wagon: The Memoirs of W. J. Braithwaite. London: Methuen.

Croll, D. A. (1979) (Chairman) Retirement Without Tears: The Report of the Special Senate Committee on Retirement Age Policies. Ottawa: Minister of Supply and Services.

Education Department (1897) Special Reports on Educational Subjects. c. 8447. London: HMSO.

Finer, M. (1974) (Chairman) Report of the Committee on One Parent Families. Vols. 1 and 2, Cmnd. 5629. London: HMSO.

Gowers, E. (1953) (Chairman) Report of the Royal Commission on Capital Punishment: 1949-1953. Cmnd. 8932. London: HMSO.

Hall, P. (1976) Reforming the Welfare. London: Heinemann.

Hall, P., Land, H., Parker, R. and Webb, A. (1975) Change, Choice and Conflict in Social Policy. London: Heinemann.

Hepworth, H. P. (1980) Foster Care and Adoption in Canada. Ottawa: Canadian Council on Social Development.

Horlick, M. and Skolnik, A. M. (undated) Mandating Private Pensions: A Study of European Experience. Research Report No. 51, Office of Policy, Office of Research and Statistics. Washington: US Department of Health, Education and Welfare.

Imber, V. (1977) A Classification of English Personal Social Services Authorities. Statistical Research Report Series No. 16. London: HMSO.

Martin, F. and Murray, K. (1981) Children Out of Court. Edinburgh: Scottish Academic Press.

Hellyer, P. (1969) (Chairman) Report of the Federal Task Force on Housing and Urban Development. Ottawa: Queen's Printer.

Merrison, A. (1979) (Chairman) Report of the Royal Commission on the National Health Service. Cmnd. 7615. London: HMSO.

Ministry of Health (1963) Health and Welfare: The Development of Community Care. Cmnd. 1973. London: HMSO.

Mommsen, W. J. (ed.) (1981) The Emergence of the Welfare State in Britain and Germany. Cited in Hennock, E. P. (1981) The Origins of British National Insurance and the German Precedent, 1880-1914. London: Croom Helm.

Robbins, Lord (1963) (Chairman) Report of the Committee on Higher Education, 1961-1963. Cmnd. 2154. London: HMSO.
Searle, G. R. (1976) Eugenics and Politics in Britain, 1900-1914. Science in History No. 3. Leyden: Noordhoff.
Seebohm, Lord (1968) (Chairman) Report of the Committee on Local Authority and Allied Personal Social Services. Cmnd. 3703. London: HMSO.

2
RESEARCH AND POLICY IN THE PERSONAL SOCIAL SERVICES

Olive Stevenson

In this chapter, the personal social services will be somewhat narrowly defined in organisational terms. The phrase can embrace a wide range of voluntary activities and agencies and there are significant administrative variants in the statutory sector between England, Scotland and Northern Ireland. There are also major differences in the arrangements for research funding. To consider all these in the context of the description and arguments which follow would be confusing. The focus here is upon the personal social services entitled 'social services departments' within the structure of English and Welsh local government. [1]

In what follows, an attempt is made to unravel the complex web of connections between research and policy in the British scene. To do so, four main issues are addressed:

- first, recent developments in research funding machinery

- secondly, the effects of political attitudes towards the social sciences on research

- thirdly, some critical elements in the relationship between researchers, policy-makers, and practitioners

- fourthly, some key issues for the future.

RECENT DEVELOPMENTS IN RESEARCH FUNDING MACHINERY

In 1973, the Department of Health and Social Security (DHSS) in England and Wales initiated a completely new structure for the support and development of research outside the department. (Other government departments, such as the Home Office, had a much more extensive programme of 'in-house' research). Kogan et al (1980) have described the DHSS relationships with researchers between 1973 and 1980 as 'exceedingly complex' and, in a preliminary report, have sought to describe the mechanisms and analyse some of the issues which arose. While it is impossible here to discuss this important innovation in depth, its significance in the overall pattern of policy and research must be clarified.

The recommendations of the Rothschild Report (1971) were accepted in a government White Paper (1972). The report made a sharp distinction between fundamental and applied research which has been much criticised — but that is another story. For the personal social services the need to develop 'applied' research was urgent. Research expenditure in the personal social services was minute in comparison with that, say, in medical care. A deliberate policy from the DHSS to stimulate research in the personal social services, in contrast to the reactive mode of the time, was welcome.

Two of the main developments proposed in the White Paper are salient for our purposes: first, the decision to introduce a 'customer-contractor' relationship, by which the DHSS would specify their needs as 'customers' which researchers as 'contractors' would then implement; secondly, the appointment of an advisory Chief Scientist, with an associated development of supporting research management services within the DHSS and of external advisers.

In translating the 'customer-contractor' principle into practice, the DHSS decided to link research, through the machinery of newly created research liaison groups, to existing branches, which were either client or service based. Thus, for example, research liaison groups for the elderly and children, for nursing and local authority social services, were set up. These research liaison groups, chaired by the civil servant who headed the branch, included representatives of the advisory professional groups within the DHSS, research

23

liaison staff, external academic advisers and (later) advisers from local government social services.

Kogan et al (1980) set out the essential purposes of the research liaison groups (RLGs):

> RLGs have several functions. First, they help customer divisions identify areas in which research could advance understanding of our policy problems. Next, they match proposals to research programmes by modifying spontaneous proposals submitted to the RLGs to be more sharply focussed on RLG topics and by working with DHSS funded units so that a unit's programme of work relates to RLG need. Third, they ensure the scientific standards of the research commissioned. Fourth, the completed research has to be evaluated, to ensure that its conclusions are scientifically valid and policy implications drawn out. Fifth, there is the issue of dissemination of results (p. 16).

Such a brief description of the formal position begs many questions for, as Kogan et al point out:

> Whilst government is unitary it is also a mass of administrative and professional groupings with great discretion within the policy framework. And that discretion has made the persuading, wooing and capturing of customer interest in research a key development in the post-Rothschild story (p. 8).

Thus, it soon became apparent that RLGs were taking on a life of their own, varying greatly in their commitment and approach to research, in their style of management and in the quality and emphasis of the external academic advice from which they drew. There were also variations in the research resources available, some RLGs being able to draw on well established units or teams; in the case of the personal social services, very few such resources existed and those which did were not regarded with unqualified enthusiasm. There is little doubt that the creation of RLGs has served to stimulate research in the personal social services. Whilst, on occasion, the constraints of the customer 'prescription' (a word at first actually used and,

prudently, later dropped in one RLG) may have been
frustrating for the researcher, researchers in
general have begun to learn how to adapt their
proposals in a way which is broadly acceptable to
both sides. If it is accepted that this is a
negotiating process which takes time and that these
preliminary discussions are in fact one of the ways
in which policy and research influence each other,
some of the tension is diminished. (Such lofty
statements, however, ignore the anxiety about the
future which untenured researchers experience and
which is bound to affect such negotiations). Even if
times were not so harsh, however, the success of the
RLG process, so far as the research for the personal
social services is concerned, rests on the
resolution of three main problems.

First, the system must allow for some
responsiveness to the proposals not defined by the
RLG as in priority areas. There is one such avenue -
the Small Grants Committee, which can offer awards
of up to £40,000. But valuable as that is, it does
not cater for the rare but potentially highly
significant more costly research initiative. It is
understandable that, having worked hard in defining
priorities, an RLG will not want these overturned.
Yet it is possible that a potential researcher will
have discovered a research need not previously
identified by the customers who are quite a long way
removed from the realities of local personal social
services. (It is not only academics who live in
ivory towers).

Secondly, the quality and quantity of external
academic advice for research in the personal social
services is vital. Here the DHSS have a problem.
Traditions of medical research are much more firmly
established; no such firm base existed in the
personal social services in the early 1970s although
the position is changing. This has made for a
situation in which a small group of academics 'took
in each other's washing' and problems of rivalry and
associated subjectivity have not been overcome. But
the problems are more basic than that. One concerns
the valid differences in approach which may exist
between advisers, perhaps particularly between some
medical and social scientific advisers.

The author, who served on the Chief Scientist's
Committee and one RLG, was acutely aware of two
difficulties. First, the approach to research
methodology advocated by most medical advisers and
apparently receiving the seal of approval from civil

servants was a relatively narrow one, firmly rooted
in the conventional experimental model. When agendas
are heavy and meetings large and conducted in a
fairly formal manner, it is difficult for underlying
differences of approach to be constructively
discussed. The danger is that when the question is
asked, 'is this problem researchable?', the answer
may be given by consideration of applicability of
traditional methods rather than by an open
discussion of the alternative modes of research
which might be appropriate to answering the
questions.

The second problem with which the social
scientific adviser has to grapple is a familiar one.
Invited to advise on the merits of proposals, on
their design, on the reliability of their findings,
and so on, there is an implicit assumption that
research is for researchers and policy for the
policy-makers. This is in fact an acceptable
division of function for some academics, notably
those from medicine. But as Rein (1976) has
powerfully argued, it does not fit the reality of
the social policy researcher, whose commitment is
not only to discovery of knowledge but to its
appropriate application. Rein takes the view that
'the meaning of social events is inextricably bound
up with the values we attach to them. Hence, fact,
value and theory are inseparably welded together.'
He suggests therefore that 'a primary function of
(policy) analysis is to submit goals to critical
review rather than treating them as given' (p. 72).

He suggests that for the academic in social
policy there is an uncomfortable but creative
compromise which he describes as 'the value critical
approach'.

> The value critical approach is itself a
> middle position because it is not
> detached, or value neutral, as the
> empirical positivists, nor as partisan as
> the radical activists – who assume one can
> only be in support of, or against, a
> social group or a social force. The
> analyst who works within the framework may
> yearn for the self assurance that the
> rigours of science or the faith of
> ideology can provide. But he cannot be
> tempted by these false idols, nor can he
> possibly undertake his work without method
> and belief (p. 79).

This view is helpful in defining more realistically the role of a scientific adviser for the personal social services on an RLG. Uncomfortable though it may be, it is much preferable to the artificiality of a role assumed to be value neutral by civil servants and by those researchers in other fields, especially medicine, whose relationship to policy is remote.

The third area of importance to the personal social services in the DHSS research machinery concerns the role of research liaison officers, standing as they do between the customers and the contractors. Whatever the theoretical significance of the RLG, it is upon the Chief Scientist's executive arm, the liaison officers, that day-to-day work devolves. The extent to which relationships with the DHSS are perceived as constructive by the researchers is to a substantial extent determined by the liaison officers who have considerable influence over the decisions in crucial matters. The liaison officers are drawn from three professional divisions, medicine, nursing and social work, although so far as the last is concerned, a number of those representing the social work arm of the department with whom the personal social services researchers liaise are not social workers. (This is an interesting anomaly not discussed by Kogan). It would therefore be misleading to assume a common professional interest and, in any case, a researcher in the personal social services may, through a particular RLG, relate to a liaison officer from another profession. For example, doctors have been liaison officers for RLGs on the elderly and physical disability which have involved extensive research in the personal social services. This highlights the importance of liaison officers having a wide view of research, an understanding of the practice issues, sometimes outside their field, which the researchers may wish to address. The oddity is that there is no built in assurance that this will be so; professionals are not necessarily thus equipped and there is no special training for the purpose.

This necessarily cursory account of a complex development at central government level sets the scene for more general discussion of the relationship between research and policy in the personal social services. Researchers looked to the DHSS rather than to the Social Science Research Council (SSRC), until the late 1970s, when the latter actively sought applications in areas relevant to the personal social services, through the use of their research initiative panels, such as that for children in care. This marked a shift of emphasis by the SSRC which blurred the boundaries of responsibility suggested by Rothschild between government departments and the research councils. A further example of blurring is in the creation of linked SSRC studentships which ensure that a research student pursuing independent work is connected to an on-going research project which may in some cases be DHSS funded. However, the longer term effects of these developments are difficult to gauge. At the time of writing, the government has invited Lord Rothschild to review the workings of the SSRC and it is well known that there is considerable ministerial hostility to the SSRC. In any case, the budget available from the SSRC for these different initiatives was small in comparision with that of the DHSS and finance for studentships has been severely restricted. Further, as Kogan (1980) points out, there are questions as to the perceived policy relevance of the SSRC initiatives, controlled as they are completely by the academic community without reference to those who actually deliver the services; 'legitimation of research choices is as important as intellectual quality' (p. 49).

POLITICAL ATTITUDES TOWARDS RESEARCH IN THE SOCIAL SCIENCES

It would be misleading to leave this account of the emergent relationship between customer and contractor without referring to the present political and economic climate. Despite financial stringency, there has been some protection of research funding for projects, although the structure described above has been seriously weakened by the reduction of RLG meetings and in research liaison staff. In any case, the structure was incomplete. Whilst arguably some economies could have been, and were, reasonably made, the system for coverage of personal social services research needs was not adequate and there is now little hope of its further development. For example, though RLGs based on client or service groupings seemed logical there are unresolved problems of gaps and overlappings in research strategy caused by these divisions.

Writing in 1982, the position looks bleak; the position of the universities, and therefore of the research community, is threatened by the effects of a severe reduction in government support. Behind financial stringency, however, lurk deeper and more worrying trends for those of us who have striven to contribute to social policy through research. Both here and in the USA, governments are presently in power which have little confidence in the contribution of social science to social policy. Similar trends in the USA and UK are evident; for example, the decision to collect fewer of the social statistics upon which many researchers rely for preliminary data. The parallel between the USA and the UK is not an exact one, for social scientists have never wielded the same degree of influence in the UK as in the USA. It is thus particularly sad for the UK if the personal social services, so slowly gathering internal research momentum, should now be slowed down again by a combination of financial restriction and lack of political interest or outright hostility. A political ideology which seeks to 'roll back the frontiers of the state' is hardly likely to encourage the identification of research in the statutory personal social services, since this is in itself a form of interference and may lead to strategies for further intervention. This is well exemplified in the recent government White Paper, 'Growing Older' (1981) which virtually ignores the place of government funded research in helping to cope with the social implications of demographic trends which are creating a very large increase in the numbers of the frail elderly. This may be contrasted with the working paper on priorities for the local autority social services prepared for one RLG, which specifically suggests, inter alia, the 'experimental evaluation of alternative caring arrangements ... the effects of different methods of intensive practical and emotional support for the very frail elderly living in the community' (p. 215).

This is not of course to ignore the potential value of the work in progress which has, so far, not been halted, although it has certainly been slowed down. It is to point to the possibility that unless or until this government falls, or a marked shift in ideological emphasis becomes apparent, the medium term future for the relationship between social research and social policy looks bleak, especially in the area of the statutory personal social services whose role is presently conceived by our political masters as diminishing.

THE RELATIONSHIP BETWEEN RESEARCHERS
AND POLICY- MAKERS

The debate concerning the relationship, potential and actual, between researchers and policy makers is, of course, of long standing, although the literature has been more prolific and the interest more intense in North America than in the UK. The post-war literature shows the swings of mood between pessimism and optimism, especially concerning the contribution which research can and should make to policy development. Writers such as Millikan (1959), Donnison (1972), Sharpe (1976), Weiss (1977) and Rein (1980) have all attempted to clarify the nature of the interaction and, in particular, have sought to distinguish between the natural and social sciences in this respect. These issues lie behind any more specific discussion of research in relation to the policies for the personal social services.

For any sophisticated discussion of the relationship between research and policy in these matters, there are two pre-conditions. First the complexity of the model must be considered; secondly, the different actors in the roles must be identified.

The Complexity of Interaction: Many authors, including those cited above, have pointed out the inadequacies of a 'linear' model, one which suggests a direct causal relationship between research findings and policy formulation. Yet the longing for a natural science model dies hard and the linear model is sometimes discussed as if it were a kind of long-term goal for social science research rather than an unsuitable explanation of the research contribution to social policy formulation. Rein (1976) cites MacIntyre:

> MacIntyre's review of the epistemological limitations of social science has led him to conclude that social science cannot aspire to provide genuine, law like, predictive generalisations. As he puts it: 'Whenever an event or state of affairs of type A occurs then an event or state of affairs of type B will occur unless (1) intelligent reflection by the agents involved leads them to change their ways or (2) unpredictable factors deriving from creative intellectual innovation intervene

> ... It follows that the type of rational consensus as to past achievement and future horizons that characterize the natural scientific community cannot be available to the social scientific community.'

> Correlations between events can be identified but there are always several possible causal linkages to account for these relationships. Policies for intervention require an understanding of these processes. But even if the theory could be specified, the external conditions under which it might apply are uncertain (pp. 53-54).

Thus many different strands of research are relevant and have to be considered together in policy formulation, either because they offer different perspectives which are complementary or because they advance fundamentally different propositions from which policy-makers must choose. Furthermore, the development of the personal social services is affected by social and political factors unrelated to research.

The field of child welfare illustrates the complexities of the policy-research interaction. The example is particularly instructive because the topic has generated more research interest and activity than any other in the personal social services and because policy and practice since 1948 have generally been regarded as amongst the most progressive and informed.

With Fuller, the author (1979) attempted to explore the impact of policies concerning child welfare in relation to the notion of deprivation. We point out that 'the population of children in care is a heterogeneous one, not only in terms of age and presenting problems but also in mode of entry to care and legal status and comprises a number of different groups whose care careers are differentially subject to a range of determinants outside professional child care'. Investigations as to why children come into care suggest that 'the need to which the care system is responding is itself a complex outcome of a number of social processes which is at risk of being oversimplified by unacceptably positivist assumptions'.

This field of research also exemplifies the issue of 'fact and value' which Rein (1976) discusses. In no aspect of social care research is the impossibility of separating out fact from value more vividly illustrated than in the question 'what is the best placement for children?'. Strong emotions, deeply held convictions and political assumptions influence what research is done, how it is done and how it is used by researchers and others. In comparison with other fields in the personal social services, the issue of substitute care for children in care and the alternative of rehabilitation to natural parents has generated considerable research both here and in North America. That the well being of children or the issue of parental rights should rouse strong emotions is not surprising. Nor is it surprising that such emotions play a part in the political processes which determine policy. In the UK, the case of Maria Colwell, who died at the hands of her stepfather, was made the subject of a government inquiry in 1974.[2] The first in a series of inquiries reflecting concern about child abuse, its distinguishing feature was that it embodied another highly charged element – the 'tug of love'. (Maria had been fostered with her aunt and uncle and returned to her mother and stepfather against the wishes of her foster parents). Although legislation to give greater security to foster parents had been mooted before the inquiry, there is little doubt that its findings facilitated the passage of the Children Act 1975, which has been praised by some and condemned by others, with academics as well as practitioners on both sides. Its proponents valued the increased security for foster parents which would give them some rights similar to adoption. They claimed that research evidence showed that most long-term foster parents and their foster children wanted the security of actual or quasi adoption and that it was in the child's best interests. Studies showing high success rates for adoption were also cited.[3] Critics saw the Act as unbalanced since it did nothing to strengthen the capacity of natural parents, usually socially disadvantaged, to retain or regain the care of their children.[4] So heated was the debate that the then Minister gave assurances that research programmes whould be launched to evaluate the workings of the Act and most of these are now coming to fruition.[5] The findings, although of considerable interest, are unlikely to end a debate in which ideological convictions and deep personal investment amongst those who engage in the research or attempt to utilise it are characteristic. The best one can attempt is to be 'value critical'.

But even without such complications, we are still left with the basic question: what should be the nature of the relationship between research and policy in the personal social services? The question may be answered on two levels, again with illustrations from the field of child welfare. First, as other social policy analysts, I would emphasise the interactive model whereby research is seen as 'part of a complex search for knowledge from a variety of sources ... a disorderly set of interconnections and back and forthness that defies neat diagrams.' (Weiss, 1977, pp. 13-14). This means inter alia, that research from a wide variety of sources has somehow to be assimilated in the search of 'good enough' solutions for children in care. The second level in the relationship between research and practice is more specific: what kind of research is most help? The evidence so far suggests that exclusive concentration on research which attempts to evaluate outcomes and develop predictive measures is unlikely to lead us very far, given the often rehearsed difficulties of controlling variables at the point of sample selection and during the process of study. One has only to think of the unique characteristics of foster children and their carers to see the problem. Yet it would be arrogant to dismiss any attempts to develop research along these well-tested lines. The plea is rather for greater tolerance and understanding by those who adopt such techniques of the value of an alternative emphasis upon the study of processes rather than outcomes alone. There is a great deal to be learnt about the delivery of the personal social services if one accepts certain moral premises which are not solely determined by measures of outcome. For example, if we care about how children and adults feel about receiving the services we offer, that becomes a subject worthy of research for practice. That is a part of the inseparability of value and fact about which Rein (1976) has written. However, there is a more pragmatic justification for study and reporting of processes. Quite simply, it may alert policy-makers and practitioners first as to what is really involved in carrying through a plan and, secondly, as good analyses of policy always show, to 'the unintended consequences of planned change.' Whilst this research contribution is not predictive in the scientific sense, it can generate in 'the actors' more responsive and sensitive attitudes for

future work. Looking further ahead, it may be that
certain generalisations about process relevant to
outcome will become apparent and this would be of
course a kind of prediction. But that is a secondary
benefit not integral to the strategy.

Examples of research sensitising others to
processes in the personal social services are not
hard to find. The author, with Hallett (1980)
undertook a modest descriptive study of the
processes in case conferences concerning child
abuse. By any standards it is relatively
insignificant as research and laid no claim to
generalisable findings. Yet it appears to have
considerable effect upon the actions of those who
formulate procedures and training programmes in
cases of child abuse; perhaps because the issues
scrutinised, the role of conference participants,
especially the chairpersons, were immediately
recognised as crucial by the participants yet
equally acknowledged as having heretofore been
neglected. Strangely, perhaps, they had paid little
attention to the processes involved in such
inter-professional co-operation. Yet the course of a
child's life may in some cases be affected by the
quality of such discussion, in which emotions and
anxieties run high and in which professional frames
of reference affect concepts of role and interaction
with others.

The Actors in the Roles: I referred earlier to the
need to identify the actors in the roles. Donnison
(1972) suggested that there were four groups of
actors on the social policy stage, not two, as the
linear model of research and policy had seemed to
imply. 'People working in four fields must be in
active contact with one another.' These fields are
'politics, technologies mechanical and social,
practice and research'. All these are 'part of a
much larger community concerned with other things',
a point which needs to be emphasised lest the
analysis becomes unreal in its specificity (in
Bulmer, 1978, p. 52).

In the UK and in relation to the personal
social services, Donnison's four fields need further
elaboration. Placed as these services are within
local government, they are subject to political
pressures both from the centre and from their own
local authorities. The practitioners, employed
within separate departments and with varying levels
of education and training, are highly variable in

their awareness of, and response to, the implications of research for their work.

Nor is the relationship between central and local government easy to analyse in relation to the promulgation of research findings. One cautious medium of communication is that of the advisory circular which has been dear to the hearts of British government until now (the present administration has cut back on this mode of communication with local authorities). Whilst rarely making explicit mention of research, the advice proffered in these documents, drawn up in consultation with DHSS professional advisers, has certainly drawn upon resarch. It is, however, surprising and disappointing how little the professional social work advisers devolved to regions by central government have involved themselves at local level in the dissemination and discussion of the implications of relevant policy in the personal social services.

Nor is research in the personal social services the prerogative of the academic community in institutions of higher education. Following the recommendations of the Seebohm Committee (1969) a number of local authority social services departments set up their own research sections, recruiting at a time of expansion in the social sciences, a number of able young peple most of whom were not professionally qualified. Such a pattern would have much to commend it if the leadership offered to them had been sufficiently expert in research and senior in the status of the departments. But the impression is that many of the more able researchers became disenchanted with the role and status assigned to them. (There was, incidentally, no adequate career structure for these staff). Their difficulties raise a more general question concerning the commitment of management and practitioners to research. Such a commitment would have implied spending time with researchers in order to formulate researchable questions from issues of concern and discussion of the implications of findings. The lesson seems to be that research in social services departments will not thrive unless it is perceived as integral, which is rarely the case. Currently, research is one of the first options to be considered for cuts when economies have to be made.

The interaction of key personnel is yet further complicated by the distinction, which in theory should be false, between those who teach and those who undertake research. The reality is that many of those now teaching prospective social workers about the personal social services are not themselves competent in research. This is bound up with the extremely rapid expansion of social work education in the 1960s and early 1970s which brought into academic life many experienced practitioners who had no experience in the practice of research. Once in post they frequently gave priority to the demands of work in the field on behalf of their students and academic pressures were not then of a kind which prompted them to acquire research skills. These matters have been competently explored by the Central Council for Education and Training in Social Work (CCETSW) and (the late) Personal Social Services Council (PSSC) (1980). Unfortunately, the recommendations of that joint working party, whose brief was to devise a research strategy for the personal social services, are unlikely to bear much fruit in the present economic climate. But the analysis of the problem of uncertainty and diffidence about research amongst many practitioners and teachers is one which will command general acceptance.

Thus it cannot be assumed that those who educate practitioners are the same members of the academic community as those who research, nor that the former will necessarily be confident and eager to impart the latest research findings to their students, as might be expected, for example, in the natural sciences. Yesterday's students are today's practitioners and some are tomorrow's policy-makers at local government level. The educational experiences they receive have a direct bearing on their subsequent attitudes to research. Thus we see how diffuse and problematical is the nature of the relationship between research and policy in the personal social services which embraces but expands the fields to which Donnison referred.

Thus far, the intention has been to demonstrate, with examples, some of the subtleties of the relationship between research and policy. For greater precision, one must also note that research can affect policies and practice at three stages: during the period of their formulation; in monitoring and evaluating their progress; or in post hoc evaluation intended to influence subsequent development.

THE RELATIONSHIP OVER TIME BETWEEN
POLICY AND PRACTICE

The period of formulation is, of course, 'messier' than it sounds. Policies do not hatch, like chickens out of eggs. They are formed and re-formed over a period of time. Programmes, the outcome of policies, are the chickens. It is possible and highly desirable for those who wish to introduce such programmes to examine the available research before doing so. A topical example concerns juvenile delinquency. Legislation has encouraged the development of 'intermediate treatment' schemes which are designed to provide alternatives to custodial care and which go beyond coventional casework intervention. Thus a new programme may be introduced by social services departments in the context of their overall policies for the care and control of juvenile delinquents. This has aroused enthusiasm and interest amongst practitioners and researchers and there is research to be drawn upon before individual social services departments embark upon their own ventures (see, for example, Waterhouse, 1978). Similarly, whilst fostering has occupied a central position in child welfare policy since the 1950s, programmes involving the use of 'professional foster parents' have developed rapidly in the past few years and some attempts to monitor and evaluate them are available to those who wish to move in a similar direction. (See, for example, Hazel, 1981).

The extent to which research findings are systematically examined in such circumstances is in fact highly variable. This raises questions as to the value placed upon research by those who introduce the programmes. It also emphasises the curious insularity which the structure of our local government personal social services encourages.

This is not, however, to underestimate the overall effect of research upon policy formulation in the personal social services. The process is more diffuse and difficult to pinpoint because some major research influences upon the personal social services are not derived from service research. Indeed, research of this kind is a comparative latecomer on the scene. For example, major studies of social work in the UK appeared a decade later than in the USA and are still sparse. The research which has played a greater part until recently in shaping policies, programmes and services, has been, broadly, from the basic disciplines of sociology and psychology. Furthermore, as Hall et al point out (Hall, Land, Parker and Webb, 1975):

> neither the theory nor its application necessarily has to be correct; it is enough that they are generally believed to be so.

These matters are illustrated in what one might describe as 'Bowlbyism', which serves to exemplify the points made above. Bowlby's research into separation, attachment and loss spans forty years. Naturally, the theories developed from it have been modified and changed over that period and have been subjected to rigorous analyses by others (see, for example, Rutter, 1972). The early impact of Bowlby's research upon child welfare services which developed rapidly in the 1950s was undoubtedly considerable, subject to filtering processes, sometimes distorting and often over-simplifying. In this period training for the child welfare field was growing with exceptional speed from a very low base. The problem of assimilation of research by practitioners was obviously heightened not the least because both educators and practitioners were largely unfamiliar with research approaches and methods. Furthermore, there is always a problem of time lag and the 'received wisdom' derived from empirical research will be running behind new challenges and new findings from on-going research. Thus, Bowlby's early findings on the relationship between deprivation and delinquency, unsophisticated by the standards of his later work, were widely cited and then criticised long after they had been superseded. The complexities of the debate concerning the reversibility or irreversibility of emotional damage resulting from separation were often insufficiently understood by practitioners. Antagonism mounted from the Women's Movement, who interpreted the 'Bowlby message' as an attack on their freedom to work outside the home and to find alternative care for their children during the day. Sociologists also argued that the theories took insufficient account of cultural variations. By the end of the 1960s, many social workers were confused as to the status of the evidence and therefore of its implications for substitute care for children. Even now, twenty years on, that confusion has not been resolved. That being said, the whole area of bonding, attachment and loss, to which Bowlby's contribution has been major, is influential in the decisions which

practitioners take concerning the removal of
children from their primary caretakers and in the
policies which were formulated for fostering and
adopting (Bowlby 1969 et seq.).

A similar, contemporary example comes from the
field of child abuse. In recent years the problem of
child abuse has generated great anxiety amongst
those who work in the personal social services and
some other professionals involved in such cases.
Amongst the consequences of this is a raised level
of interest amongst practitioners and policy makers
about research findings. (It is common for day
conferences on such topics to be over-subscribed at
a time when others are sparsely attended). But, not
surprisingly, those who expect confident answers
especially about causative factors, are doomed to
disappointment. For as Weiss (1977) remarks:

> Even as research in a subject accumulates
> and its methodological and conceptual
> quality improves, it may provide no
> further basis for choice (p. 10).

Rigorous analysis of the implications of research
for policy, updated frequently and presented to the
practitioner in a form which can be understood and
utilised is an extremely difficult task, even when
there is interest and willingness to learn. For
example, in the UK, there are interprofessional area
review committees whose task is to formulate policy
on procedures in cases of child abuse at a local
level. One element in their procedural guidance
concerns the calling of these conferences at
critical points. Defining a 'critical point' may be
usefully related to research evidence. Yet there is
no firm predictive evidence that would enable
researchers to say - 'if thus and thus, the child is
very likely to be injured or re-injured' - all one
can do is to point to different strands of evidence
which, when woven together, suggest that those at
the sharp end will be prudent to convene a
conference. (See, for example, Kempe, 1962; Gil,
1970; Lynch, 1976).

If the interpretation of research focused on a
specific issue and discipline is difficult, how much
more difficult is the reality that research for the
personal social services is drawn from a variety of
sources and from many different disciplines? The
point is well illustrated from the field of mental
illness. Psychiatry in Dissent (Clare, 1976)
analyses a dilemma which is acute for social workers

as well as psychiatrists. Given the sharply contrasting views of mental illness propounded by psychiatrists themselves and the associated disciplines of, _inter alia_, sociology and biochemistry, it is small wonder that those who must devise policies for the care of the mentally ill may be confused about the implications of research for their work. Perhaps for this reason work such as that of Brown and Harris (1978) which accepts that mental illness exists but firmly locates it in a social context is more valuable to those who must plan services than that of the wild men at each end of the continuum.

FACTORS AFFECTING THE IMPACT OF RESEARCH ON POLICY AND PRACTICE

There remains the more specific issue of the impact of social services research (social work being only one component) upon policy and practice. For such research to be valued by those who deliver services it must be seen to relate closely to the values and structures which are familiar to them. In a sense, it must be local though 'local' in this context may range from national to the area covered by one area team in a local authority, depending on the questions which are being studied. It is not usually easy to extrapolate research findings from one country to another, even when some general matters such as social work effectiveness are under scrutiny. Social work, at the interface of personal problems and social structure, is indigenous and its practitioners often remain intellectually unconvinced or even apathetic about the findings 'from abroad'. To the extent that such findings do have general applicability, they often need translation into a more familiar social context.

An example of this is of _Girls at Vocational High_ (Meyer et al, 1965) whose findings are said to have had a marked impact on the profession of social work in the USA. The reverberations just reached academics in the UK but, by and large, were not felt by practitioners or policy-makers, many of whom would not even recognise the title of the book. Indeed the very title, with its specific North American terminology, is alienating to the British reader. By contrast, _The Client Speaks_ (Mayer and Timms, 1970), a modest and methodologically shaky study of consumer reaction to social work service in one atypical voluntary agency in the UK, had a disproportionate significance, at least among those who teach and learn about social work. The reasons for this merit exploration. Published in 1970, its findings suggest that the perceptions of interaction between worker and client as to the nature of the exchange might differ widely and that this might be related to social class. This was in the period in the UK when the sociological critique of social work was reaching a peak and the findings were congruent with that. Eagerly espoused by the critics of social work, there was little critical appraisal of its status as research or even of the arguments derived from its conclusions. Not until 1975 was there a complementary study published by Sainsbury, methodologically much superior and more stimulating in its discussion of findings. This study dealt with client and worker perceptions of each other and of the helping process in a family service unit for so-called 'multi-problem families'. It received far less attention that the work of Mayer and Timms.

Is research more eagerly scrutinised by those who wish to attack the welfare professionals? Is the task of sifting carefully weighed empirical evidence too complex for the professionals to whom nonetheless its implications are so important? Is it just that there are times when research falls upon deaf ears? The answers are not certain but if the relationship between research and action is to be more profitable than heretofore, the issues must be further examined.

Reference has been made earlier to the difficulty of transplanting social services research from one country to another. However, two exceptions are instructive. The first concerned social work and the research by Reid and Epstein (1972) on brief and extended casework. Although widely read by teachers and students, it is doubtful how much impact it would have made upon practice and hence ultimately on policy had it not been taken up by Goldberg, an established social work researcher who sought to apply it to British agencies and attempted various forms of replication. Again, it is important to recognise the climate in which the British research took place. Concern about lack of purposefulness in social work activity was being expressed following the reorganisation of the personal social services and it had become clear that rapid expansion of social work activity at that time had not been accompanied by clarification of the social work task (see, for example, Parsloe and Stevenson, 1978). Thus research which sought to contribute to that debate fell upon fertile ground.

In summary, then, consideration of the impact of research upon the formulation of policy and practice is extremely complex to analyse. This is for three main reasons. First, it is impossible to stop the clock. Policies and programmes roll on and it is rare indeed for there to be a point at which the messages from earlier research can be formally considered at the point of implementation. Secondly, much of the influence is derived from the basic disciplines, notably those of sociology and psychology, whose influence is pervasive but difficult to pinpoint and at times contradictory in the messages which it gives to those who must act. Thirdly, the service-based research has been slow to develop in the UK and there have been resistances and difficulties in the utilisation of relevant research from abroad. This is further complicated by the local organisation of personal social services which contributes to insularity within the country.

MONITORING AND EVALUATION

Another stage at which research and policy become involved is in the monitoring and evaluation of specific programmes. Researchers within social services departments have played a significant part in this and their work, because of its local commissioning, has not always received the attention it deserves. The initiatives for this research have different origins. In some, research enthusiasm has generated the idea of an experiment and associated evaluation. In others, central or local government have looked for researchers to examine a particular scheme. The balance between monitoring of process and evaluation of outcomes is important and will depend, as has been suggested earlier, by the view of research taken by both researchers and consumers. Furthermore, difficulties of rigorous scientific evaluation in fields such as the personal social services are formidable and not always appreciated by the more enthusiastic practitioners. Nevertheless, one detects a growing awareness amongst both policy-makers and practitioners that possibilities exist for a more rigorous on-going scrutiny of developments. One example recently completed and awaiting publication, is of a scheme in a large Midlands town to test the effects of 'unlimited' home help time to a given locality. This research had a number of important facets; for example, the effect on home helps and their families of the changed and extended role had to be taken into account and a theory of insatiable demand in a locality tested (and, incidentally, refuted). In south eastern England, at present, evaluation is in progress of a scheme which gives to social workers a sum of money each week to spend as they wish on supports for the frail elderly in the community, the sum being below that which it would cost to provide residential care. Recently, the author has been approached about the possibility of monitoring and evaluating day centres catering for families where the children have been abused. Many other examples could be cited and it is notable that more social service evaluation seems to be in progress or nearing completion than has been formally reported in published work.

Earlier work of this kind centred more upon social work intervention and its effect on policy is doubtful. Goldberg's Helping the Aged (1970) was a landmark in British empirical research. It set out to test the effectiveness of trained social workers who work with the very old. Whilst it did not demonstrate the relevance of training per se, it did show, in a carefully controlled experiment, that the morale of very old people could be improved in measurable terms by the input of skilled social work (not extra time alone) even though many of their problems were by definition irremediable. Yet the research had little impact upon policy at central or local government level and it is only recently, now that more serious attention is being paid to the needs and problems of the very old, that the channels of communication for research messages on this subject seem to be opening.

This is perhaps an illustration of the importance of a relationship which had begun to develop between policy-makers and the research community through the Chief Scientist's machinery and of the potentiality for similar relationships at local level. The timing of research is of critical importance in determining the extent to which it is used. Sometimes this is a matter of luck. But in general researchers who have a commitment to influencing policy (and incidentally who are keen to acquire research grants) would be wise not to swim against the tide of current interests but rather to swim with it. In the field of the personal social services where so little systematic evaluation has been done, this is not difficult provided that one accepts that the tide may on occasion have turned again by the time the research is completed or that the tide may go out too fast and leave the researchers stranded!

RETROSPECTIVE ANALYSIS

The third and final point at which research and policy may interact is in the retrospective analysis of the effects of policies and programmes. Defined programmes with beginnings, middles and ends are relatively rare in the United Kingdom and it is even rarer for them to have been set up in a manner which permits systemative evaluation unless the researchers have been involved from the outset. Where they have not, retrospective research dependent on the accuracy of statistical material and record keeping is doomed to failure. The only way to come at such evaluation in the personal social services is through direct contact, often face to face, with the actors, be they clients or practitioners. This means that the type of information obtained and the style of research will inevitably be 'softer' than some would wish.

Examples of policy evaluation on a large scale are rare in British research in the personal social services. But one in recent years raises a number of interesting issues and is concurrent and retrospective and prospective. This concerns the Children Act 1975, discussed earlier. The research commissioned is retrospective in the sense that the Act has been passed and many of the decisions under scrutiny have been taken. It is concurrent because in some instances it was possible to agree with the agencies involved that they would collect data in ways which would facilitate analysis and because some 'decision making on the spot' was also to be studied. It is prospective because the implementation of certain sections of the Act has not yet taken place and research findings might still have a bearing on that. (It has to be admitted, however, that resource constraints are probably a more powerful factor).

THE FUTURE

It is a depressing and confusing task to examine the next phase of the relationship between policy and research in the personal social services at the present time. The political climate at central government level is antagonistic to growth in the statutory sector. Since that antagonism is further evident in attitudes to social science research in higher education, there seems little chance in the next decade of developments such as we have witnessed in the 1970s. For even if the recession eases and the government changes, it will take time to regenerate the impetus and reconstruct the structures upon which a creative partnership rests.

Furthermore, as has been fully discussed earlier in this paper, the complexities of the relationship were always such as to need careful and subtle fostering. One particular area of interaction - that of researchers and practitioners - was in urgent need of review, even before the present political winds blew so cold. There has been apparent in the social work profession, who are to a very large extent the natural consumers of research in the personal social services, a fear of elitism which seemed often to lead to an anti-intellectual stance. This in turn has affected the willingness of the profession to accept forms of specialisation which, the author (Stevenson, 1981) has argued elsewhere, is the only way in which practice expertise can advance. One of the major reasons for specialisation is precisely the subject of this chapter - that it offers an opportunity to assimilate and utilise a body of research knowledge relevant to that specialisation. Without this, social workers retreat, defeated and overwhelmed, from the edge of a forest in which they know they will get lost.

It is too early yet to say whether alternatives to central government support will be sought and found for research initiatives of various kinds. Just as the arts now look to commercial sponsors, it may be that social sciences will seek to develop closer and wider links with commerical enterprises, not all of whom have a particular axe to grind in the monies they disburse. There are ideological pills to be swallowed, but a mixture of altruism and self interest may drive researchers in the personal social services to look elsewhere if the faltering progress of the past decade is not to be halted.

If, then, we should plan for a future, what should be the priorities? It is instructive now to look at Pinker's [6] report presented to the SSRC in 1977 on research priorities for the personal social services and to compare this with the working party [7] chaired by Goldberg which reported on priorities for the local authority social services to the research liaison group in 1979.

Pinker makes a courageous plea for research concerned with 'that large part of the personal social services ... which is concerned with protection, care and commitment' (p. 14). He suggests:

> that SSRC research priorities should be accorded to investigating the provisions made for those persons in each of the major need groups whose social status is lowest, whose prognosis is poorest and whose conditions of need are likely to be long term (p. 15).

This is a theme conspicuously lacking in the LASS report which, in its emphasis on evaluation and output, perhaps illustrates Pinkers's concern that:

> the key conceptual distinction should not be between medical and social care but between success and failure as it occurs in both models (p. 15).

Whatever constraints are in fact placed upon research activities, it seems clear from a consideration of these recommendations and the not insubstantial research literature of the past decade that three themes could most profitably be pursued and elaborated.

First, the relationship of the statutory personal social services to alternative formal and informal support systems in the society which they serve is in need of more detailed exploration. Such studies have many components, ethical, organisational and financial, and require a closer examination of the notion of community than is conveyed by political sloganising. The author (Stevenson, 1980) has drawn on the work of Abrams (1977) on the meaning of community to stress the need for greater precision in the use of the term. Without it, service planning may be right off target.

Secondly, as has been made clear by studies such as those by Goldberg (1980) and Parsloe and Stevenson (1978), social work in the personal social services has suffered from a lack of clarity about its task and the organisational framework best suited to the task. Research is needed into objectives, the best means of achieving them, the limitations and the potential contribution of others to the work of the personal social services.

It is argued in this paper that such a complex array of research problems requires alternative research approaches and that too narrow a definition of research is unhelpful. For example, the distinction between research and development, if too tightly drawn, is constricting. Most of the problems we need to study are dynamic - they change as we examine them. It is therefore better to seek some control over their behaviour through the framework of action research.

Thirdly, the whole area of residential care is still seriously under-researched. Residential care is expensive in money, demanding of staff and some of our most dependent members of society live in such institutions. Recent work, such as that of Wilkin and Jolley (1981) commissioned by the DHSS, to study the perceptions of residents and staff in three old people's homes, holds promise for the future. Like its predecessor, by King, Raynes and Tizard (1971), on care for the mentally handicapped, it is a serious attempt to apply scientific criteria to the less tangible but vital questions concerning the quality of life for such residents. But, perhaps in this aspect of the personal social services more than any other, it is not enough to discover institutional behaviour and attitudes if we do not know how to change them. It is a particular challenge to the 1980s which cuts across all client groups of the personal social services.

There is so much to be done; the 'value critical' stance of most researchers in the personal social services is one which should not be rejected by any developed society concerned about the quality of care it offers to its most vulnerable citizens.

NOTES

1. The statutory personal social services are administered by local government in Scotland but the departments are entitled 'social work departments' and, unlike in England and Wales, where it is administratively separate, include the Probation and After Care Service. In Northern Ireland, there is presently no system of local government as in the rest of the UK and the personal social services are within 'Health and Social Service Boards', of which

there are four in the Province. Research funding for the personal social services in Scotland and Northern Ireland is less formalised than in England and Wales and, of course, planning in the Scottish and Irish systems is from a much smaller population base.

2. Report of the Committee of Inquiry into the care and supervision provided in relaton to Maria Colwell, (HMSO, 1974).

3. See for example: Shaw, M. and Lebens, K. (1976), 'Care between families', Adoption and Fostering, 84, 2; Raynor, L. (1980), The Adopted Child Comes of Age, (Allen & Unwin); Lambert, L. and Streather, J. (1980) Children in Changing Families (Macmillan Press); Seglow, J. et al (1972), Growing Up Adopted (National Foundation for Educational Research).

4. R. Holman has been one of the main proponents of this argument. See, for example, his articles in New Society, 1 May 1975, pp. 268-69 and Community Care, 8 October 1975, p. 12.

5. The work, commissioned and nearing fruition, has been undertaken by D. Fruin (National Children's Bureau and British Association of Adoption and Fostering), J. Packman (Exeter University), J. Rowe (previously director of British Association of Adoption and Fostering) and Olive Stevenson (Keele University).

6. Pinker, R. (1977), 'Research Priorities in the Personal Social Services' (Research Report to SSRC).

7. 'Report to DHSS RLG for Local Authority Social Services' in British Journal of Social Work, vol. 10, no. 2, 1980.

REFERENCES

Abrams, P. (1977) Social Care Research: Some Research Priorities and Problems. London: Policy Studies Institute.

Bowlby, J. (1969 et. seq.) Attachment and Loss (Vols. I, II and III). Hogarth Press.

Brown, G. W. and Harris, T. (1976) Social Origins of Depression. London: Tavistock.

CCETSW and PSSC (1981) Research and Practice. London: Central Council for Education and Training in Social Work.

Donnison, D. (1978) "Research for Policy", in M.

Bulmer (ed.), Social Policy Research. London: Macmillan.

Framework for Government Research and Development (1972) Cmnd. 5046. London: HMSO.

Fuller, R. and Stevenson, O. (1979) The Impact of Social Policy upon Transmitted Deprivation. Unpublished Research Report to the SSRC. (Forthcoming as: Policies, Programmes and Disadvantage. London: Heinemann.)

Gil, D.G. (1970) Violence Against Children: Physical Child Abuse in the USA. Cambridge, Mass.: Harvard University Press.

Goldberg, E.M. (1970) Helping the Aged. London: Allen and Unwin.

Goldberg, E.M. and Warburton, R.W. (1980) Ends and Means in Social Work. London: Allen and Unwin.

Growing Older (1981) Cmnd. 8173. London: HMSO.

Hall, P., Land, H., Parker, R. and Webb, A. (1975) Change, Choice and Conflict in Social Policy. London: Heinemann.

Hallett, C. and Stevenson, O. (1980) Child Abuse: Aspects of Interprofessional Co-operation. London: Allen and Unwin.

Hazel, N. (1981) A Bridge to Independence. Blackwell.

Holman, R. (1975) "The Place of Fostering in Social Work", British Journal of Social Work, 5(1), 3-29.

Kempe, C.H., Silverman, F.N., Steele, B., Droegmueller, W. and Silver, H. (1962) "The Battered Child Syndrome", Journal of the American Medical Association, 181, 105-112.

King, R.D., Raynes, N.V. and Tizard, J. (1971) Patterns of Residential Care. London: Routledge and Kegan Paul.

Kogan, M., Korman, N. and Henkel, M. (1980) "Government's Commissioning of Research: A Case Study", Unpublished Paper, Department of Government, Brunel University.

Lynch, M.A. (1976) "Child Abuse: The Critical Path", Journal of Maternal and Child Health, July.

Mayer, J. and Timms, N. (1970) The Client Speaks. London: Routledge and Kegan Paul.

Meyer H., Borgata, E. and Jones, W. (1965) Girls at Vocational High. New York: Russell Sage.

Milikan, M. (1959) "Inquiry and Policy: The Relationship of Knowledge to Action", in D. Lerner (ed.), The Human Meaning of the Social Sciences. New York: Meridian Books.

Organisation and Management of Government Research (Rothschild Report) (1971) Cmnd. 4814. London: HMSO.

Parsloe, P. and Stevenson, O. (1978) Social Service Teams: The Practitioner's View. London: HMSO.

Pinker, R. (1977) Research Priorities in the Personal Social Services. Unpublished Research Report to the SSRC.

Reid, W. J. and Epstein, L. (1972) Task Centered Casework. New York: Columbia University Press.

Rein, M. (1976) Social Science and Public Policy. Harmondsworth: Penguin.

Report of the Committee of Inquiry into the Care and Supervision Provided in Relation to Maria Colwell (1974) London: HMSO.

Report of the Committee on Local Authority and Allied Personal Social Services (Seebohm Report) (1968) Cmnd. 3703. London: HMSO.

Rutter, M. (1972) Maternal Deprivation Reassessed. Harmondsworth: Penguin.

Sainsbury, E. (1975) Social Work with Families. London: Routledge and Kegan Paul.

Sharpe, L. J. (1978) "Governments as Clients for Social Services Research", in M. Bulmer (ed.), Social Policy Research. London: Macmillan.

Stevenson, O. (1981) Specialisation in Social Service Teams. London: Allen and Unwin.

Stevenson, O. (1981) "The Realities of a Caring Community", University of Liverpool, Eleanor Rathbone Memorial Lecture.

Waterhouse, J. (1978) "Group Work in Intermediate Treatment", British Journal of Social Work, 8(2).

Weiss, C. H. (1977) Using Social Research in Public Policy Making. Lexington Books.

Wilkin, D. and Jolley, D. (1981) The Management of Mental and Physical Impairment amongst Old People in Residential Settings. Unpublished Research Report to the DHSS.

Yelloly, M. (1978) Independent Evaluation of 25 Placements. Kent: Kent Special Placement Project.

Part I

RESEARCH AND POLICY-MAKING

(b) Policy-making and the Assumptive Context of Research

3

LAW REFORM AND SOCIAL CHANGE: COMMUNITY AND SOCIETY, *SOCIAL* WORK AND SOCIAL *WORK*

Hans Mohr

DIMENSIONS OF DISCOURSE

A critical enquiry into Law Reform and Social Change must start with the assumptions and preconceptions built into the very terms signifying the subject. In common speech, the terms seem unproblematic. Law reform is what it says - the activity of reforming the law. In the second half of this century law reform has gained official status in the creation of Law Reform Commissions throughout the common law world (as well as in other legal systems). Federated States such as Canada and Australia do not only have Federal Commissions but also Commissions on a province or state basis. It is in fact by now almost impossible to follow the work of the many Commonwealth commissions. [1] What motivates this activity after almost a century of slumber? Social change has become a key word at about the same time, informing not only the social sciences but public consciousness. By now, we can see that both, the renewal of law reform and the demand for social change, have their roots in the nineteenth-century idea of progress, as expressed in Marx's eleventh thesis on Feuerbach:

> Philosophers have only interpreted the world in various ways; the point, however, is to change it.

The models (paradigms) adopted for law reform commissions and inherent in notions of social change are basically nineteenth-century models. After the enormous impetus provided by the changes and experiments of the now proverbial sixties, these models reveal themselves as inadequate; or more correctly, inappropriate in the context of the social, economic and political conditions of the latter part of the twentieth century. This is graphically expressed in an imaginary encyclopedia entry by one of the new philosophers, Levy (quoted in Turkle, 1978):

> Socialism (masculine noun) born Paris 1848. Died, Paris 1969.

The nature of the immense variety of notions concerning law reform and social change can be analyzed by making problematic the relationship between the two concepts hidden in the conjunction "and". Is it - as is often stated - that law is an instrument of social change and therefore that law reform will produce social change? Or is it - as is equally often stated - that social change has taken place and can readily be perceived around us and that the law has to adapt to this change? If we examine the influences that guide our thoughts and actions we find that we are in the grip of directional linearity, cause and effect, the means-end paradigm. We perceive law reform as a conscious activity of formulating and formalizing legislative enactments even though the common law has always prided itself as the kind of flexible instrument which can meet and resolve new problems in its ongoing praxis. Social change too is not seen as being historically determined (not even by historical materialists who have to invoke "dialectic") but as something which has to be made. And we believe above all that reform and change are good things and will augur a better future. Yet, at the same time we desire social stability and we expect the law to offer us certainty.

What makes words like "reform" and "change" so attractive, is their inherent call for activity and the production of new things or states of affairs. Increasingly, during the last decade, the wisdom of this commitment to production has been questioned (see, for example, Meadows, et al., 1972; Illich, 1973; Schumacher, 1973; Rotstein, 1976; Leiss, 1976). [2] There are now second thoughts about the imperative of increased production and limitless growth which have been made possible by our technological capabilities. Science and technology have added disaster to promise and the application of scientific, technological approaches to human affairs is rapidly losing its lustre. The danger and disaster points have been recognized, [3] but are still counterbalanced by the perceived danger of nihilism and paralysis. Having lived with and based our intentions and expectations upon action, passivity is experienced not just as neutral, but as dangerous. This can be demonstrated by examining the active and passive form of basic verbs. To have turns into being had, to possess into being possessed; taking - which in its active form has to be augmented by "fraudulently and without colour of right" to become theft - shows this quality very simply in its passive form: being taken. Using becomes being used and buying being bought.

There is no such asymmetry of meaning in words like loving - being loved, respecting - being respected, giving - being given, although if we give carelessly as in giving away, we are being given away. The insidious character of 'being helped' has been discovered over recent years, as well as the consequences of the passive form of 'to reform', 'to correct' and 'to change'. The critique of psychiatry by Laing (1965; 1967; Laing and Esterton, 1964), Szasz (1962, 1970) and others, as well as the demise of the "correctional ideal" provide illustrations in point.

Law Reform and Social Change are, at least on the surface, conceived and perceived as beneficial actions (for what and for whom remains in question). The gap between actors and recipients is almost total, not because there is no correspondence (of which there is little) but because the very gap is not recognized. What is seen as reform and positive change at one stage may only later be recognized as oppression. The history of juvenile delinquency is a case in point. The substance of discourse has changed in this area but the form has not. Today's child savers can easily be seen as fashioning consequences similar to those which the child savers of yesterday produced without recognizing essential similarities.

Positivism which conceives of society as a natural form upon which we can act as if we stood outside it has become problematic not only as a scientific vision but in its very metaphorical connotation. The corresponding social response is Negativism - that is, resentment as ressentiment.

SOCIAL WORK AND SOCIAL WORK

Social action, which implies that social change can be directed, is not only problematic in terms of the meaning of action but also the meaning of 'social'. Although the difference is clear to us whether we are at a social gathering or are assigned to a social class, the adjective "social" itself hides its two fundamentally different reference points: community and society. [4] We increasingly use the word community to express a sense of longing and the need for belonging. It has not found adjectival expression of any currency. 'Communal' is neither a form of everyday speech nor does it have conceptual location. Communes and communism are not everybody's idea of community. On the other hand, although 'society' is clearly recognized, 'societal' has some conceptual location but no place in common speech. Reference may be made to 'formal', 'institutional', 'structural' in scientific languages as well as everyday speech. But their reference point (indexicality) is increasingly unclear as can be demonstrated with 'structural' which has very different meanings in the context of 'structural-functional' and 'structuralism'. [5]

The same unacknowledged division and resultant tension appear in the conceptual structure of a field such as social work. Social work, taken literally, surely is what actors accomplish in loving, fighting, speaking, teaching, learning, getting married and divorced, having children and so on and so forth. Social work, although initially conceived as an aid to social work, was invariably drawn, conceptually as well as in its practice, into the normative institutional framework and has become societal work. The literal meaning of social work, although recognized by anybody who lives in any relationship, neither makes conceptual sense nor is it a part of common speech. Although there are ingenious reminders in humanistic advertising, such as 'have you hugged your kid today?", moral action and moral speech are too close to doing good and to sermonizing to reveal their character as necessary work to produce the good rather than the goods.

Sociology, although it does not accept social work as its praxis (nor social work) cannot escape the division and tension between the two forms of social either. Ostensibly born in positivism (in acknowledging Comte's paternity), the tension becomes obvious in Durkheim, even though he opts for the normative paradigm which makes possible the scientific study of what he sees as social science. "The Rules of Sociological Method" instils the clearest expression of Durkheim's project, which has largely become the project of sociology (Durkheim, 1964a). Weber himself is close to an ideal type of the dilemma and although he too opts for rationality, he has no illusion about the disenchanted world and the iron cage as the price to be paid for an order-ly world. Parsons attempted to diffuse the tension and kept American sociology naive (and full of bad faith). The study of the life world, coined by Husserl, found sociological expression in Schutz, but did not capture the sociological imagination until recently, as reflected in the impact and growth of Harold Garfinkel's "Ethnomethodology" (Garfinkel, 1967). In Canada this direction is represented in the works of Allen Blum and Peter McHugh (see, for example, Blum, 1970; McHugh, 1970) among others.

Social Work which now is used as a designation of a discipline and a profession has a long tradition in western societies. Michel Foucault (1965, 1977) [6] has painstakingly explored the archaeology as well as the genealogy of this tradition. He has increasingly shown that the legacy of Marx and Freud which led us to focus on repression, political or psychological, is insufficient to explain the nature of what I here call social work. Even 'surveillance' as developed in "Discipline and Punish" (Foucault, 1977) and as extended by Donzelot (1979) to "The Policing of Families" is still too closely linked to repression to make intelligible what is hidden in Aristotle's assertion that man is a political animal. Foucault's (1980) issuing of Herculine Barbin as well as Garfinkel's Story of Agnes (in Garfinkel, op. cit.) are illustrations of the nature of social work and its conflict with social work.

COMMUNITY AND SOCIETY

The split between the life world and the rationalized world, between the social and societal, community and the state, is also apparent in the split between science and praxis. The material to fill in these increasing structural fissures is provided by two projects: ideology and technology.

If we reflect on the period since the Second World War, a period which encompasses John Spencer's work, we can readily see that the solution of social problems has increasingly been sought in ideology and technology. The war itself was conducted primarily on those two grounds. Technology (in spite of some contrary voices) has been almost universally accepted as the official road to salvation.

Technology as a solution to social problems stands in need of an ideology to cover up the alienation it entails. Conversely, ideology stands in need of a technology to fashion the life world in its image. This point has been covered exhaustively, for example, in the work of Jurgen Habermas (see especially Habermas (1974)) and Jacques Ellul (see especially Ellul, 1964a, 1964b, 1967).

Both, ideology and technology, when subjected to critical thought are far less clear in their means-end propositions. Is law an instrument (technology) of social change (ideology)? No doubt, numerous illustrations can be cited in which this is in fact the case. Most illustrations, however, if critically pursued, will show the ambiguous if not nefarious character of the means-end relation which effectively excludes the human-social particularity. Legislation governing juveniles and the discussion of 'child savers', fair or unfair, provide a case in point. Although the main illustrative basis of this paper is the reform of criminal law and family law, other areas of welfare law and social planning may be cited.

C.K. Allen (1964, p. 1), in speaking of the sources of law, puts the dichotomy we have pursued very clearly:

> In the one [source of law] the essence of law is that it is imposed upon society by a sovereign will. In the other, the essence of law is that it develops within society of its own vitality.

The sovereign will is no longer a personal will (if it has ever been one) but the will of the State, the will of institutionalized forms of social management. This source of law now coincides almost totally with the common sense notion of law. Law reform is therefore primarily seen as legislative reform and for those closest to the subject it may in addition mean administrative and institutional reform. The second source of law, although still operative as ever, has now hardly any conscious or conceptual grounds. It is in fact nothing less than a scandal that jurisprudence in the late twentieth century has not taken a resounding position on this matter. The Law Reform Commission of Canada entitled its Second Annual Report "The Worst Form of Tyranny". It found in its initial searches that citizens were subject to about 40,000 federal and provincial offences, most of them of strict liability. Law has indeed become an instrument of social control and law reform, at best, looks for clues to social management concepts.

Can we still make sense of Allen's second source of law, where law "develops within society of its own vitality"? Here the conception of social change is not that it is made but that it happens and in the happening forms its own rules. We do profess, at least in the social sciences, that all social behaviour is rule governed, but we are not sure about the status of these rules. They are rarely explicated in everyday life. [7]

Nevertheless, the social work of members in community is expressed in notions of justice, fairness, equity, promise and consideration, restitution and compensation, reference to precedence, sanctions and other operations which are conceptualized in the formal law. Every family is an example of a legal system in operation and breakdown can be interpreted as a lack of consciousness that this is so. The Law Reform Commission of Canada, for instance, has undertaken a project in which public school students were introduced to basic legal concepts which they tested against everyday occurrences. Even these young children were quickly able to perceive and conceptualise rule-making and conflict resolution in their everyday observations.[8] As evidenced, for example in the work of Jean Piaget, even the play of children can be seen as members' vitality as a source of law, since interactive play cannot proceed without rule making activity. [9]

LAW REFORM AND SOCIAL CHANGE

Institutional societal work and members' social work are indeed different forms of work, even though the second is usually not incorporated in our concept of work. [10] The division of labour, so successful in the mode of industrial production, has not achieved the organic form Durkheim (1964b) expected; and Durkheim's legal argument linking criminal law to mechanical solidarity and cooperaive law to organic solidarity, although logically sensible, is historically unjustified. The amount of alienation which our society must tolerate in order to adhere to rationalized modes of organization and production can now barely be defended on the basis of economic necessity. Its social (communal) consequences are obvious. [11]

Legal and social work as institutionalized forms could hardly escape this development. In law the state was already acknowledged, at least in part, as the source of authority. Social work needed the welfare state before it could appear in a rationalized form. Common law and case law were increasingly replaced by legislation and administrative decision-making; and case work by social planning and social service administration. Weber's predictions have thus largely come to pass.

There is a contradiction in this development which, because it is not generally acknowledged, also constitutes a vicious circle. The notion of social change must surely arise from dissatisfaction with existing social conditions. It is here that a differential analysis between the social and societal, community and society, Gemeinschaft and Gesellschaft is all important. If social problems are identified as structural and organizational problems, then the remedies will be sought in structural and organizational changes. If, on the other hand, problems arise from a lack of attention to members' _social_ work, structural and organizational changes directed to improved systemic functions will become counter productive because they will tend further to reduce that social work of members. Even 'case work' which leaves the ground of self-determination because it is bound to institutional aims becomes a contribution to systemic work and not an aid to members' _social_ work.

Two areas of law reform (in both of which John Spencer was deeply engaged) should illustrate the propositions made so far. The materials used will be mainly Canadian, but the processes we want to identify are at work in other jurisdictions as well. The areas are the reform of family law (see, for example, Law Reform Commission of Canada, 1974a; 1975a, b, and c; 1976a) and criminal law (Law Reform Commission of Canada, 1974b, c, and d; 1975d and e; 1976b, c, and d). There is no doubt that in family law the very rule structure governing family relations in terms of property, maintenance and the custody of children (or even the legal status of children, such as illegitmacy) were historically outmoded and in need of reform. To the extent that the family is a political structure (see, for example, Mohr, 1978), role and power relations had indeed changed, creating stresses which had increasingly led to the de facto dissolution of families. The legal regime was an obstacle to de jure dissolution not only in terms of divorce but in terms of consequences of property divisions and support obligations tied to inappropriate moral judgments. This aspect of law reform, which can be seen as a mixture between the adaptational and instrumental mode of relationship of law reform and social change, has now been accomplished either explicitly or implicitly in most jurisdictions.

Can the claim be made that it has improved family relations? Hardly. We do not want to assume that it has contributed in a direct sense to family breakdown although some data such as increasing divorces seem to point in this direction. These data may only make officially visible what has in fact socially occurred in any case. The claim can be made, and must be acknowledged, that law reform in this area has made the dissolution of families easier. If we value families, as we generally still do, this can only be seen as a detriment if it contributes to the de facto situation. If it does not, then to make dissolution easier is certainly better than making it harder. Whatever this interaction may be, we can already see that ease of dissolution is confined to what can in fact be dissolved. Property can be divided on an equity share basis, maintenance can be settled on the basic principle that everyone is responsible for his own maintenance and adjustments are only necessary where one member has become disadvantaged in his or her economic equity through marriage. But children cannot be divided in this way and the battle for children seems to replace (and make up for) all the traditional battles. The battle for children becomes representative of the unaccomplished human-social work of the parents.

Little attention has been paid in this reform to marriage and family formation. Had this been done, the paradox of the reformed family law regime would have become visible. As we are going to argue later, the meaning of law is not exhausted by instrumental or adaptational transformations. Law must also, on its own grounds, mediate the tensions between surface and deep structure, or at least make these visible (see, for example, Smith and Weisstub, 1979). The beginning of family in marriage is still by and large in the intention of the actors a commitment to duration. Duration of human-social relations can only be achieved through social work. The lack of perception of this work as work and not as a self-propelling process makes relationships brittle as recognized in social work devoted to marriage and family counselling. This work is not accomplished by applying moral precepts and normative assumptions, a tendency which has given marriage and family counselling a bad name, but by making human social work between members possible. It is the only work that can yield social satisfaction in a context of family, work place or community at large.

Could law reform have proceeded otherwise? Given a social rather than a societal perspective, it could have explored families as legal systems in which the vitality of their members is the source of law by which they govern their everyday activities. Ignoring members' legal work means that differing assumptions of equity and justice are ignored leading to the sense of injustice (and guilt) which can finally be met only with dissolution. Dissolution in turn aids the forgetting of unaccomplished work which in aggregate leads to reduction of the social product, increasing anomie and narcissism. [13]

Dissolution, the focus of family law reform, is dissolution of the community (however deformed it may have become). Dissolution of community involves an increased dependency on institutions and the state, the replacement of the social by the societal. In this context, even our measures of social well-being become contradictory if not paradoxical. For example, the work of parenting and other work performed in the home is not counted in economic measures such as the G.N.P. Only when parenting is performed institutionally by paid workers is there an increase in the G.N.P., only when food is prepared outside the home rather than inside and so on and so forth. [14] If prostitution were legalized then even sex outside the home would contribute to the measure of economic health.

Reform of criminal law, in spite of great efforts, has not shown significant results. Resistance to change could be seen as the resistance of vested interests, class and power differences. There is no lack of pressure for social change since the common assumption is that crime has drastically increased in industrialized societies. There has been in fact an institutional response as can be measured by the growth of such agencies as police and corrections. Although both are seen as necessary in the face of perceived change they do not inspire general confidence in their contribution to social change. This is still expected from law reform as legislative reform. It is true that the criminal process increasingly turns to 'community' for legitimation as in community policing and community corrections. What 'community' means in this context remains, however, highly questionable. At best it means the involvement of community members (volunteers) in the managerial task of the agencies. They are an aid to <u>social</u> work rather than to social work.

Causes of crime, if one is not too embarrassed even to mention them any more, have run the course from individual to societal factors. Ideologically, some changes have occurred in the perception of institutional responses, as expressed in the demise of the rehabilitative ideal, the return to due process considerations, the critique of the New Criminology and the identification of psychological management as political control. This, however, has not in any way reduced the phenomenal growth of the anti-crime industry. Calls for reduction of the formal system as in de-criminalization and diversion have hardly made an impact on the size of the formal system; if anything the latter may, in fact, contribute to further expansion. Any de-criminalization that may take place is more than outweighed by an increasing sanction orientation in the public law area.

Even though the criminal law is basically constituted as enforcing the interests of society rather than those of particular members, we also recognize that much of what we term criminal behaviour is in fact comprised of members' transactions. Even (or particularly) serious crimes, such as crimes of violence, happen to a large degree in the context of familial and communal relationships. It is interesting to see that in cases of homicide, the most readily measurable and therefore best-measured offence, the data have been clear for a long time but also have been consistently ignored. In fact, cases of homicide are consistently used to strengthen institutional intervention which on the face of the majority of occurrences must remain blatantly ineffective.

THE INDIVIDUAL AND THE STATE

Family law reform has thus opted for the individual; criminal law, because of its very nature and history cannot do so and remains linked to societal operations in spite of attempts at de-institutionalization and di-version. The results are paradoxical. The family, which needs to be taken seriously, not only as a nexus of psychological satisfactions but as a social bond, has been legitimated in its atomization. Law reform in this area has responded to social change and has recognized shifts such as the changing roles of women and the changing authority structure within families. It has focussed, however, on individual rights which leads us to the present concern with children's rights and the recognition that the alternative to familial responsibility is state intervention.

Criminal law reform, on the other hand, has consistently called for a sense of community, a sense it cannot constitute as an expression of the state. At best it can control the limits of social work and its most blatant failures. As law reform commissions are eager to say, criminal law is the law of last resort.

Both law reform and instrumental/adaptational social change seen in their surface textures seem to ehance the eclipse of community rather than to redress it. Paradoxically it is the very decline of community which has given rise to this conception of law reform and social change in the first place.

Ideological differences so pronounced in our world today seem to disappear at this point. The utilitarian-liberal-democratic paradigm which ostensibly governs our political operations has historically relied on a dialectic between the community and the state and not between the individual and the state as generally expressed; community was taken for granted. [15] If not located in some form of community, the individual is powerless against the state. On the other side, in the Marxist model, Hegel already missed his own point when he proclaimed the state as the expression of the spirit of its people rather than their dialectic over-against. Marx let the matter rest there although he did express some vague hopes that the state would wither away, which has not been the case in the states which adopted his name.

What has become visibly problematic now, and has to be critically examined, is the legitimacy of the state and its political and institutional processes and the status of the individual in what is now frequently termed his narcissistic pursuits. Community in any real sense (and not as wishful thinking which attests to its necessity but not to its nature) can only emerge when the critical foundations of law as well as the social have been purified from their mutual contamination.

THE PARTICULAR AND THE GENERAL

To recapitulate this discourse in its formal elements: In the common speech proposition "law reform and social change" the conjunction "and" has been made problematic in the following way:

```
Law   Reform   AND   Social  Change

      ------------------->
^   ¦ for the purpose of        instrumental
¦   ¦ as a means to             structural-functional
¦   ¦
¦   ¦ <-------------------
¦   ¦ necessitated by           adaptational
¦   ¦ adapting to               functional-structural
¦   ¦
¦   ¦ <----------------->
¦   ¦ as an instance of         expository
¦   ¦ reflecting                structuralist
¦   ¦                           (surface structure)
¦   ¦ >-----------------<
¦   ¦ mediating                 dialectical
¦   ¦ reflexively grounding     critical
^   ¦                           (deep structure)
```

In the terms presented in this diagram, common language recognizes the instrumental purpose of law reform: there ought to be a law. It also recognizes the adaptational function: the law is out of date. It tends to pass over that law reform is in itself an instance of social change as an activity of and in society. It hides the point that "law" and "social" are dialectically related and determine and explicate each other. We acknowledge that no social group exists without a rule/law structure. It is more difficult to understand today in the absence of an ontic or metaphysical location that law/rules have their own autonomy. Law is not derivative from the social; nor is the social intelligible without a rule/law notion.

Law does stand in relation to society but also in relation to itself. The social also stands in relation to the societal (rule governed) but must have first of all a grounding of its own, a grounding which is not reduced or deduced from formal operations. The two natures which emerge in the adjective "social" also represent different sources of law of which only one, the societal, is commonly recognized. The impotence of law lies in the crisis of authority which in forgetting (if not repressing) the true authorship of the social has only access to instrumental and adaptational means. Law, to be of value and to speak of values, has to mediate between community and society, between vitality and form. Law in its purely formal elements can only speak to the eternal recurrence of the same. Law as purely a social product can only be the culmination and endorsement of power and brute force.

Community is not self evident; for its creation and maintenance it needs social work. The surplus value of this work is society, now more or less embodied in the state. In its organic form social work constitutes the familiar; yet: "the familiar, just because it is the familiar, cannot be recognized". [16] Hence, the familiar, the everyday, the life world has to be mediated by and reflexively grounded in The Concept. Law is the expression of The Concept par excellence (in science as well as society). Law cannot be derived from the natural attitude; it must remain over-against, the objective which objects, the medium of estrangement (alienation) in which the social world recognizes itself. In this sense law makes sociology and social work possible.

Finally, it has to be admitted that this discourse focussed on the movement of the general to reopen the ground of and for social work. The movement of the particular of social work in the activity of law reform and social change has to proceed in reverse.

NOTES

This text was developed from the Catriona Gibson Memorial Lecture - Law Reform and Social Change: Inquiry, Rules, Membership - delivered at Queen's University in 1975. John Spencer had commented on the initial text which was a tribute to an exceptional student of law; this version is addressed to an exceptional teacher of the social sciences and social work.
1. The Bulletin of the Australian Law Reform Commission "Reform", edited by Mr. Justice Kirby, provides the most useful references and commentaries

on developments not only in Australia but other commonwealth countries as well. The Law Reform Commission of Canada provides annual reports which survey the work done and in progress. In spite of the immense amount of work which has been produced by the different commissions there is increasing uncertainty about its value. Sir Michael Kerr, the Chairman of the English Law Commission characterized the achievement of his Commission over the past fifteen years as "a drop in the ocean". (Edward Bramley Memorial Lectue, Sheffield, as reported in The Times, 20 June 1980.)

2. The Vanier Institute of The Family (with which John Spencer had a close association) is involved in ongoing work on the "Familial Economy".

3. The images of Huxley's Brave New World and Orwell's 1984 preceded this new development by decades. Their images were, however, mostly associated with political dictatorship. Chaplin's Modern Times was much closer to the point.

4. These two forms of sociation were given prominence by Ferdinand Tonnies as early as 1887, in his Gemeinschaft und Gesellschaft; the first English-language edition did not appear until 1957 (Community and Society, Michigan State University Press, Lansing, Michigan).

5. The attempt to formulate common language expressions such as "convivial" (Illich, 1973) and "familial" (Vanier Institute) have not attained wide currency. There is a revival of "co-operative" after the rise and fall of "transactional" which has become widespread in the psychological and sociological literature but has not entered common speech.

6. These two works illustrate the argument made here. Further, more theoretical explanation may be found in Foucault (1966, 1972, 1973).

7. Erving Goffman's work such as the Presentation of Self in Everyday Life (Doubleday Anchor, New York, 1959), Interaction Ritual (Doubleday Anchor, 1967), Strategic Interaction (Basil Blackwell, Oxford, 1970) and Relations in Public (Basic Books, New York, 1971) attempts to explicate the rules of everyday behaviour. The last has the significant subtitle of Micro Studies of the Public Order and assists us in observing behaviour but its grounding is finally psychological rather than social.

8. A text was developed by Patrick Fitzgerald: This Law of Ours (Prentice-Hall, Scarborough, Ontario, 1977) to assist in the formation of a

different perception of law in the schools than has been traditionally the case, if law was touched upon at all.

9. Already in Piaget's work, but even more so in subsequent endeavours of "Ages and Stages" such as by Erikson and Kohlberg, an hierarchical ordering takes place in terms of "maturation" which clearly moves from psycho-social observation to normative judgements.

10. Professors James Porter of York University and Michael Lustigman of Bishops University have made a closely argued and imaginative attempt to interpret "The Co-operative Bond" (Paper presented to the Canadian Sociological and Anthropological Association, Montreal, June 1980).

11. Marx located alienation mainly in the ownership of the means of production i.e. private property and not in the nature of the means themselves. Capital, however, is only one form of the rationalization of production. Thus, given the same means of production and their organization, the dissolution of private ownership is followed by what is appropriately called state-capitalism.

12. In this sense Weber's work is less a critique of Marx than an augmentation.

13. The term narcissism is now over used as e.g. in C. Lasch's Culture of Narcissism (Norton, New York, 1978). The concerns expressed in the overuse are nevertheless a valid expression of social dislocation.

14. These points are further documented in the ongoing work of the Vanier Institute of the Family, Ottawa, Canada.

15. This proposition is developed at greater length in "Individual Rights and the Common Good: The Social Location of Legal Forms" (paper presented to the Western Association of Sociology and Anthropology, Lethbridge, Alberta, February 1980). This paper asserts that the development of legal forms during the past two centuries can be best understood as the bifurcation of communal forms into forms composed of the individual on the one hand (private law) and the state on the other hand (public law). The underlying philosophical strands have been utilitarianism, liberalism, and the concept of democracy derived from those positions. This development also involved the centralization and the removal from a communal context of legal institutions under the Rule of Law. The destruction of pluralism of legal forms as well as institutions is developed in the work of H. A. Arthurs (cf.

Arthurs, H. A. (1979) "Rethinking Administrative Law: A Slightly Dicey Business", Osgoode Hall Law Journal, 17.).
16. The word "familiar" is supplied by W. Kaufmann in: Hegel: Texts and Commentary (Doubleday Anchor, New York, 1966) but Hegel's das Selbstverstandliche may also be translated as the taken-for-granted.

REFERENCES

Allen, C. K. (1964) Law in the Making. Oxford: Oxford University Press.
Blum, A. and McHugh, P. (1970) "On the Failure of Positivism", in J. Douglas (ed.) Understanding Everyday Life. London: Routledge and Kegan Paul.
Donzelot, J. (1979) The Policing of Families. New York: Random House.
Durkheim, E. (1964a) The Rules of Sociological Method (trans. S. A. Solovay and J. H. Mueller). New York: Free Press.
Durkheim, E. (1964b) The Division of Labour in Society. London: Collier-Macmillan.
Ellul, J. (1964a) The Technological Society. New York: Alfred Knopf.
Ellul, J. (1964b) Propaganda. New York: Alfred Knopf.
Ellul, J. (1967) Political Illusion. New York: Alfred Knopf.
Foucault, M. (1965) Madness and Civilisation. New York: Random House.
Foucault, M. (1966) The Order of Things. London: Tavistock.
Foucault, M. (1972) The Archaeology of Knowledge. London: Tavistock.
Foucault, M. (1973) The Birth of the Clinic. London: Tavistock.
Foucault, M. (1977) Discipline and Punish. New York: Random House.
Foucault, M. (1980) Herculine Barbin (introduced by M. Foucault). New York: Random House.
Garfinkel, H. (1967) Studies in Ethnomethodology. New York: Prentice-Hall.
Garfinkel, H. (1967) "The Story of Agnes", in H. Garfinkel, op. cit.
Habermas, J. (1974) Technik und Wissenschaft als Ideologie. Frankfurt: Suhrkamp Verlag.

Illich, I. (1973) Tools for Conviviality. New York: Harper and Row.

Illich, I. (1974) Energy and Equity. New York: Harper and Row.

Laing, R. D. and Esterton, A. (1964) Sanity, Madness and the Family. London: Tavistock.

Laing, R. D. (1965) The Divided Self. Harmondsworth, Middlesex: Penguin.

Laing, R. D. (1967) The Politics of Experience. Harmondsworth: Penguin.

Law Reform Commission of Canada (1974a) The Family Court. Ottawa: Information Canada.

----- (1974b) The Principles of Sentencing Disposition. Ottawa: Information Canada.

----- (1974c) Restitution and Compensation. Ottawa: Information Canada.

----- (1975a) Family Property. Ottawa: Information Canada.

----- (1975b) Maintenance and Divorce. Ottawa: Information Canada.

----- (1975c) Divorce. Ottawa: Information Canada.

----- (1975d) Diversion. Ottawa: Information Canada.

----- (1975e) Imprisonment and Release. Ottawa: Information Canada.

----- (1976a) Report to Parliament, Family Law. Ottawa: Information Canada.

----- (1976b) Report to Parliament, Dispositions and Sentences in the Criminal Process. Ottawa: Information Canada.

----- (1976c) Mental Disorder in the Criminal Process. Ottawa: Information Canada.

----- (1976d) Our Criminal Law. Ottawa: Information Canada.

Leiss, W. (1976) The Limits to Satisfaction. Toronto: University of Toronto Press.

McHugh, P. (1970) "A Commonsense Conception of Deviance", in J. Douglas (ed.) Deviance and Respectability: The Social Construction of Moral Meanings. New York: Basic Books.

Meadows, D. H., Meadows, D. L., Randers, J. and Behrens, W. W. (1972) The Limits to Growth. New York: New American Library.

Mohr, H. (1978) "The Politics of the Family and the Family in Politics", Canadian Journal of Family Law, 1(2).

Rotstein, A. (ed.) (1976) Beyond Industrial Growth. Toronto: University of Toronto Press.

Schumacher, E. F. (1973) Small is Beautiful: Economics as if People Mattered. New York: Harper and Row.

Smith, J. C. and Weisstub, D. N. (1979) "The

Evolution of Western Legal Consciousness", International Journal of Law and Society, 2(2).

Szasz, T. (1962) The Myth of Mental Illness. London: Secker and Warburg.

Tonnies, F. (1957) Community and Society. Lansing, Michigan: Michigan State University Press.

Turkle, S. (1978) Psychoanalytic Politics. New York: Basic Books.

Part II

POLICY AND PRACTICE

(a) Obstacles to Planned Reform.

4

KNOWLEDGE AND CITY PLANNING: A CASE STUDY OF THE ROLE OF THE ENVIRONMENTAL HEALTH OFFICER

Norman Dennis

John Spencer's academic base and personal commitment were in social administration. He was therefore necessarily involved throughout his working life with the relative suitability of different arrangements for attending to human needs. In what circumstances ought social arrangements to incorporate foresight and planning? In what circumstances ought such foresight and planning to be the duty specifically of agents of the state endowed with powers of legal compulsion and financed by obligatory taxation? In what circumstances, on the contrary, ought the process to be left to trial and error? The principal argument for the supersession of a voluntaristic, laissez-faire or market system by a collectivistic system of regulation through the binding powers of the state or of some other form of associated decision-taking, is the ability of the regulating agent to base action upon knowledge. Early in his career (certainly by the time of his Bristol Social Project in the mid-1950s) John Spencer became aware that the 'knowledge' created, claimed, utilized and propagated by decision-takers was not a straightforward concept. Contributing to this awareness was his interest in sociology, especially through Parsons, Goffman and the writers on community power structures. John Spencer's interests in the 'knowledge' used by takers of decisions continue to be pursued in at least one place, the University of Newcastle upon Tyne, by 'members of what we have come to call in our more grandiose moments the North East School of political sociology' (Green, 1981, p. xi). This chapter will present first a case study of 'knowledge' and decision-taking in the city, and will then deal with the general sociological background of these interests.

THE ENVIRONMENTAL HEALTH OFFICER IN MILLFIELD

The case study is concerned with the creation of slum-clearance data in Millfield, an area of single-storey cottages in terraced streets built in the 1870s - an inner-city district of Sunderland, a ship-building town on the north-east coast of England. The specialized officer in the collection of slum-clearance data is the environmental health officer. At the time of this case study he was called the public health inspector, and will be referred to as such here. The public health inspector works in several fields. He is concerned with food hygiene, smoke control and other aspects of environmental control, and individual houses, as well as with slum clearance. In 1971, when Sunderland contained about 20,000 pre-1914 dwellings and three-quarters of them were classified as 'unfit by 1981', though not by the public health inspectors, [1] the establishment of public health inspectors was twenty-two. The actual number in employment was fifteen. The establishment of district health inspectors (the men most likely to be allocated the work of classification for slum clearance) was five, but there was one and only one employed. Repeated advertisements for a district public health inspector failed to attract a single enquiry. [2] The sheer scale of the task to be carried out, against the number of colleagues and the time available in a working week for actual inspections in the field, were important aspects of the circumstances within which a given public health officer had to operate.

For nearly a decade, among the occupiers large numbers contested the public health officer's classification of their homes. B.T. Robson's Urban Analysis: A Study of City Structure (Robson, 1969) is in fact a study of Sunderland. Robson, an academic geographer, totally uninvolved in any slum clearance issue in the town, remarks in passing that many of the houses in East Millfield had been renovated and modernized. Although the living quarters were 'rather cramped', he writes, in the late sixties energy was being spent on modernization, a reflection of the increasing number of occupiers who were buying their cottages (Robson, 1969, p. 190). Several other outside observers reported favourably on the fitness for human habitation in common sense or lay terms of Millfield's dwellings.

What was the public health officer's knowledge - what did he believe he 'knew' - about the slum clearance areas of Millfield? More immediately, can what the public health officer 'knew' be set against what was 'so'? Is there some way of concluding that one or other version of the facts about Millfield's housing was certainly correct on the point of statutory fitness for human habitation? The answer to this question must be, no, it is <u>not</u> possible to compare and contrast the public health officer's account of reality with any decisive alternative description. What we do have, instead, are data which throw a flood of light upon the public health officer's knowledge and epistemology in this case. For the streets of Millfield, over a period of several years, we may trace the <u>varying</u> assessments of the responsible public health inspectors, confirmed or unchecked elsewhere within the local authority structure. These data show the persistent and lavish production of what Marx termed 'quantitative incongruity' (Marx, 1958, p. 102).

The same basic story could be told about every street in the area, but for purposes of clarity even more than for brevity only one small area will be dealt with in this chapter, 102 cottages in Millburn Street and Ravensworth Street, Millfield, Sunderland.

Millburn Street and Ravensworth Street were part of a larger area containing 688 dwellings, only 62 of which (9 per cent) were estimated in 1965 to be fit for human habitation. [3] On the basis of this estimate by the Medical Officer of Health (the chief public health officer) and the chief planning officer, these 688 dwellings were included in the approved 1965-70 programme of slum clearance for the county borough of Sunderland. In 1969 another report was produced which incorporated a new set of findings from the public health inspectors. It was claimed that <u>detailed</u> internal inspections had been carried out by them in 1,200 dwellings, including <u>all</u> the cottages of Millburn Street and Ravensworth Street. <u>Detailed</u> information on repair, stability, dampness and maintenance had been obtained. [4]

There is a record which throws light on the character of these 'detailed internal inspections' of 'all' the cottages.

1-41 Millburn Street, 1-30 Ravensworth Street, 42-53 Millburn Street. Surveyed by

Wilson/Cope/Cook 50% sample - properties
NOT ripe for clearance - delete from
programme. 30 i 69: 63-80 Millburn St. -
generally could be included but more
detailed inspections required. 31 i 69:
63-80 Millburn St. - suggest leave out
entirely from slum clearance programme -
preliminary thoughts in excluding first
ten - i.e. 10 fit, then 4 poor, then 2 fit
- 3 no entry properties. [5]

In the record they produced of a meeting they held
at Millfield, the planners stated that the public
health officers carried out 200 of the detailed
inspections of all cottages between Monday, January
27th 1969 and Tuesday, February 4th 1969, seven
working days. [6] 'Every property inspected by a
public health inspector was inspected internally.'
[7] The 102 cottages of 2-80 Millburn Street and
2-30 Ravensworth Street were removed from the
clearance programme.
    In June 1974 the public health officers
reported that, after another new inspection by a
public health inspector and a 'technical officer',
ninety-nine of the 102 dwellings had been
classified. Thirty-nine of them were fit for human
habitation. Among the others, only twenty were so
defective that the only practical way of dealing
with them was by demolishing or closing the
properties. [8] Nevertheless, the first of the three
possibilities listed by the public health officer
was yet again slum clearance. Though it was a
decision considerably more favourable to the
occupants than any recommended by the public health
officer, under public pressure the area was approved
by the Council as one in which full improvement
grants might be awarded, i.e. it became what may be
roughly described as an area with a remaining life
of thirty-years-plus.
    Within a very short time Millburn Street and
Ravensworth Street were once more under
consideration for slum clearance. A report entitled
'The Millfield Study' came before the town's Housing
Committee in November 1975. It stated that even
where discretionary ('thirty-year-life') grants had
been awarded in the area of improvement, in certain
cases the main body of the cottage had 'remained'
unfit. [9] The residents referred this particular
passage to the District Auditor. Was the statement
correct? If so, the local authority had conducted

itself illegally in making the grants, and the councillors were liable to be surcharged for the thousands of pounds involved. Or was the statement an untruth? The District Auditor informed the residents that it was the latter. The passage was 'not a correct summation of the situation'. [10]

'The Millfield Study' stated quite clearly that no further surveys had been carried out in Millburn Street and Ravensworth Street since that reported in June 1974. For all of East Millfield and West Millfield, 'The Millfield Study' stated,

> to obtain an up-to-date indication of housing conditions ... it was decided for the purposes only of this study to carry out a random survey of the properties in the area excluding ... Millburn Street/Ravensworth Street where detailed inspections had recently been made. [11]

Otherwise, 'The Millfield Study' asserted, a 1:10 sample had been taken in most of the area; a 1:5 sample had been taken in part of the area called the Pilot Study area (which apparently for other purposes than that of taking the 1:5 sample included Millburn Street and Ravensworth Street). The map which showed the results of the public health officer's surveys gave the June 1974 classifications of the 99 dwellings surveyed in that month (but the 1:5 sample results in the rest of the Pilot Study area, and the 1:10 sample results elsewhere in Millfield). These observations were supported by the residents - they said that they had not been resurveyed.

The residents protested vehemently at the state of affairs in which the thirty-years-plus life of their homes was threatened by yet another recommendation that they be included in a slum clearance area (with Millburn Street and Ravensworth Street actually scheduled for first-phase clearance), without new evidence which indicated that the position had changed. These protests were followed by a claim by the public health officer that a sample survey in Millburn Street and Ravensworth Street had been carried out in 1975. The manner in which this claim was made is recorded in the Council officer's report of a meeting held between the residents of Millburn Street and Ravensworth Street and the Older Housing Working

Group of the Council, at which the public health officer principally concerned at this stage was present. The Council officer's report notes that it was contended at the meeting that no resurvey had taken place, and that the Chairman of the Housing Committee acceded to a request from a protester in the body of the hall that he be shown a copy of 'The Millfield Study'. (The Council officer's report does not record with what reluctance the Chairman did so, nor for how long he held out against the cries of the Millburn Streeters to supply it.) The officer's report continues the story at the point at which the protester at last receives the document:

> When handed a copy of the Millfield Study report [the protester] read out Section 4.1. on Page 3 which he alleged confirmed that the survey had been made in June 1974 but that no survey had been carried out in June 1975.
> The Chairman refuted this statement and in turn read out Sections B2 to B4 of Appendix B (Page 16) which indicated that a 1 in 5 survey had been made in properties in the Pilot Study area and which the Public Health Inspector confirmed had been carried out in June 1975. The Public Health Inspector confirmed that all the properties in Millburn Street and half of those in Ravensworth Street had been inspected in June 1974; random surveys had been carried out in June 1975 ... [he] confirmed that he had been inside most of the properties. (emphasis added)[12]

In the case of all other streets in the 1:5 and 1:10 sample surveys, the councillors had been supplied with the location of each individual house surveyed, but this was not so for Millburn Street and Ravensworth Street. Eventually, the location of the dwellings claimed to have been inspected in a 1:5 random survey in June 1975 were supplied to residents. [13] In the information supplied to the residents, sixteen of the twenty properties (80 per cent) claimed to have been surveyed were classified as unfit for human habitation. (It is not known whether or in what form councillors ever received any information on the contents of this claimed 1975 random survey of Millburn Street and Ravensworth Street.) Twelve of the thirteen properties claimed to have been surveyed in Millburn Street were classified as unfit for human habitation, including both the properties in the sample taken from the '10 fit' of 1969, and all but one of the properties which had been described as "NOT ripe for clearance" in 1969.

Early in 1976 another full survey of 2-80 Millburn Street and 2-30 Ravensworth Street was conducted by the public health officer. The findings house-by-house were not revealed. The report of the public health officer stated that 'the ratio of fit to unfit had slightly deteriorated' [emphasis added]. The proportion of unfit dwellings had been 60 per cent in 1974; 80 per cent in the questioned survey of 1975; and 67 per cent now in 1976. Thus the comparison was drawn with 1974 (a 'slight deterioration' from 60 per cent unfit to 67 per cent unfit) not, as would have been expected if it had been carried out, a comparison with the more recent survey of 1975 (a remarkable improvement from 80 per cent unfit to 67 per cent unfit). [14]

The public health officer was party, too, to purported evidence on the readiness of Millfielders to improve their own properties. 'Judging from previous experience of high level grants where they have been available', 'The Millfield Study' stated, 'it is possible to estimate that approximately 25 per cent to 30 per cent of the owner occupiers will improve voluntarily.' To achieve a high level of improvement 'a significant local authority initiative' would be required, especially among those with a 'low motivication' [sic.] to improve. [15]

In the event, the residents of these cottages and of other Millfield streets were successful in removing the threat of clearance. Millburn Street and Ravensworth Street became part of a Housing Action Area of 368 houses, all of which had been saved from among the 688 houses of the slum clearance area of 1965-70. Within a year, the local newspaper headlined the story that the response on Millfield grants was 'staggering'. [16] One hundred properties had already been improved and another ninety had obtained or were seeking grant approval. Except for very few landlords indeed, there was no question of any need for compulsion. Eventually more than 90 per cent of the properties were fully improved to the thirty-year standard.

Ian Nairn, a nationally well-known journalist on architectural and town-planning topics, came to Millfield in 1977. It was a surprise visit as far as the occupants were concerned and he seems to have depended on chance meetings with passers-by. His main informants were Council officials. Indeed the main informant may have been the public health officer who had himself been responsible for some of the surveys of the 1970s. (He had been appointed to give residents advice on grant applications.) 'Millfield', wrote Ian Nairn, 'is the happiest story I've had to report in a couple of decades ... Don't trust me - but please, please go and see for yourself'. [17] He was writing about the Millfield that had shaken itself free of the powerful definitions of the situation which emerged from the 'knowledge', mode of perception and value assumptions of its public health officers.

The next section deals with the sociological mode of analysing and interpreting these findings - the action frame of reference.

THE ACTION FRAME OF REFERENCE

John Spencer's Legacy

John Spencer was devoted to a multidisciplinary approach to the understanding and solution of problems people experience in contending with their own and others' conduct. Long before sociology in this country became a commonly-taught university subject, Spencer had incorporated it into his way of looking at the world. In 1956 the University of Edinburgh's arrangements for assisting authors who were commercially unattractive but academically worthy resulted in the printing of a re-write of a graduate thesis (in a suitably modest edition as a Social Sciences Research Centre Monograph). I remember John Spencer's enthusiasm for this book, the importance of which he recognised as soon as it appeared. It was Erving Goffman's The Presentation of Self in Everyday Life, now one of the best-known works in sociology (Goffman, 1956). Its subject matter is the deliberate construction of falsehoods by word and deed among social actors - society viewed 'dramaturgically' or, more crudely, as an enormous and elaborate series of scams. John Spencer was among the first academics in this country, not simply to know about and teach to students, but to use in his supervision of research and in his directorship of practical projects the sociology of Talcott Parsons. Immediately upon their publication in this country, Parsons' The Social System and

Family, Socialization and Interaction Process were grist for his mill (Parsons, 1952, 1956). His interests were Parsonian in his acceptance of 'social action' in Weber's sense as a usable frame of reference for the study of individuals as they interact with one another. The social action frame of reference is one specification among many of how observations may be limited, organized, related to one another, understood, interpreted and communicated. If only at the lowest level of enabling the observer to make some sense of the infinite complexity of empirical social life and assisting him in the task of reporting his findings it is useful to consider social conduct for its bearing on one or more of four simple matters, the subjects of this section: the actor, his intentions, his situation and the results of his actions.

The Actor

Who are the individuals involved in any example of interaction under study? By placing this question first, the action frame of reference shows that it is not merely a convenient standpoint from which the objective social world is viewed in a particular perspective and that a different perspective is obtained on the same world from other convenient standpoints. It involves a highly individualistic theory of social life. The only acting, choosing, creating force is the individual human being, the author (augere, to originate), the agent or actor (agere = do, drive, act). For Weber it is not possible to study a collective personality that acts – the proletariat, the state, the family, the local authority – because 'there is no such thing' (Weber, 1978, p. 14). What can be studied are sets of individuals in typically similar circumstances. Users of the social action frame of reference study individuals if and in so far as they are engaged in such creative action. In the panorama of human existence, the social action frame of reference selectively focuses upon and magnifies for purposes of examination this particular type of conduct. In practice, the 'typically differentiated human (and only human) individuals' (Weber, 1978, p. 18) studied by researchers who have adopted the action frame of reference have been actors in social roles: 'bureaucrats', 'politicians', 'school inspectors' or 'professional thieves'. Of central importance are (i) the actor's 'knowledge' of what he thinks he

83

knows about the world in which he acts, and (ii) how that 'knowledge' is created for him and for others.

The Actor's Intentions in Relation to an Issue

The second of the four matters to which the action frame of reference directs the researcher is the intention of the actor in relation to an issue. As people co-operate with those with similar or harmonious intentions and struggle against others with intentions which conflict with theirs, much of their behaviour is <u>not</u> directed by the more or less deliberate intention to bring about a certain state of affairs in the future. The Weberian or Parsonian sociologist chooses to restrict himself to those examples of social interaction which <u>are</u> characterized by conduct governed by the deliberate intentions of the participant actors.

His Situation

Thirdly, the action frame of reference is concerned with the situation of the actor. The actor's role is one such situation, and is frequently synonymous with 'occupational role'. The action frame of reference owes to both Weber and Parsons the theory that the ways in which other individuals perceive the world will always be important and can be decisive for the actor. The action frame of reference concerns itself with what is seen by 'situational' actors as honourable or disgraceful, good or evil, virtuous or vicious. It emphasizes, that is, the importance of morality as such as an independent and powerful influence: the content of a given moral code and the strengths or weakness or morality among a given set of actors. Weber and Parsons make the distinction in the actor's situation between those aspects of it which are available to him as means to the realization of his intentions, and those which are not available to him as means. Parsons adopts as the motto of both volumes of <u>The Structure of Social Action</u> Weber's statement that, for him, every thoughtful disquisition on the final elements of meaningful human conduct is ultimately tied into the two categories of the actor's intentions, and the means the actor utilizes to realize them (Parsons, 1968, p. xxix).

In detail, the means available to actors are

multitudinous. The action frame of reference directs particular attention, at a high level of generality, to two main types of means used by actors to attain their ends. One is rational voluntary exchange of surpluses between individuals. The other main type of means is the direct control of one actor by a second actor, through the first's willing submission to the force or other sanctions the second actor is able and ready to use in the event of disobedience. This is the very specialized type of social power Weber calls legitime Herrschaft and Parsons usually calls authority. Clearly, Weber's and Parsons' interest in 'voluntary exchange' versus ' imperative control' is closely bound up with issues variously formulated as capitalism versus socialism, laissez-faire versus government regulation, class membership versus party membership and individual liberty versus bureaucratic control.

Here too John Spencer, in his time, was in the vanguard. He was greatly interested in what was about to become fashionable in the United States, the exposure of 'community power structures'. Floyd Hunter's book on authority and power in Atlanta, Goergia, was published in 1953 (Hunter, 1953). It was the first of a sudden flood of monographs on power in the local community, addressing themselves to Lasswell's question 'Who gets what, when and how?' (Lasswell, 1958). Miller's study of Bristol's power structure, conducted on the Floyd Hunter model, was carried out and published during the life of John Spencer's Bristol Social Project (Miller, 1958).

In developing his ideas about the actor's conditions, the unalterable part of his situation which yield no means for the fulfilment of the actor's purposes, Parsons distinguished four systems. There is, first, the system of physical objects, the actor's material environment. There is, secondly, the system constituted by other people - the actors whose intentions become relevant to the given actor in relation to a particular issue, either as his collaborators or opponents. Sometimes Parsons uses the term 'social system' in a very wide way; but when he specializes the use of the term it is this second system of other actors he signifies. There is the system, thirdly, of ideas and rules, which have been produced by actors at some time and are still being created by actors at any given point of time, but which have become 'objectified'. They are separated from their original producers, human individuals. They exist in the form of books, films,

consititutions, languages, laws and so forth. Much
of the action of the actors in the social system
narrowly defined is governed by such elements of the
cultural system. (Although a whole generation might
totally neglect the plays of Shakespeare, Bassanio's
words, 'What damned error but some sober brow will
bless it, and approve it with a text ...?', would
still objectively exist in the sense that, on
turning to Act I, Scene I of a play called 'The
Merchant of Venice' by William Shakespeare, the
future reader would find those potentially
influential thoughts which had been penned centuries
before.) The most important part of the .cultural
system at any point of time is, of course, that
which is carried by and actively at work in the
conduct of the actors in the social system. In
Parsons' scheme, the last of the systems which form
the environment or situation of action is the
actor's own personality system. At any given time,
the individual's perceptions, his capacity for
pleasure or pain in relation to given stimuli, and
his system of moral values, are environmental data
for his central choosing 'ego'. What is so, what is
seen, what is experienced as pleasurable and what is
defined as virtuous are analytically and empirically
separate issues. Thus, what is seen may be what is
so; what is seen and so may be experienced as
pleasurable; what is pleasurable may be embraced as
morally laudable. But equally, what is seen may not
correspond to what is so and what is pleasurable may
be shunned as evil.

The Results of the Actor's Actions

The results of the actor pursuing his intended
course of action within the constraints of his
physical, social and cultural environment, including
the possibilities and limitations of his own
personal capacities, is the fourth of the major
categories that the action frame of reference
includes. Of salient interest is the emergence of
consequences not predicted or intended by either the
actor or his allies. One of the main premises of
such an interest, a premise not usually articulated,
is that future states of affairs are resistant to
efforts to predict them with any hope of certainty,
confidence or accuracy. Weber's and Parsons'
preoccupation in the realm of means derived no less
from their recognition of the problems created in
large-scale societies by a system of voluntary

exchange than from their antagonism to the implacable advance of bureaucratic institutions. But their emphasis on the idea that 'no one can know who will live in this cage' of the future (Weber, 1930, p. 182), is a reflection of their scepticism not only about the promises of laissez-faire ideologues, but also about the claims - of authoritative decision-takers that they possess the integrity, altruism, power and <u>knowledge</u> to create a situation which will conform to their model of a good society.

In order to interpret his conduct in social action terms, therefore, the next section places the Millfield public health inspector within his situation - in many respects a situation he shares with all other public health inspectors in England and Wales. At no point is the intention to generalize from the Millfield material outward to public health officers and their conduct nationally. On the contrary, the intention is to understand and interpret the conduct of the public health officer in Millfield by placing him within the concentric circles of cultural ideas and rules, and of other social actors. Where the Sunderland public health officer's conduct would appear in the distribution of the slum-clearance conduct of public health officers in this country over a given period, whether his conduct was peculiar to this place and time, are questions to be answered only by empirical investigations designed with this purpose in mind (English, Madigan and Norman, 1976).

THE ENVIRONMENTAL HEALTH OFFICER'S SITUATION

Other Actors

In these Millfield streets the occupants opposed his intention to bring about slum clearance whenever the public health officer envisaged it as an area 'ripe' for it. They hindered him in his preliminary intention of presenting to the councillors, the authoritative decision-takers, a convincing representation of the facts about unfitness. The occupants had their own intentions, their own physical situation, their own situation in terms of alters and their own ideas and values. (The intentions of the <u>occupants</u> were eventually realized - not to be cleared, and to win a secure future for themselves in the existing cottages and streets.)

Also in the public health officer's situation

were his immediate colleagues, reinforcing his
feeling of rectitude, feeding his sense of
indignation that his professional findings and
judgments should be questioned by the occupants and
their supporters. Beyond that immediate circle were
fellow-professionals inside and outside local
government service, in Sunderland and elsewhere.
Officers of his professional association were ready,
if necessary, to shed light if any shadow fell
across his claims, qua public health officer, to
special competence, '... a serious accusation
against public health inspectors who are required to
base their professional judgment on matters
prescribed by the Housing Act, 1957'.[18] Local
government planners, engineers, architects, housing
managers and lawyers were important actors in the
environment of the public health officer. The
planners, for example, were at one stage the main
propagandists for slum clearace. In publicizing the
idea that 15,250 houses in Sunderland would be
'unfit by 1981' a spokesman for the planners' Joint
Consultative Council as to Regional Planning said
the Consultative Council was 'concerned' lest
renewal - conservation by repair and improvement of
existing property - was substituted as a policy for
redevelopment - slum clearance - in the North East.
[19] Ten years later the planners were advocates of
the opposite. (The policy was then to 'rehabilitate
where possible, redevelop where absolutely
necessary'.[20])

Potentially and legally a key figure in his
situation was the local government councillor. It
was he who at a crucial juncture had to be satisfied
that what the public health officer reported was
correct. The role played by the councillor in
practice is a complex topic which shall not be dealt
with here: the Chairman of the Health Committee, the
Chairman of the Housing Committee, the Leader of the
Council, the councillor for the slum clearance ward,
and others. But the most striking thing in broad
outline, was the councillor's 'velleity' - the
feebleness of his intentions, the absence of actions
by him, in relation to the public health officer
(although as interesting if not as important, were
the exceptional councillors). The same striking
absence of control was also evinced, broadly
speaking, by the actors in central government whose
task it was to scrutinize the public health
officer's evidence on slum clearance. Attention will
now be concentrated on the public health officer's
cultural situation, the broad system of ideas and

rules within which he operated, as did other public health officers in this country.

The Cultural Situation

Data for decision-taking: Let us consider first the ideas and rules relating to the gathering of data by the public health officer in order to assist the councillor and the Minister to arrive at an authoritative decision about the future of houses of questionable fitness for human habitation.

All modern legislation on slum clearance has laid upon the councillor responsibility for verifying the representations made by the public health officer. The Housing Act of 1890 said that the local authority had to take into consideration the representations made to it, and "if satisfied of the truth thereof" had to pass the appropriate resolution. The Local Government Board had to confirm the scheme, if necessary after its own inspector had satisfied himself on the truth of the representations. [21] Behind these actors has loomed the formidable figure of the High Court judge. Not indeed for negligence in slum clearance inspections, but for negligence in inspections of other types, the courts have stepped in to protect the victim. Recent cases have been Dutton v Bognor Regis U.D.C. (1972), Sparham-Souter and Another v Town and Country Developments (Essex) Ltd. and Benfleet U.D.C. (1976), and Anns and Others v Walcroft Property Company Ltd. and Merton L.B.C. (1976). [22] There has, however, been a strong counter-tendency to attribute great significance to the views of the public health officer himself - the significant point here.[23]

The statutory rules current at the time of the controversies in Millfield in the 1960s and 1970s required the local authority to cause inspections to be carried out with a view to ascertaining whether any house in its area was unfit for human habitation. [24] The statutory rules specifically required that the medical officer of health make official representations whenever he was 'of the opinion' that any house was unfit for human habitation, or that any area should be dealt with as a clearance area. The local authority had to take these representations into account 'as soon as may be'. [25]

In addition to the statutory rules covering all

local authorities and all public health oficers, public health officers were governed by working rules and instructions applying to their own local authority only. In Sunderland the public health officer was made responsible for estimating the residual lives of dwellings, as well as classifying them as fit or unfit. [26]

Instructions to inspect properties were not always obeyed (perhaps being informally cancelled by powerful councillors). This was the case with most of the East Millfield district which became the Housing Action Area. [27]

Ideas about authority as a means: In relation to planning and the authoritative control of the production and consumption of dwellings the public health officer is of particular importance. Public health was the first and most damaging missile to be hurled at the citadel of laissez-faire. The public health officer has been outstandingly successful in gaining acceptance for his claim that he can and does place disinterested technical expertise at the service of the community. The objective and technical nature of his function is demonstrable. His public service motive is clear. When slum clearance is based upon the classification of the dwellings of an area as unfit for human habitation, expert and exact assessment appears to be especially appropriate and feasible.

In the first half of the nineteenth century the prevailing doctrine was that the sole purpose of state interference was to disestablish state interference. In this country cultural resources had been accumulating which could be readily placed at the disposal of the liberal form of economic organisation for the exploitation of the technical possibilities of the industrial revolution. In their contempt for and suspicion of the state Proudhon, the French anarchist, and Herbert Spencer, the English Bourgeois philosopher, were at one: the fecundity of the unexpected far exceeds the statesman's prudence. (Even when sanitary conditions and the housing of the poor had clearly established themselves as exceptions to the benign work of the invisible hand, the local authority was forbidden to undertake any housebuilding on its own account. It was not until the passing of the Housing, Town Planning, etc. Act, 1909, that this feature of the liberal, laissez-faire, state was discarded.)

The great name at the beginning of the sanitary movement was that of Edwin Chadwick, and his Report on the <u>Sanitary Conditions of the Labouring Poor</u> of 1824 is among other things a sustained attack upon 'the interests'. It laid the foundations for the public health officer's assurance that the position he was taking was the correct one. Disease was the result of bad sanitation. Bad sanitation was reparable by public action. The application of known principles and methods of sanitation came into conflict with private pecuniary interests, with inertia, with gross ignorance and with plain stupidity. What was required was 'the highest science and skill, and the strongest establishment' (Chadwick, 1842, pp. 338-39). Ingrained in the public health movement from its modern inception by Chadwick was a deep sense of being embattled and right.

The public health officer in Millfield and elsewhere operates within a broad cultural environment which is still rich in ideas generated by the sanitary movement's attack upon laissez-faire as a mode of social organization for providing men with the benefits of city life. Like most professional groups, the public health officer is exposed to his own profession's version of what Herbert Butterfield labelled the Whig view of history - the treatment of the past as a series of episodes in which errors from its point of view have been progressively reduced and in which history culminates in the current practice of the profession or at least its present demands for reform. Any set of public health officers will be differentially distributed along any scale of intelligence, any scale of insight and achievement, and in relation to their grasp of historical materials put before them in their courses. Without evidence on the particular point, on general grounds it might be supposed that some public health officers assimilate their profession's assumptions imperfectly and uncritically, that some lack motivation to look critically at conventional views, and that some are inattentive to the question of the precise applicability of their professional preconceptions to the time and place of their own daily work.

<u>Statutory rules</u>: The statutory rules current at the time of the Millfield controversy - rules as distinct from the cloud of other ideas connected with the task of classification of dwellings and areas - stated that, in determining whether a dwelling was unfit for human habitation regard had to be had to its condition in terms of repair,

stability, freedom from damp, natural lighting, ventilation, internal arrangement, water supply, drainage, sanitary cnvenience, facilities for the preparation and cooking of food, and facilities for the disposal of waste water. The house was deemable as unfit for human habitation if and only if it was so far defective in one or more of those conditions that it was not reasonably suitable for occupation. [28]

Was there in Millfield, then, and has there ever been a 'standard' of unfitness available to be referred to and applied by public health officers? Simon's report of 1866 mildly remarks that 'there seems to be some difference of opinion' whether serious constructional faults such as want of access of light or air, dampness, ruinous condition, or very serious constructional faults 'which in their higher degrees ought absolutely to disqualify premises from being inhabited', were under the law of that time technically a nuisance (Medical Officer to the Privy Council, 1866, p. 16). But the Housing Act, 1957, established by law a 'uniform and comprehensive' standard, according to the Milner Holland report (Ministry of Housing and Local Government, 1965, p. 235). (Even so, the Milner Holland report dismisses the number of dwellings actually classified by this standard as slums by the London local authorities (43,000 dwellings) as 'not a very enlightening statistic', because among other things, the definition of a house unfit for human habitation and incapable of being made fit at reasonable expense depends 'in large measure' on 'subjective judgments' (Ministry of Housing and Local Government, 1965, p. 21.) Ten years after the designation of this 'uniform and comprehensive standard', the Central Housing Advisory Committee of the Ministry of Housing was asked to consider the practicability of specifying objective criteria 'for the purposes of slum clearance, rectification of disrepair and other minimum tolerable standards of housing accommodation' (Ministry of Housing and Local Government, 1966, p. 1). In 1967 David Eversley's blunt opinion was that 'at present there is no uniform basis for the periodic returns of houses classifiable as slums'. The note on definitions relating to slum clearance provided by the Ministry, he wrote, did not confirm that such a standard existed, but simply sidestepped the question (Eversley, 1967, p. 14).

Part of the system of traditional ideas (coexisting with planners' contrary ideas about the

enormous dimensions and endless re-creation of the
slum problems through a combination of neglect and
rising expectations) is the persistent notion that
the problem of the slum is on the point of solution
- that the next bit will see us through. Thus,
Marx's 'admirable Dr. Hunter' (Marx, 1958, p. 658)
took the view in 1866 that unfit and overcrowded
houses were 'not numerous in proportion to the whole
country'. Therefore 'a gentleman of upright
principle and sober judgment' if he were
'practically left to himself' would be able to bring
substantial benefits 'by slow annual process well
matured' (Medical Officer to the Privy Council,
1866, pp. 61-62). 'In very few years', Simon himself
believed, with compulsory powers like those he
advocated and which were granted in the Cross Act,
together with authoritative powers to raise funds
for the construction of new dwellings, local
authorities would be able to ring within conditions
of decency and comfort 'myriads who now subsist
under conditions which it is dreadful to
contemplate' (Medical Officer to the Privy Council,
1866, pp. 16-17).

The statutory rules governing the clearance of
an area of dwellings, current at the time of the
Millfield case study, were contained in section
42(1) of the Housing Act, 1957. The clearance of an
area was crucially different from the clearance of
an individual cottage in the following respect -
where the grounds for the clearance of the area were
straightforwardly unfitness for human habitation,
there was no opportunity for either the
owner-occupier or the landlord to remove the threat
to a home by undertaking to remedy the offending
defects of condition. The local authority had to be
satisfied that the most satisfactory way of dealing
with the conditions in an area was by way of
demolition of all the buildings. That is to say that
a majority of councillors meeting in Council had to
signify by vote that they were so satisfied. On the
basis of any information in their possession
(including official representations from the
authority's own medical officer) they had to be
satisfied either (i) that the houses in the area
were unfit for human habitation, or (ii) that the
bad arrangement of the houses or streets, or the
narrowness of the streets, meant danger or injury to
the health of the inhabitants of the area. As with
the unfitness of individual houses, the unfitness of
houses to be included in clearance areas has been
revealed as an uncertain matter, both under the 1957

Act and under previous statutes. Prior to 1957 the courts had considered on several occasions the appropriate degree of unfitness. Lord Macmillan's dry summary of the results was that the decisions 'are not all in complete agreement' (Lord Macmillan and others, 1940, p. 306).

RESULTS

The results of the environmental health officer's social action in his slum clearance role must be reviewed at two levels.

On the surface is the straightforward matter of his getting his own way, of succeeding in realizing his intentions in relation to an issue, even against opposition. Intending to clear slums, did the public health officer succeed in clearing slums? As his classification of any particular house as 'unfit for human habitation' was so unstable, and the legal concept itself is so lacking in any empirical referent which possesses any degree of definiteness, the question is unanswerable. We cannot go back to all the demolished houses and endeavour to apply more rigorous standards; the evidence has disappeared for ever. This is one of the things that makes Millfield a precious and prized scientific exhibit: if in 1982 it had not existed, the possibility of its existence in 1982 could have been with perfect plausibility denied. It is certain, however, that in Sunderland the environmental health officer up to the emergence of community opposition in Millfield was extremely successful in realizing his intention to have cleared those dwellings that he defined as suitable for inclusion in a clearance area. Until the emergence of Millfield's protests, no clearance area was ever saved by occupants' objections once it had been put before the Council as suitable for inclusion in a clearance programme, much less again when it was actually represented as a clearance area under the formal provisions of the Housing Act. Suggestions that the chances were anything but negligible that occupants' opposition could win at the stage of the Public Inquiry - the 'opportunity to "fight at the proper time" (i.e. at a future public inquiry)' [29] were ill-founded. Given the proven instability of classifications purporting to relate to the fitness of the same dwelling over short periods of time, the chance of a given dwelling within a clearance area being reclassified from unfit to fit was extraordinarily

low. The average for twenty Public Inquiries in
Sunderland was claimed to be only one chance in
fifty. [30] It is known that national figures were
equally unreliable (Dennis, 1970, pp. 120-21), yet
the chance of success in defeating slum clearance
proposals on the one hand, and having a given house
in a slum clearance area reclassified on the other,
was comparably low.

Nationally the success of the public health
officer in securing the demolition of areas he
defined as clearance areas shows, as English,
Madigan and Norman demonstrate, 'a remarkable
continuity' from the introduction of modern
procedures in 1930 up to the mid-1970s (English,
Madigan and Norman, 1976, pp. 38-40).

At a deeper level, however, there was the
intention, not merely to demolish, but to replace
offending dwellings and areas with better. The
direct pursuit of this intention had been left
entirely to other actors than the environmental
health officer. But actual results in these terms
are closely implicated in his slum-clearance role,
which derives its rationale from this ultimate
objective.

Many dwellings were built to the high standards
suggested in 1961 by the Parker Morris report
(Ministry of Housing and Local Government, 1961).
Architects were employed to design local authority
housing (Malpass, 1975). Councils with the greatest
housing pressures built the most houses (Boaden,
1971; Pinch, 1978). Houses were allocated according
to need (Murie, Niner and Watson, 1976).

Nevertheless an as yet unmeasured but sizeable
segment of replacement housing has produced
important and unforeseen problems. The basic design
of some of the new dwelling complexes seems to
generate problems, especially in conjunction with
existing and probably seriously declining cultural
standards. In recent years there have been several
critical studies of high flats, notably that by
Elizabeth Gittus (Gittus, 1976; see also Sutcliffe,
1974). In Sunderland the dwellings built in the
1950s that would have been the destination of some
Millfielders (from their 'irredeemably unfit' homes,
which 'technically' could not have lasted until the
end of the 1970s), by the end of the 1970s, when
Millfield was flourishing, were having to submit to
drastic and expensive surgery to make them
habitable. £22,000 were spent on demolishing the top
two storeys of the three storeys of Railway Court to
provide (at the cost of £367,535, plus £500 a

dwelling for redecoration) thirty-two houses from the ground-floor remnant. [31] Winners of a design award, 678 flats elsewhere in Sunderland at Sulgrave, by October 1979 were completely vacated and all-but-completely vandalized, eleven years after they were built. The Council arranged to renovate them and sell them to private buyers at prices ranging downwards from £5,500. [32]

Nationally, poor construction standards resulted in remedial work requiring expenditure running into several hundred millions of pounds. [33] When the local authority at Easington inherited Peterlee's housing from the Development Corporation in 1978, it claimed that as compared with the average of £113 a house it spent on its own houses annually, £1,800 a house would have to be spent in Peterlee's new town houses. [34]

Heating systems proved a particular bug-bear. In the 1960s the new flats at Gilley Law were a destination for Millfielders who were in those years reluctantly rehoused. A much-publicized feature was the pioneering district heating scheme, inaugurated by the Chairman of the National Coal Board (Dennis, 1970, p. 234). After a history of complaints about the inefficiency and expense of the system an expenditure of £211,000 was approved in 1976-77 for repair or total replacement. [35]

Adam Smith was proud to say at the end of the eighteenth century that 'it may be true, perhaps, that the accommodation of a European prince does not always so much exceed that of an industrious and frugal peasant as the accommodation of the latter exceeds that of an African king, the absolute master of the lives and liberties of ten thousand naked savages' (Smith, 1974, p. 117). As Runciman would point out, however, the significance of these facts would depend upon whether the peasant compared himself with his own prince or the African king. An attempt to understand unexpected housing problems in terms of 'the tenant's point of view' has been made by the sociologically-minded geographer Peter Taylor at the University of Newcastle upon Tyne (Taylor, 1979). In Sunderland different areas of council housing have over all very different powers of attraction to tenants. In 1965 Carley Hill estate was attracting 1,190 requests for transfer to the estate for every 100 requests for transfer out; Fulwell was attracting 1,050 requests in for every 100 requests out. Town End Farm, at the other end of the scale, was attracting 724 requests out for every 100 requests in (Dennis, 1969, p. 12). Forty per cent of the households interviewed at Town End Farm said they would have preferred to have stayed in their previous, perhaps now demolished, dwellings (Dennis, 1969, p. 11).

Council houses failed to attract the vast majority even of Millfield's private tenants in their constantly threatened 'slum clearance' homes. A 10 per cent sample was drawn from the waiting list for Sunderland council houses in the mid-1970s. In one of Millfield's two wards 74 per cent of the private-tenant households were not on the waiting list; in the other 83 per cent were not. [36] Unmodernized properties in Millfield were commandng twice the price of otherwise similar properties in other parts of the town. [37]

By the late 1970s public complaints about housing in Sunderland were restricted almost entirely to those coming from council tenants. When Railway Court was being restructured the reported attitude of residents in the neighbouring court was 'demolish the lot'. [38] The 1950s flats which the Council had proposed as promises, but Millfielders had perceived as threats, were by the late 1970s and early 1980s the subject of furious demonstrations at the Civic Centre by their tenants: 'Shock treatment in the form of photographs depicting dilapidated coalsheds, neglected buildings and collections of black beetles aroused great interest'. [39] Extreme measures were sometimes adopted to secure rehousing from council accommodation. In an arson case in Newcastle Crown Court the defendant said that he set fire to his council flat because he was sick of it and wanted to be rehoused. [40]

Interest has switched from the 'classic slum' (Roberts, 1971) to the 'new slum'. In contrast to the 1950s, when John Spencer was working in the then notorious Southmead estate in Bristol, and when – it is scarcely an exaggeration to say – right-minded liberal citizens regarded the canard about 'coals in the bath' as a disgraceful libel on the council tenant, the 'new slum' is increasingly acknowledged to be a problem of considerable dimensions. The facts are no longer seriously disputed. The division between left-wing and right-wing views hinges on the origin of the problem and the solution. Difficult housing estates have now established theselves as a topic of considerable priority in housing management – one which is likely to engage the attention of the local authorities concerned and the Department of the Environment for some time to come (Wilson and Burbridge, 1978). Peter Taylor has studied the problem of the 'new slum' at Killingworth new town on the northern outskirts of Newcastle upon Tyne (Taylor, 1979). The building of Kirkby in the 1960s was to have been the opportunity (as Barbara Castle, the prominent Labour politician, said) to build the new Jerusalem of Blake's hymn. The subsequent story has been told, with vivid pictures, as 'new Jerusalem's self-destruction by its inhabitants'. [41] In 1978 Liverpool, to save itself the cost of demolishing them, proposed the sale of 1966-built maisonettes to any singe buyer at a price of a few pence each - the 'Piggeries' of Everton. In Manchester the social problems of Hulme have been exposed by the Hulme People's Rights Centre (Hulme People's Rights Centre, 1977). At Gilley Law, Sunderland, allegations are made of a 'reign of terror' with pensioners, in particular, as targets. [42] Similar complaints are made in other areas of the town. [43] At Edith Avenue (Sulgrave), the complex of 678 Council flats referred to above, the residents' association, in direct contrast to Millfield, was the Edith Avenue Rehousing Group, demanding that the accommodation should be speedily vacated. [44] John English has studied the problem from the point of view of housing allocation (English, 1976), as has Peter Taylor, with special reference to the power of different categories of claimant in their competition for the Council's housing stock (Taylor, 1979). Peter Taylor is a Labour councillor as well as being an academic; and Sean Damar's study of Wine Alley, the 'dreadful enclosure' of Govan, is not a right-wing treatise (Damar, 1974).

One result is the number of council dwellings which are unlettable for long periods. At the beginning of 1981 Sunderland had 412 council dwellings which had been vacant for more than a year. Manchester had 1,869. Thirty-seven local authorities had at least 100 dwellings of this sort (House of Commons, 1981, vol. 997, No. 20, col. 202). In Northern Ireland the most celebrated case of unlettable council property is Craigavon. [45]

The final result is some council property in extremis. Glyndwr demolished 140 ten-year-old houses on the Maes Hafod estate at Ruthin. [46] In 1979 Knowsley Council, according to Community Action, had 2,300 of its Kirkby flats either under contract for demolition or awaiting government approval for demolition. [47] In Newcastle upon Tyne the Noble Street flats, built in 1956, were demolished at the end of the 1970s. The East End flats at North

Shields, housing nearly 1,800 people, were built in 1958 and subject to a decision of the North Tyneside Council in 1979 to demolish them. In 1977 North Tyneside council demolished six of Longbenton's five-storey blocks of flats of about the same age. Oak Gardens and Eldon Gardens, Birkenhead, were built in 1959 (240 flats). In 1979, at the cost of £150,000 they were razed to the ground. [48] In 1981 Liverpool Corporation decided to demolish three high-rise blocks of flats on the Netherley housing estate, and 450 vandalized flats and maisonettes at Belle Vale. The Netherley dwellings had been built ten years before. The dwellings at Belle Vale had been built eight years before at the cost of £3 million; for fifty years into the future the total cost in resources for them - annual loan charges - would amount to over £20 million. [49]

CONCLUSION

The programme sketched and inaugurated in Bristol by John Spencer remains the programme of the North East school of sociology. It is a study of authority in the context of the local community. It is interested in the main claimants to the possession of accurate and relevant knowledge of the world of physical, social and cultural objects - the custodians of authority themselves. It is especially interested in the two sets of problems introduced by Goffman and received with so much enthusiasm by John Spencer. The first remained a preoccupation for Goffman, the ways in which a world is created 'dramaturgically' by those who have the power to do so. The second was developed by Harold Garfinkel (Garfinkel, 1967) and the ethnomethodologists (before too many of them became merely eccentric) as a central problem for modern society - in a world in which most knowledge for most people most of the time is not first-hand, what convinces actors that they know enough about something to act upon their 'knowledge'? What is their epistemology?

The study of an actor in his social role; of the physical, social, cultural and personality situations he typically confronts; of his personal values and knowledge and his mode of distinguishing between what is certain, dubious and erroneous; and of the results of his actions - these are the research topics of a project within the actor's frame of reference. This contrasts with all forms of structuralism. Structuralist criticism in literature demotes the author to scripteur. Structuralist anthropology strives to demonstrate that, behind the varieties of institutions and concrete social behaviour of individuals, are driving forces referable to certain decisive elementary structures. Structuralist Marxism enjoins that attention be paid not to the individual, and a fortiori not to his own consciousness of his intentions in relation to issues, but to the society's underlying material forces of production and its corresponding social productive relations. Parsons himself, of course, switched his own interest soon and drastically, from action-frame questions to structuralist-functionalist questions. For the action frame of reference the centre of interest is the individual and what he does with his given world insofar as he is actor, not acted upon; as author not amanuensis; as subject, not object; as object, not reflection; as instigator, not instrument.

It has been usual to undertake research within the action framework on criminals, the mentally ill, drug addicts, the unemployed and members of minority groups, with the intention of arriving at an interpretative understanding of their life predicaments and their conduct. But the actor in a position of responsible authority in society is as entitled to be sympathetically understood within the action frame of reference, by those over whom he exercises control, as is the inmate of a prison or a mental hospital.

From the point of view of the recipient of the products of responsible authority, in this case slum clearance and rehousing, the action frame of reference provides a mode of making sense of his interaction with the agents of such authority, of ordering and grasping otherwise extremely complicated and confusing data. It can also put in his hand a means to assess the validity of the claims to superior rationality with which those in authority constantly confront him, and to combat with greater confidence the irrationality which can issue from even the most benign, knowledgeable and efficient servant of authoritative power.

NOTES

1. The document which contained this concept of 'unfit by 1981' was produced by town planners. Joint

Consultative Committee as to Regional Planning, 'Final Report of the Working Party on a Method of Assessment of North East Housing Need', February 1965.

2. Minutes, Health Committee, June 9th 1971, Minute No. 34. Less than two years earlier, in justifying a claim that within a remarkably short period the district inspectorate could have and had examined at least 1,200 dwellings internally and in detail, the reference was to a 'team' of trained District Inspectors; see below, footnote 6, at para. 2, sub-para. 3.

3. County Borough of Sunderland, 'Second Five-Year Slum Clearance Programme 1965-1970', February 15th 1965. Approved by Council, May 19th 1965.

4. J. E. Barlow, 'Pre-1914 Housing: First Report', March 1969, para. 12, p. 2, and para. 32, p. 6. The new five-year programme was approved in April 1969.

5. PO 50 - GP CEB/PC, letter dated October 24th 1969.

6. 'Minutes of Meeting held with Millfield Residents' Association on October 6th 1969'. Sunderland C.B. Planning Department, October 9th 1969, para. 4, sub-paras. 2-6, p. 3. Sub-paras. 4 and 6 give an account of the inspections in Millburn Street and Ravensworth Street.

7. Medical Officer of Health, AM/BP, letter dated July 4th 1972.

8. Housing Committee, June 11th 1974, 'Inspection of Properties in the Ravensworth Street/ Millburn Street Area'; and 'The Millfied Study', Plan 6. 'The Millfield Study' came before the Housing Committee on November 11th 1975. It had been produced by a working group that 'comprised officers of the Council and representatives of the D.O.E.' (p. 1).

9. 'The Millfield Study', Appendix A, para. A.3.

10. District Auditor, letter dated December 8th 1975.

11. 'The Millfield Study', para. 4.1., p. 3.

12. 'Report on Meeting between the Older Housing Working Group and the Residents of Millburn Street and Ravensworth Street on February 23rd 1976'. (Older Housing Working Group, February 25th 1976.)

13. Director of Public Health, AA/CEC/PER/10, letter dated March 10th 1976.

14. Director of Public Health, 'Millfield Study

Area la', February 25th 1976. (Older Housing Working Group, February 25th 1976.)

15. 'The Millfield Study', Appendix C, paras. 1, 2.

16. Echo (Sunderland), May 3rd 1977.

17. Sunday Times, April 24th 1977.

18. K. J. Tylor, Assistant Secretary, Association of Public Health Inspectors (now the Environmental Health Officers Association), answering criticism printed in New Society. New Society, July 6th 1972.

19. Echo (Sunderland), July 29th 1966.

20. The Times, July 8th 1976.

21. Housing of the Working Classes Act, 1890, Section 4.

22. The Times, February 10th 1976 and March 5th 1976. The cases concerned negligence in inspections leading to the approval of foundations.

23. As early as Model Bye-Law No. 27 of the pre 1865 Local Government Act, the occupation of a building could be prohibited if it was 'certified' by the local inspector of nuisances to be unfit for human habitation.

24. Housing Act, 1957, section 3.-- (1).

25. Housing Act, 1957, section 157.-- (1).

26. See, for example, the Agenda of the Housing Committee of August 16th 1971, where the 'lives' of forty properties are given jointly by the Medical Officer and the Planning Officer (the two officers agreeing exactly in all forty cases).

27. The resolution to resurvey streets such as Granville Street and Westbury Street was passed by the Older Housing Working Group at its meeting of November 20th 1975, but the resolution was not complied with.

28. Housing Act, 1957, section 4.-- (1), as amended by the Housing Act, 1969.

29. 'Minutes of Meeting held with Millfield Residents' Association on October 6th 1969', Sunderland C.B. Planning Department, October 9th 1969, para. 7, sub-para. 4, p. 4.

30. "A check had been made on the last twenty Inquiries in Sunderland and only 2 per cent of the total properties had actually had their classifications changed by the Minister." Ibid., para. 6, sub-para. 3, p.4. (In fact the chance would have been much higher if it had been calculated on the basis of houses the subject of contest at Public Inquiry. The intention of the above statement, however, was to demonstrate that the public health officer's classification was objective, accurate and

replicable by other independent experts.)

31. Echo (Sunderland), September 11th 1979.

32. Echo (Sunderland), July 16th 1979; November 14th 1979.

33. The Times, January 14th 1980. This is partly a report on a number of surveys carried out throughout Britain by Building Design.

34. The Times, October 16th 1978.

35. The consultant's report was considered at the meeting of the Housing and Estates Committee in June 1975.

36. A. Reid and P.B. Kershaw, 'The Need for House Building', Sunderland M.B., 1974, Appendix F, p. 7.

37. Ibid., Appendix C, p. 4.

38. Echo (Sunderland), January 16th 1980.

39. Echo (Sunderland), September 4th 1980.

40. Ibid.

41. Observer, March 11th 1979. See also 'Hooligans, Vandalism, Theft, Make New Town Disaster Area', The Times, December 3rd 1975.

42. Echo (Sunderland), November 11th 1979.

43. 'Flats of Fear: Teenage Gangs Terrorizing Residents', Sunderland and Washington Times, July 24th 1980.

44. Echo (Sunderland), July 16th 1979. See also, 'Last Families Quit Hell of Edith Avenue', Echo (Sunderland), October 18th 1979.

45. '657 Houses Go Begging as Dream Crumbles', The Times, September 5th 1980.

46. The Guardian, March 14th 1979.

47. Community Action, No. 42, March–April 1979, p. 10.

48. Daily Telegraph, August 16th 1979 and October 1st 1979.

49. The Times, April 28th 1981. The Guardian gave the figure as £36 million. The Guardian, April 29th 1981.

REFERENCES

Boaden, N. (1971) Urban Policy Making. Cambridge: Cambridge University Press.

Chadwick, E. (1842) Report of the Poor Law Commissioners to the Secretary of State on an Inquiry into the Sanitary Condition of the Labouring Population of Great Britain. London: HMSO.

Damar, S. (1974) "Wine Alley: The Sociology of a Dreadful Enclosure", Sociological Review, 22.

Davies, J. G. (1972) The Evangelistic Bureaucrat. London: Tavistock.

Dennis, N. (1969) "Mass Housing and the Reformer's Myth", Planning Outlook, 6.

Dennis, N. (1970) People and Planning. London: Faber and Faber.

English, J. (1976) "Housing Allocation and a Deprived Scottish Estate", Urban Studies, 13.

English, J., Madigan, R. and Norman, P. (1976) Slum Clearance: The Social and Administrative Context in England and Wales. London: Croom Helm.

Eversley, D.E.C. (1967) "The Economics of Regional Planning", Report on Town and Country Planning School 1966. London: Town Planning Institute.

Garfinkel, H. (1967) Studies in Ethnomethodology. Englewood Cliffs, New Jersey: Prentice-Hall.

Gittus, E. (1976) Flats, Families and the Under-Fives. London: Routledge and Kegan Paul.

Goffman, E. (1956) The Presentation of Self in Everyday Life. Edinburgh: University of Edinburgh Research Centre for the Social Sciences.

Green, D. G. (1981) Power and Party in an English City: An Account of Single Party Rule. London: George Allen and Unwin.

House of Commons (1981) Parliamentary Debates [Hansard]. London: HMSO.

Hulme People's Rights Centre (1977) Inner City Crisis: Manchester's Hulme. Manchester: Hulme People's Rights Centre.

Hunter, F. (1953) Community Power Structure. Chapel Hill: University of North Carolina Press.

Lasswell, H. D. (1958) Politics: Who Gets What, When and How: With Postscript. New York: Meridian.

Lord Macmillan and others (1940) Local Government Law and Administration in England and Wales, Volume XII. London: Butterworth.

Malpass, P. (1975) "Professionalization and the Role of Architects in Local Authority Housing", Journal of the Institute of British Architects, 82.

Marx, K. (1958) Capital, Volume I. Moscow: Foreign Languages Publishing House.

Miller, D. C. (1958) "Industry and Community Power Structure", American Sociological Review, 23.

Medical Officer to the Privy Council (1866) Eighth Report of the Medical Officer to the Privy Council 1865. London: HMSO.

Ministry of Housing and Local Government (1961) Homes for Today and Tomorrow. London: HMSO.

Ministry of Housing and Local Government (1966) Our Older Homes. London: HMSO.

Ministry of Housing and Local Government (1965) Report of the Committee on Housing in Greater London. London: HMSO.

Murie, A., Niner, P. and Watson, C. (1976) Housing Policy and the Housing System. London: George Allen and Unwin.

Parsons, T. (1952) The Social System. London: Tavistock.

Parsons, T. and others (1956) Family, Socialization and Interaction Process. London: Tavistock.

Parsons, T. (1968) The Structure of Social Action: A Study of Social Theory with Special Reference to a Group of Recent European Writers. New York: Free Press.

Pinch, S. (1978) "Patterns of Local Authority Housing Allocation in Greater London 1966-73", Transactions of the Institute of British Geographers, 3.

Roberts, R. (1973) The Classic Slum. Harmondsworth: Penguin.

Robson, B. T. (1969) Urban Analysis: A Study of City Structure. Cambridge: Cambridge University Press.

Smith, A. (1974) An Inquiry into the Nature and Cause of the Wealth of Nations. Harmondsworth: Penguin.

Sutcliffe, A. (1974) Multi-Storey Living. London: Croom Helm.

Taylor, P. (1979) "Difficult - to - Let, Difficult - to - Live - in and Sometimes Difficult - to - Get - out - of: An Essay on the Provision of Council Housing", Environment and Planning, 11.

Weber, M. (1930) The Protestant Ethic and the Spirit of Capitalism. London: George Allen and Unwin.

Weber, M. (1978) Economy and Society: An Outline of Interpretive [sic] Sociology. London: University of California Press.

Wilson, S. and Burbridge, M. (1978) An Investigation of Difficult-to-Let Housing. London: Department of the Environment.

5

ANOMIE, RITUALISM AND INERTIA AMONG CUSTODIAL STAFF IN CANADIAN PRISONS: SOME IMPLICATIONS FOR RESEARCH AND POLICY

Terence Willett

In this chapter I want to do four things: first to pay tribute to a great teacher and friend, John Spencer to whom I am ever grateful for directing me to an enjoyable life in the academe; second to draw attention to a neglected area of penology: the analysis of a key role at the lower levels of power in prisons. Third I want to discuss the problem of inertia, or inherent resistance to change, in prison systems, the contribution to it by interest groups low in the hierarchies of rank, and the extent to which this can be explained by the theoretical concept of anomie. Finally I want to discuss some problems of relating research to penal policy that have arisen from my studies of penology in Canada, and to suggest that these may be of more general application.

It was in the nature of my tutelage under John Spencer that I should be driven always to find the gaps in sociological knowledge and to explore them despite the overt reason for their existence: possibly that they are too full of potential trouble for the gatekeepers of policy, and too peripheral or mundane to attract the latter's counterparts in the academic world ... the publishers of books. Unless they are totally unamenable to research I can see no other explanation for these areas being left virtually untouched at a time when, in the UK and in North America, nearly everything and everyone is over-researched and graduate students are still hungry for thesis topics. Certainly the perils of probing politically sensitive issues with full sociological rigour were all too evident when, as a fledgling sociologist, I observed Spencer's difficulties in wrestling with the sponsors of the Bristol Social Project while maintaining, as he did to the end, his notable integrity as a researcher.

It is an indication of Spencer's genius as a
teacher that he managed to fuse the interests that I
had developed as a professional soldier with some of
the central concerns of sociology, of which one is
the ideology or ideologies that influence the use of
coercive force by modern States. Hence I was led to
research on the main agencies of coercive control:
the military, the police, and the penal services so
that I might understand better the belief systems of
members, and the relationship of these with the
structures of power-relations that may seem to
distinguish the agencies from each other, but which
they may share collectively.

KEY ROLES AND POWER-RELATIONSHIPS: SOME THEORETICAL
CONSIDERATIONS

My experience in the British Army, including a
brief period as a junior non-commissioned officer
(NCO), and an early acquaintance with Goffman's
(1961) work on power in total institutions made me
sceptical of postulations that are common in
penological literature suggesting an hierarchical
distribution of power, albeit polarised between the
senior staff command on the one hand, and the
prisoners on the other. According to these
conceptions, key roles were identified mainly in
these higher sectors and the space between was given
scant attention. To some extent this is justified if
one thinks of key roles as those that determine
policy within the particular institutional setting;
certainly policy is determined at the highest
levels, and action is made or broken by, inter alia,
the reactions of its targets. But there is a
particular set of roles that Goffman (op. cit.) saw
to be crucial in converting policy into the action
that is felt by the targets, be they called inmates
or prisoners. To grasp this one might use the
analogy of the reflex arc, according to which
impulses or forces are said to flow through a
nervous system to "synapses", or junctions of
several conductors ("effectors") along which the
impulses travel to result in action. Similarly with
power in formal organisations, policies and their
resultant stream of directives pass through a system
of linkages between hierarchies of stations until
they reach the equivalent of a synapse, which is
usually the last point in the chain of action where
the decision is taken either to act as directed, to
modify action in some way unintended by the

originators, to "muffle" the effect so that it is lost, or to ignore it altogether.

In the agencies of social control such synapses can be found without much difficulty; Goffman (op. cit.) cited the nursing aide in the mental hospital who had considerable power over patients, and one might say the same of the correctional officer in charge of a group of prisoners, or the junior NCO in the military. All these could be seen as "synaptic roles", though only to the extent that supervision from above is too distant or trusting. Hence there is, in effect, a marked concentration of power at a very low level, so it is not surprising that, when power in the prison context has been seen from the receiving end its real agent has been the "guard", "warder" or "screw". The past tense is used deliberately here since, as we shall see below, the power of the captors has been believed by them to suffer serious erosion in favour of their captives during recent years.

It would seem that these synaptic roles have much more significance for understanding of agencies of social control than the interest of researchers in them suggests. This is especially with regard to custodial staff, upon whom I wish to focus this chapter since, by comparison with the amount of literature on prisoners, material is vary sparse indeed, even in the USA. Hence Thomas' (1972) historical study of the English Prison Officer since 1850 was quite a landmark; so was another British study by T.P. and P. Morris (1963) of the sociological dynamics of the great London prison, Pentonville, which gave considerable attention to the basic grades among staff, besides adding considerably to the older penological research that is mostly American. Both studies illustrate two points which are relevant to this paper; one is the importance of cultural differences in styles of effecting control, and especially supervision which, it would appear, is much closer by superiors in Britain than in North America. The other is the effect of research on social policy in "tender" areas, like those of social control.

In the North American tradition, control seems to have been dominated by the conception of prisoners as highly dangerous, hence the marked reliance on perimeter defences manned by armed guards, and on sequences of barriers controlled remotely, leaving the areas for prisoners to congregate relatively free from penetration by staff whose contact directly with prisoners was limited.

This contrasts with Britain where prison walls are not usually studded with armed strongpoints, and where the emphasis is on security within the walls and relatively close proximity between captors and captives. It would seem that each of these two approaches to control reflects significant differences in the degree of fear and inter-group tension that prevails in the prisons, and the receptivity of the responsible authorities to critical research into what they do.

This "sensitivity" and the "tenderness" of the area might explain to some extent the curious lack of research on the lower levels of prison staff mentioned above, but this is not enough to convince. More plausible is the traditional pre-occupation of social scientists with what they perceive to be deprived groups among which prisoners have an especially strong appeal to those whose concerns about "problems of power" are affected strongly by preconceived ideas about injustice and oppression. It is not, therefore, surprising that the captors, especially those who seem actually to apply the oppression, should be unattractive to researchers who may be justifiably apprehensive about the prospects, or indeed the consequences, of being accepted as "friendly" or "trustworthy" by groups which are stigmatised by their (the researchers') peers.[1] An instance of this is the paucity of uncommitted research on the National Front in Britain or Ku Klux Klan in North America. There is also the obvious problem that many authorities subjected to heavy and constant criticism by civil libertarians seem very defensive, or even hostile to research.

Custodial workers in particular are not helped to acquire a satisfying self-perception by the almost totally negative bias of history when it touches on their role. Guards, gaolers and warders are usually depicted as willing agents of an oppression that is often expressed by torture and execution: the more especially heinous since the majority of the victims are from their own social class. It would not seem too extreme to accuse historians of setting these people apart as a pariah group, and to have paid little or no attention to finding the many "good guys" among them who must have existed in no small number. Hence these workers have no positive tradition to bolster their self-respect among a public whose interests are often vicarious in a disturbing way (or so it seems to some of my research subjects).

There are, therefore, some gaps in research on prison communities that are sufficiently great to damage its credibility, especially to those in the neglected areas, e.g. the custodians, "guards", "prison officers" or whatever they are called. Their image of themselves and what they do is mirrored in forms that are distorted by research and by other kinds of information (e.g. the findings of official inquiries) that may often be biassed. Hence some role incumbents have great difficulty in making sense of their relationship with the wider world.

Realising these gaps in knowledge inspired a researcher in 1973 to study the effect of selection, induction training at the Canadian Correctional Staff College, and the subsequent experience in the prisons on an intake of 20 aspirants (Willett, 1974,1977). Though this had to be a pilot project owing to limited resources, we aimed to outline the origins, at least, of the prison guard's "world view". The subjects were interviewed on tape by a research assistant who went through the course in uniform as "one of them", though his identity as a researcher was known to them; he interviewed them at length twice during the course, and on a further six occasions at intervals of about six weeks in their homes after work. In six of the last interviews we made a special point of supplementing the picture by interviewing the men's wives, though in many cases the women and other members of the family were present during all the later sessions. The findings are too complex and lengthy even to summarize here, but they seem to have been successful in depicting credibly the view from the base that is so badly needed in total institutions. Also of interest was the picture that emerged of the subjects' relationships with their families, friends, neighbours and the wider public as it was perceived by the men themselves. In some respects it was similar to that of police officers, as reported in the now abundant literature, but there were special differences in that the subjects' work was in a hidden and secret world that they are not only forbidden to discuss, but are disinclined to do so anyway. Surmounting all the evidence is an impression of frustration with their inability to "change things" in a system that seemed to them beyond anyone's control, and the most appropriate concept that comes to mind to describe this is inertia: a condition in which there is an in-built resistance to change. The situation is very familiar to students (and to members) of modern bureaucracies in which the checks and balances against any input of power great enough to induce major changes are so diffuse and embedded that all that really changes are the names of things.[2]

Making sense of one's role is clearly of crucial importance for one's overall social adjustment, hence the ongoing interest of sociological theorists in what Durkheim (1951), and later Merton (1968) called "anomie". Though there are differences between the two conceptions, both involve an inability to make sense of one's place in one's social world and a feeling of irritation at the contradictions between one's essential values and those to which others appear to pay lip-service only. But, particularly relevant to penal work is the frustration set up by conflicts between the objectives (often "value-loaded") prescribed by penal policy, and those that peer pressure and local conditions make possible. The goals set by policy seem impossible to reach, so incumbents "manage" the anomie situation by utilising one of the following "modes of adaptation" proposed by Merton (op. cit.):

1. Conformity where there is willing and behavioral acceptance of both the officially prescribed goals and the officially prescribed means of attaining them. Things are taken as given, and inconsistencies are (conveniently) ignored;

2. Innovation where prescribed goals are accepted but, prescribed means are circumvented, and others less legitimate, but ostensibly more effective, are used;

3. Ritualism where the prescribed goals are not understood, or are understood but rejected, yet the prescribed means are followed by "just going through the motions";

4. Retreatism where goals and means are rejected and the actor "drops out";

5. Rebellion where goals and/or means are targets for elimination and replacement by others.

Merton's paradigm was used by the Morrises (op. cit.) to amplify the different ways in which the

Pentonville prisoners adjusted to the conditions of imprisonment (they added also a further type proposed by Sykes (1958) - "manipulation" where the actor "plays the system", using it without supporting its goals, and exploiting its weaknesses fully). Though the Morrises did not apply it to custodial staff, they emphasised the extent to which the latter were like the prisoners in their "world view" (Morris and Morris, op. cit., p. 100). Hence it seems justifiable to use the paradigm, as we did in our Canadian study, to understand the reactions of custodial staff to the pressures of the penal environment, and especially their marked discontent with it. It would, however, be naive to interpret all expressions of discontent as indicating low morale. Colvin (1977) in a more recent study of English "discipline officers" showed that "grousing" can also reflect comparisons between high standards and the status quo; yet these seem more likely to be concomitants of the conditions of incarceration, of which "censoriousness" - an excessive concern with criticising supervisors - is one of what Mathiesen (1962) called the "defences of the weak".

In an unusually perceptive study by participant observation of three Norwegian prisions, Mathiesen demonstrated the vulnerability of prisoners and staff to the confusion that stems typically from attempts to maintain regimes that are trying to mix therapeutic treatment (amorphously conceived), with custody and the administrative orderliness, to which administrators appear to be dedicated. The response of the prisoners is "censoriousness", i.e. criticism of those in power for not following in their behaviour the principles that are established as correct within the social system in question" (ibid., p. 23).

It would seem that censoriousness is a peculiarly apt concept to convey the sense of powerlessness and frustration that has become perceptible among custodial staff at the lower levels. From our interviews we have a persistent set of pleas for even the slightest positive recognition to offset the blame and abuse that is seen as "their lot". A remark from a respondent in one of our research interviews expresses the point aptly: "when things are going okay no one notices us, but when they aren't you get all the heat there is". And again, "if only someone in authority would give you a bit of appreciation and listen to what you think, this job would be easier to take". The comment is the more significant when the strain conveyed from our interviews is realised, and it seems to be due mainly to the constant mixture of rejection, abuse and "censoriousness" to which custodial staff are exposed from day to day; after all, to the prisoners they are the most salient symbols for their captive condition which, despite all the defensive contrivances of the "prisoner subculture", is one weakness.

Though the custodians may occupy synaptic roles, their power relationships with higher authority are conditioned by their sense of inferiority, vulnerability and a constant need to defend their status against erosion. Especially is this so when concessions to prisoners are thought to have been excessive, and at the expense of staff to whom it seems - from our research interviews in Canada - that the principle of "less eligibility" has been turned upside down (Willett, op. cit.).[3] This "principle" is almost sacred to prison workers though it is questionable whether they know its venerable lineage; it is reflected in Thomas's account (op. cit.), and more recently in the Report of the May Committee on conditions in the United Kingdom prison service (Committee of Inquiry into the U.K. Prison Services, 1979). It also confirms the proposition that the values expressed by staff are not dissimilar to those of most Canadian citizens not involved with prisons, whose views on penal conditions appear to be far less liberal than advocates for changing them (Singh, 1979). But in manifesting a conflict about values and objectives, this concern about "less eligibility" is at the core of the anomie that seems to be endemic in penal systems.

ANOMIE, RITUALISM AND INERTIA

I would suggest that there is much in the ideas of Merton and Mathiesen, referred to above, that explains the combination of anomie, ritualism and inertia that seems to characterise most prisons whatever is done to change things. It seems all too evident that censoriousness is a vivid expression of ritualism since, stopping short as it usually does of outright rebellion, it contributes to a passive resistance to change. And change in the highly routinised world of the prison seems to be regarded with either ambivalence or hostility. Personal security, whether among staff or prisoners, seems to depend on "knowing where you stand" in relation to

the rival interest groups, and it is all too evident
from our research work that this concern, with its
perilous consequences if there is misunderstanding,
is as great among staff as it is among inmates. In
such a situation initiative or innovation are risky,
and there is a pressure towards "protection" from
either that is manifest in the curiously limited
nature of the union movement among custodial staff.
In Canada the union seems uninterested in other than
material benefits, and activity in it is eschewed by
many staff who fear the label of "disruptive" or
"trouble-maker"; in effect its activities seem to
contribute to the status quo since their success in
narrowing differentials of pay between grades has
discouraged movement; as one respondent put it "why
take on more responsibilities when you can earn as
much or more as you are with a bit of overtime".
Hence inertia is compounded by the system itself,
though it is often disturbed by the kind of rivalry
that is generated by suspicion that those who do
move from the grooves of ritual behaviour have
unworthy motives. Indeed suspicion that others are
getting unfair advantages is another seemingly
permanent feature of prison life.

That there is rivalry between groups is
instructive since, hypothetically, this contradicts
the notion of a "system" which is, by definition,
something integrated (Perrow, C., 1961; Grainger, B.
1978). But if our research in Canada and our
interpretation of penological literature are
credible, the term "system" is a euphemism which
hides a chaos of organisational elements whose
relationship is definitely not integrated, but at
crossed purposes.

For the 1973 research we postulated, among
other models, one for a prison system whose raison
d'etre was to provide a means of containing
prisoners in humane and constructive conditions. For
this we set out four conditions: first that
objectives had to be clear and unambiguous, and that
the three key elements --- training, selection and
operations --- should be geared to the objectives
and be integrated; particularly in that the
personnel of each should be interchangeable and
interchanged often.

Our findings showed a very different situation
in which the conditions conducive to anomie and
ritualism were all too evident. The selection,
training, and operational elements were not
integrated nor, compared to the model, were they
related to any clear objectives cited in penal

policy. Selectors were untrained, unaccustomed to working together and at variance about the purpose of imprisonment, especially as between the more punitive custodians and the "degree people" e.g. clinical psychologists; moreover the processes were geared towards selecting candidates for counselling roles rather than that of a "guard", and this gave a misleading impression of the job. The training given at the Staff College was undermined intensively before and after by the custodial staff in the operational element - the prisons - who exhorted trainees to regard it as a holiday and to forget what was taught as mainly irrelevant (especially as many of the teachers were said to be "guys who couldn't hack it in a real institution").

Though "operational" personnel were on selection boards, the training element was not represented, and it seemed that it was discrete from the operational element also. Hence our view that this particular relationship between elements could not conceivably be called integration.

On returning to the operational prisons, where most trainees had been conditioned before attending the Staff College, they found a situation that was quite opposite to the co-operative model projected at the Staff College where the overall objective was said to be "rehabilitation". Asked about objectives after returning to the prisons, the men were confused, but most thought that the real aim was to punish and to deter against further criminal behaviour: crude views that did not match official policy at all.

Our research suggests that the problems inherent in the prisons, and especially the inertia which tended to neutralise efforts towards change, were due in large part to the absence of theoretical models from which trials could be run before changes were implemented generally. Hence we proposed a model prison at which selection could be carried out in a prison setting, and training could be done with "real" prisoners, but by a staff selected because they were outstanding and, through frequent "rotation" with the field, proof against charges of remoteness.

The absence of models was evident also in regard to the staff unions which were growing in size, frustration and in militancy. In Canada and, it seems, in Britain unionism has grown in the penal services in a climate of ambivalence and uncertainty as to what kind of organisation is appropriate to a type of work, style of life and occupational environment that is unique. Hence the tendency of the unions to follow industrial or civil service models concerned almost exclusively with material benefits.

A good example of inappropriate models is found in Canada where the union for federal penitentiary staff is a minor part of the Public Service Alliance of Canada whose concern is primarily with white collar civil service employees, none of whom are even approximate to prison workers. Indeed it would seem that the latter cannot fit models for office or shop floor workers, nor even the police, and need an entirely new model. As regards ambivalence towards trade unionism, British and Canadian prison staff include many from the military who are not usually well disposed to trade unionism since its ethos is seen to confuse loyalties, to erode discipline and to put individual (and usually material) needs before those of the Service; hence strikes and other forms of extreme industrial action are abjured. Because many ex-Service prison workers are apathetic, and even hostile, to their unions their anomie is amplified by a working environment that is in some respects more military than civilian, and in others subject increasingly to the tensions of the civilian work place. However, "things change" and, during the 1970s, industrial action by the lower grades of prison staff became more frequent and disruptive, e.g. the May Report cited examples of staff refusing to admit prisoners from the courts, and to distribute prisoners' mail. Other developments in staff representation contributory to anomie are the conventions which presuppose that an incumbent's loyalties and attitudes to the job change drastically when promoted across the arbitrary barriers between "line" and "staff" i.e., "management" or (in Canada) "administration". While such divisions are common in most civilian occupations, they induce unusually sensitive situations in those where crises demand total co-operation regardless of rank.

Also conducive to anomie and to inertia are such frequent occurrences as "re-organisations in name only" when role titles change but little else, and there is excessive resort to euphemisms. As one of our research subjects said "in prison nothing is what it is called: the Environmental Control Area isn't to do with the heating system - it's the hole". Solitary confinement is now "isolation" or "segregation", as if the truth is disagreeable to those imposing it - again reflecting guilt and confusion, which are also concomitants of anomie.

Hence change tends to be at a superficial level, usually in response to media or parliamentary pressure after crises. So it is generated by expedience, though the real need is for measures directed at the fundamental issues.

But all this is to beg questions and avoid sensitive core areas of penal policy i.e. those from which the anomic frustration about objectives stem. These are the areas where, to use a trite simile, "fools may rush in where angels feared to tread"; and indeed they <u>are</u> intimidating, as manifest in the reactions of knowledgeable people to the simple questions, what <u>are</u> prisons for; and what <u>should</u> they be for?

ANOMIE, INERTIA AND POLICY

It seems that one basic characteristic of penal policy has to be recognized: like defence policy (and perhaps moreso, as it is projecting power on humans continuously, and not only in emergency) it is designed, if needs be, to kill or to incapacitate. Hence it is loaded heavily with crucial values and, to paraphrase a speech by M. Rector, President of the National (US) Council on Crime and Delinquency, it shows the world "what kind of people we are" (Conference on Alternatives to Imprisonment, 1980). There is, therefore, a political aspect to all major penal policy that projects well beyond domestic boundaries. An example of this is the discussion in Canada about establishing "remote access communities" for prisoners serving sentences of 20-25 years (Parliamentary Sub-Committee on Canadian Penitentiary System, 1977). Needless to say the parallels with "gulags" were inhibitory, and a conversation with a Russian refugee with experience of penal colonies left no doubt as to the impression such a policy would have outside Canada. Moreover the existence of international organisations to watch over national penal policy and action - e.g. The Human Rights Commission of the UN, and Amnesty International - promotes very cautious approaches to change.

At domestic levels it seems obvious that sound policy in any area depends basically on competent research. And here we might add that it shoud not be inhibited by dependent constraints, e.g. by secrecy, fear of consequences, or by entrenched polcies and practices. But here again we meet head on the special difficulties of the penal domain and its sensitivity to political pressures, including, inter alia, the tendency for ministers to be committed personally and publicly to particular policy positions; e.g. The Solicitor General of Canada in 1972-76 committed himself to oppose reintroducing the death penalty in Canada, whatever the view of parliamentary colleagues or the electorate. Another instance is the substantial study by Mohr et al (1971) of optimum prison populations which argued against "big prisons" and economy of scale, but seems to have been "buried". Moreover it seemed that the Commissioner of Penitentiaries during the same period was committed personally to instituting the "living unit" concept which, in effect, divided the lower ranks of the penitentiary service into "guards", concerned only with security, and living unit officers with primarily a counselling function who would be paid more than the "guards" and not wear uniforms. In such circumstances there may have been an unwillingness to hear counter-arguments, and to suppress research findings that were "inconvenient"; this was the case with our research report of 1973 which a new regime has now disinterred and, with commendable courage, has proposed more extensive research.

A problem with research that is related directly with policy is the extent to which it is controlled by the policy-makers themselves through the process of inquiry. In Canada there are some causes for concern in that there is a noticeable increase in the use of "in house" researchers by government departments which have burgeoning research organisations. Where work is done outside, it is invariably by contract with either a researcher in a university, or a private research agency (of which there is an increasing number in North America) from which research is literally "bought". It seems that government agencies are reluctant to give grants in the light of bitter experience of failure to "produce" at all, or according to promises given, or within the terms of reference agreed originally.[4] In Britain there seems to be more flexibility and readiness to offer grants rather than contracts, but it is evident from a recent article in the Home Office Research Bulletin that the issue of independence is affecting adversely the demand for grants by university researchers (Croft, 1980). Hence the Home Office may, like its counterpart in Canada, rely increasingly on "in house" research and work contracted outside the universities. This will leave only Foundations for truly independent research. Hence, in both Canada and Britain, the latter are becoming vital to the maintenance of radical incentives and credible research.

CONCLUSION

It is perhaps fitting to end the chapter with a reminder about the close relationship between credibility and anomie. For efforts to achieve change at the deeper levels of penal organisations will get nowhere unless the reasons are credible to the incumbents of synaptic roles, and especially those at the lower levels who are as deeply suspicious of research as of directives from above. And there has been some justification for this because researchers - and especially "social scientists" - have not only neglected these people, but have been too ready to dismiss their views with such adjectives as "authoritarian" and "simplistically punitive" without giving them the consideration that their proximity to the social reality of prison life deserves. Hence there is a real need for researchers to reorientate their attitudes if their work is to be credible and not one-sided. The same is true of sponsors, especially those with vested interests in policy, whether apparent or real, since there is also profound suspicion among penal workers of inquiries, including research, that seem merely to support policies to which sponsors were known to be committed beforehand.

Hence it is evident that considerable changes of approach and of attitudes will be needed if the principle of maximum credibility is to be applied to research and to the social policy that emerges from it. With such changes and some fearless leadership there would be, at best, some hope of dissipating the fog of anomie and inertia that have obscured the prison world for so long, despite the many brave attempts to break through it.

(I am grateful for the help of Mrs. C. Hider and Professor H. Mohr in preparing this chapter.)

NOTES

1. For an interesting discussion of these issues see Devereaux (1967).

2. In this connection one is reminded of a private communication from a senior military officer about problems of effecting changes in the Pentagon. He quotes a Chief of Staff as saying that "even at the top one can give this vast system only a nudge before it's time to move on". And again, citing a military setting, "the only guys with real power to change things in this set-up are battalion commanders". Apparently the check on the power of generals by competing groups is so great that they are almost powerless in effect.

3. It was a salient principle of the English Poor Law Commission, 1834, that the lot of the pauper should always be "less eligible" than that of the worst paid honest worker (Slater, 1939, p. 319).

4. These views are difficult to document, but arise from quite extensive participation in committees set up in agencies of the Canadian federal government to administer research grants and contracts.

REFERENCES

Colvin, E. (1977) Prison Officers: A Sociological Portrait of the Uniformed Staff of an English Prison. Unpublished Ph.D. thesis, Cambridge University.

Committee of Inquiry into Prison Services in the United Kingdom (1979) Report. Cmnd 7673. London: HMSO.

Committee on the Design of Federal Maximum Security Institutions (1971) Report. Ottawa: The Solicitor General of Canada.

Croft, J. (1980) "The Universities and the Home Office", Home Office Research Bulletin, 9.

Department of the Solicitor General for Canada (1980) "Conference on Alternatives to Imprisonment", Liaison, 6.

Devereaux, G. (1967) From Anxiety to Method in the Behavioral Sciences. The Hague: Mouton.

Durkheim, E. (1951) Suicide. Glencoe, Ill.: Free Press.

Goffman, E. (1961) Asylums. Garden City: Doubleday

Anchor.

Grainger, B. (1975) "Unity in the Criminal Justice System: A Rhetorical Question", Canadian Journal of Criminology, 20,324-329.

Mathiesen, T. (1962) The Defences of the Weak. London: Tavistock.

Merton, R. K. (1968) Social Theory and Social Structure. Glencoe, Ill.: Free Press.

Morris, T. P. and Morris, P. (1963) Pentonville: A Sociological Study of an English Prison. London: Routledge and Kegan Paul.

Parliamentary Sub-Committee on the Canadian Penitentiary System (1977) Third Report. Ottawa: Queen's Printer.

Perrow, C. (1961) "The Analysis of Goals in Complex Organisations", American Sociological Review, 26, 885.

Singh, A. (1979) "The Attitudes of Canadians towards Crime and Punishment", Canadian Journal of Criminology, 21, 463-466.

Slater, (1979) The Growth of Modern England. London: Constable.

Sykes, G. (1958) The Society of Captives: A Study of a Maximum Security Prison. Princeton, N. J.: Princeton University Press.

Thomas, J. E. (1972) The English Prison Officer Since 1850. London: Routledge and Kegan Paul.

Willett, T. C. with Wale, J. (1974) Becoming a Correctional Officer in The Canadian Penitentiary Service. Unpublished Report. Ottawa: Office of The Solicitor General of Canada.

Willett, T. C. (1977) "The Fish Screw", Queen's Law Journal, Summer.

6

THE MYTH OF PREVENTING DELINQUENCY THROUGH EARLY IDENTIFICATION AND INTERVENTION

Jack Byles

INTRODUCTION

My thesis is that the notion that delinquent behaviours in children can be prevented by employing techniques based on assumptions derived from the medical model, is a chimera. The medical model assumes the existence of a "disease", which if diagnosed at its inception and treated appropriately, can be arrested or cured. The perpetuation of this myth does considerable harm to children, first, by routing children into agencies of social control for unnecessary treatment of misdiagnosed conditions, and second, by impeding efforts to find truly effective approaches for dealing with the very real problem of juvenile delinquency. This position is based on accumulated evidence from the research in the field of delinquency over the past twenty years and is supported by a study conducted by the author which is reported below. Two major conclusions can be drawn from the abundant research conducted on delinquency to date. These are: (1) our present knowledge of the causes of delinquency is not sufficient to permit making an early accurate diagnosis of the condition; and (2) even if diagnosis were possible, our present technology in behavioural change is not able to deal effectively with this condition. My purpose here, then, is to acquaint the reader with the evidence for these conclusions, and to suggest some of the implications of this position for social policy as it relates to the problem of juvenile delinquency.

The belief that delinquency can be prevented through "early intervention" is still held tenaciously, not only by the general public but by most professionals in the field -- despite the absence of any supporting evidence and, in fact, mounting empirical evidence to the contrary. While the old adage about "an ounce of prevention" being worth a "pound of cure" might be the basis for much of this belief, the conviction more probably stems from two relatively recent and interrelated developments. First has been the impressive success of medical science in controlling the communicable diseases such as smallpox, diphtheria, infantile paralysis, etc. by means of the medical model. Second is the "medicalization" of delinquency; that is, the adoption of the view that the delinquent is "sick" and in need of "treatment". The success of the medical model not only gave its practitioners great power and prestige but also instilled the hope that other problems of mankind — including social problems such as delinquency — might also eventually be solved by recourse to this model. Consequently, professionals in other disciplines such as social work and psychology adopted this model as their own. Thus, starting with the assumptions of the medical model, the belief evolved that the way to bring delinquency under control was to "screen" the would-be delinquents at the early stages in the development of their problematic behaviour and "inoculate" them with the appropriate treatment. Pioneers in this endeavour to predict delinquency and develop a screening instrument were Sheldon and Eleanor Glueck (1950, 1972) whose work has dominated research in the field for the past several decades. The "medicalization" of delinquency was in part, an effort to humanize some of the more callous practices in dealing with delinquent children. Labelling the child as "sick" rather than "bad" provided political leverage for keeping children out of adult jails and contact with adult criminals. Together, the adoption of the medical model by non-medical disciplines and the medicalization of the problem gave credence and support to the view that delinquency could some day be ameliorated through "early intervention". This is both a powerful and a pervasive belief, which has influenced policy makers in both the United States and Canada. In the United States, it is reflected in the billions of dollars allocated by the federal government over the past two decades to programmes identified as "delinquency prevention". In Canada, its influence is evident in the Young Persons in Conflict with the Law legislation proposed by the Solicitor General in 1975 to replace the existing Juvenile Delinquents Act. That legislation expresses the essence of the preventive belief in its statement that:

> This philosophy of prevention is contingent in part, upon the early identification of children who are experiencing conflict in their homes, schools, and other areas and the application of appropriate services before the child is brought within the juvenile justice process (Solicitor General's Committee, 1975, p. 4).

The basic tenet of prevention then, is that by the "early identification" of children experiencing difficulty at home, school, or in the community, plus the "application of appropriate services", the disturbing behaviours (symptoms) will either be eliminated or so reduced that recourse to the justice system will be unnecessary. The translation of this tenet into practice is, however, confounded by many problems.

DIFFICULTIES INHERENT IN PREVENTION PROGRAMMES

The first and rather awkward problem is that there is no consensus as to what, specifically, should be prevented. This arises from the fact that there is as yet no generally agreed upon definition of the term "delinquent". Thus, programmes intended to prevent delinquency have many differing goals and objectives, depending upon the chosen definition of delinquent. The term is used in two quite different ways. It is used frequently to refer to the behaviours of children -- that is, behaviours which violate the norms or legal codes of society. But more often, it is used to refer to the legal status of a child -- that is, a child who has been found guilty in juvenile court of committing an offence is called a delinquent. Thus, some programmes are intended to modify behaviours only, whilst others are intended to affect the legal status of children. While most children at some time commit offences or exhibit behaviours which might be considered delinquent (inasmuch as they violate social norms), only a very small percentage of children ever appear in juvenile court.

Although there are many theories about the causes of delinquency, none have as yet been verified by empirical research. Without a theory of causation, the application of appropriate services is largely a matter of chance. Of the thousands of delinquency prevention programmes conducted in the United States during the last two decades, only a few have been predicated on any causal theory of delinquency. The multi-million dollar "Mobilization for Youth" project was based on "opportunity theory" as formulated by Cloward and Ohlin (1960); unfortunately, all research efforts to validate that theory during the course of the project were unsuccessful. During the planning stages of their Seattle project, Berleman, Seaburg and Steinburn (1972) undertook the testing of a set of hypotheses derived from a number of prominent theories of delinquency. The only theory to receive any empirical support was Sutherland's (1947) theory of "differential association"; that is, boys who admitted associating with known delinquents were more likely to commit delinquent acts themselves than were boys who did not associate with known delinquents. But these authors found no support for the hypotheses derived from any of the other theories tested which included "anomie" (Merton, 1957), community disorganization theory (Glueck, 1952; Nye, 1958) and self-concept theory (Scarpitti, 1960). They report that their results put them in a quandary:

> the inability to confirm a range of theoretical positions meant that the selection and service procedures for the test phase could not be enlightened by specific and verifiable concepts that would help explain the well-springs of delinquent behavior.

As if it were not already difficult enough to think about preventing an undefined condition having an unknown aetiology, another problem is the selection of the target group for the prevention programme. That is, who should be the recipients of the service? Primary prevention (Caplan, 1964) would require that the programme be directed at all the children in a community. But not only would the cost of such a programme be prohibitive: it would also be strategically impossible. Thus, most programmes of prevention are directed at children who have been selected by some criteria as already exhibiting symptoms of the condition perceived as delinquency; that is, "secondary" prevention. Many programmes have drawn their subjects from children referred to juvenile court; others have selected their subjects from children reported as manifesting behavioural problems in school; and still others have selected their subjects from referrals made by a variety of community agencies. No two programmes have been directed at target groups drawn from comparable populations using the same selection criteria. This both reflects the lack of consensus among people in the field as to what constitutes delinquency, and makes comparison of results across programmes very difficult.

Despite these and other problems, a great deal of effort and money has been spent on delinquency prevention programmes over the past two decades, particularly in the United States where, during the fiscal year 1970, the federal government alone spent 11.5 billion dollars in juvenile delinquency and related youth development programmes (U.S. Interdepartmental Council to Co-ordinate All Federal Juvenile Delinquency Programs, 1972). In their review of identified "delinquency prevention" programmes in operation between the years 1965 and 1974 in the United States, Wright and Dixon (1977) examined reports on approximately 6,600 programmes. In only 96 of these did the reports contain any form of empirical data about the project efforts, and of these, only nine:

> used random assignment of subjects,
> inferential analyses of their data, and
> outcome measures of delinquent behavior,
> and at least six months follow-up after
> the subjects had left the project.

Wright and Dixon conclude from their review that "... no delinquency prevention strategies can be definitively recommended". Lundman et al. (1976) arrive at a similar conclusion from their assessment of delinquency prevention projects reported in the professional literature. Out of nearly 1,000 citations they found "only 25 that contained information on the nature and results of the prevention venture". But after examining the research methods employed in the evaluation of these projects, they conclude:

> In the small number of projects where the
> design and measurement techniques permit
> reliable assessment of results, it is
> clear that there were no differences
> between the experimental and control

groups. As a consequence, <u>it</u> <u>appears</u> <u>unlikely</u> <u>that</u> <u>any</u> <u>of</u> <u>these</u> <u>projects</u> <u>prevented</u> <u>delinquent</u> <u>behavior</u>.

Indeed, those programmes which have been most carefully managed and subjected to the most rigorous evaluations have all been demonstrated to have produced no significant effects. These include the exemplary Cambridge-Somerville project (Powers and Witmer, 1951), the Seattle Atlantic Street Center Experiment (Berleman, et al., 1972) and the Juvenile Services Project in Hamilton, Ontario (Byles, 1979). No programme has as yet been shown to be successful in consistently reducing the anti-social behaviours of juveniles or preventing their entry into the formal juvenile justice system. A technology for changing children's anti-social behaviour to pro-social behaviour has yet to be developed.

The study reported below shows the effects of efforts to provide "early intervention" in one Canadian city, for children whose behaviour brought them into repeated contact with the police.

THE USE OF COMMUNITY RESOURCES IN THE PREVENTION OF JUVENILE DELINQUENCY

This study differs from those mentioned above, in that it is not an evaluation of a specific programme to prevent delinquency. [1] Instead, it assesses the overall impact of a wide range of community services on the anti-social behaviours of children. Canada differs appreciably from the United States in many ways, one of which is the relative lack of governmental concern with the problem of juvenile delinquency. While there have been a number of programmes intended to improve the effectiveness of treatment and rehabilitation of adjudicated delinquents, there have been very few programmes aimed specifically at the prevention of delinquency. To the extent that it exists, "prevention" is attempted mainly through efforts of the police to prevent children from going to juvenile court; the extent varies according to the philosophy and the structure of the municipal police department. In Hamilton, Ontario (population 309,000), as in most Canadian cities, this informal "diversion" is the rule rather than the exception. That is, the police are reluctant to lay charges against children which would require them to appear in court, unless they have committed serious offences or they have committed a number of offences and seem to be developing a pattern of delinquent behaviour. For first and minor offences police prefer to use other alternatives at their disposal, such as giving the child a "police caution and release". Or if the child appears to be having problems in the family or community, the police may refer him to a community health or social agency for help. As much as possible, the police use the court only as a last resort. Thus, in Hamilton as elswhere, children showing the beginning signs of anti-social behaviour are usually referred to those agencies in the community that can provide specialized help with child and family problems.

The objectives of this study were:

1. To measure the nature, extent and intensity of services provided by community agencies to pre-delinquent children and their families;

2. To determine whether the impact of these services significantly reduced the tendencies of these children toward continued anti-social behaviour.

For this study "pre-delinquent children" are those who have come to police attention two or more times because of misdemeanours, but who have not been charged to appear in juvenile court. Thus, at the time of entry into the study, none of these children had appeared in court, but all had two or more police occurrence reports filed on them for alleged offences. The sample consisted of 305 children (264 boys and 41 girls) under the age of 14. (Mean age at entry of boys = 11.5 years, mean age of girls = 12.5 years.) Most (63%) came from Protestant families, 33% came from Roman Catholic families and the religious affiliation of the other 4% was unknown. Two-thirds of the children came from intact, two-parent families and the other one-third from single-parent families, most of whom were "mother-led". In nearly half of these families (45%) one or more juvenile siblings of the target child also had police occurrence reports on file. Most (74%) of these children came to police attention for committing offences against property (mainly "theft under $50.00" or "wilful destruction") but 13% had committed offences against persons (assault) and 12% had committed "status" offences (that is, an act that would not be considered an offence if committed

The Myth of Preventing Delinquency

by an adult).

Two main kinds of data were collected. First, information on the nature and extent of all services provided to the child and/or any member of his family by all of the health and social agencies in the community were collected for a two-year period. Second, data were obtained on all offences known to the police for a two-year period following the child's entry into the study, plus court charges and dispositions. (Figure 1.) Two measures were devised from these data; first, an "intensity scale" for measuring the intensity of all services provided to a child and/or his family by all community agencies, and second, a "seriousness scale" (based on the work of Sellin and Wolfgang, 1964) to measure the seriousness of the offences committed by juveniles.

FIGURE 1: Data collection periods monitoring agency services and delinquent behaviours of a sample family

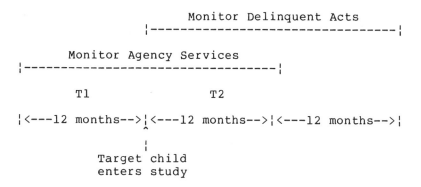

The agencies and services included in the study were all those that provide social-psychological help to children and families in the community. These included two Children's Aid Societies, two out-patient mental health clinics, three hospital departments of psychiatry, two residential treatment centres, the psychological and counselling services of two school systems, and two Family Service Associations. Not included were private physicians, the clergy, or other individuals that might be used as sources of help. The Hamilton Region is well provided with a wide range of services available to help its citizens with personal and family problems, and compares favourably with other Canadian cities

Table 1: Multiple Use of Services (by Category) by
Families and Target Children during Two-Year Period

	Number of Families	Number of Target Children
Not served by any agency	121 (39.7%)	150 (49.2%)
Served by one category only:		
Schools (PAS)[a]	40	31
Health [b]	21	22
CAS/CCAS	15	22
Private [c]	7	13
Sub-Total	83 (27.2%)	88 (28.8%)
Served by (any) two categories	64 (21.0%)	45 (14.8%)
Served by (any) three categories	25 (8.2%)	17 (5.6%)
Served by all four categories	12 (3.9%)	5 (1.6%)
Totals:	305 (100.0%)	305 (100.0%)

a = Pupil Adjustment Services of two Boards of
    Education
b = Inpatient and Outpatient units of hospital
    departments of psychiatry; mental health
    clinics and residential treatment centres
c = Family Service Associations and group homes

of similar size.

It was found that one or more members in 184 (60%) of the 305 families in this study received service from one or more of the community agencies during the two year interval for which services were monitored (the year prior to and the year following the target child's entry into the study). Of the target children in these families, 51% had received service of some kind from one or more of these agencies during the same period. Of these (155) target children who received service during this time period, 42% were judged to have received only "low intensity" service (no more than two interviews), 28% were judged to have received "high intensity" service (at least six months of continuing out-patient treatment, or two weeks of in-patient treatment), and the other 30% were judged to have received "medium intensity" treatment -- anything more than "low" but less than "high intensity". Briefly, the findings on the patterns of utilization of these community services by the 305 families and their target children, showed that:

1) about 40% of the families and 50% of the target children were not seen by any of these community agencies during this two year interval -- a period when at least one child (the target) in the family was in repeated trouble with the police;

2) agencies in the "mental health" sector provided the largest portion of "treatment" services to both families and children;

3) the amount of service given to most families and children was relatively modest;

4) there was no evidence of a significant overlap or duplication of services given to these children and/or families. (Table 1)

It was thought that services (such as marital counselling) given to family members other than the target child might influence the behaviour of the target child. Therefore the relationships between the continued delinquent behaviours of the target children and the use of community services were analyzed separately, by services given to any or all family members and services given to the target children. But the results revealed no significant differences in recidivism rates of the children,

Table 2: Recidivism Rates for "Served" and "Unserved" Target
Children during T1, by Number of prior police occurrences

| | | Some Service | | | No Service | |
Number of prior "Occurrences"	N	Number of Recidivists	Rate of Recidivism	N	Number of Recidivists	Rate of Recidivism
One [a]	63	36	57.1	145	67	46.2
Two	33	24	72.7	34	23	67.6
Three or more	17	16	94.1	13	13	100.0
Totals [b]	113	76	67.3	192	103	53.6

a
Chi-square = 2.09; 1 df, ns.
b
Chi-square = 5.43; 1 df, p.<.05.

depending on whether the rates were calculated from all services given to the family, or from only services that included the target child. Thus, the following results are based on services given to the target children in the sample. Three hypotheses were generated from the assumptions usually made about the benefits of early intervention:

1) Children who receive services from community agencies will exhibit significantly less anti- social behaviour than children who do not receive service.

2) The earlier that services are initiated in the development of a pattern of anti-social behaviour, the greater the probability that such behaviour will be reduced.

3) The greater the intensity of service given, the more likely the anti-social behaviour will be reduced.

During the year prior to their entry into the study (T1) 113 target children (37%) received service from one or more of these community agencies. During the following two years, 76 of these children had one or more police occurrence reports filed on them, a recidivism rate of 67.3% (Table 2). However, of the 192 children who were not served by any of these services during T1 only 103 had police occurrences filed on them during the follow-up period, a recidivism rate of 53.6%. During the year following their entry into the study (T2) another 41 children received some service from one or more agencies. Thus, for the two-year period during which services were monitored, 154 children received services to some degree, and 151 received no service from any of these agencies. Of those who received service, 106 had further police occurrence reports filed on them during the follow-up period (69%) compared with only 73% of those children (48%) who had received no service (chi-squared = 13.2, p<.001). These results are significant and in the opposite direction to the first hypothesis; therefore the first hypothesis must be rejected.

For 208 target children, the offence that brought them into the study was only their second; 67 children had had two police occurrence reports filed on them prior to the offence bringing them into the study, and the remaining 30 children had

Table 3: Severity of Offences Committed during Follow-up Period (Total Seriousness Scores) by Juveniles, and the Extent of Service Given by Community Agencies

Intensity of Service [b]	Total Seriousness Scores				
	0 [a]	1-3	4-9	10+	
No service	78 (62.9)	43 (60.5)	19 (31.7)	11 (22.9)	
Low service (1 - 2)	23 (18.3)	11 (15.5)	20 (33.3)	10 (20.8)	
Medium service (3 - 4)	16 (12.7)	9 (12.7)	14 (23.3)	8 (16.7)	
High service (5+)	9 (7.1)	8 (11.3)	7 (11.7)	19 (39.6)	
Totals	126 (100.0)	71 (100.0)	60 (100.0)	48 (100.0)	

a
A total seriousness score of zero identifies non-recidivists.
b
Values of intensity of all services received during T1 and T2 (chi-square = 52.68, df = 9, p < .001)

134

Table 4: Frequency and Seriousness of Offences Committed by the "Most Delinquent" Recidivists [a] and the Intensity of Service Given Families.

Intensity of Service to Family	N	Number of Occurrences		Total Seriousness Scores	
		Mean	s.d.	Mean	s.d.
None	6	9.8	4.07	25.0	10.45
Low (1-2)	6	10.8	5.80	29.5	9.45
Medium (3-4)	6	12.2	3.87	27.0	4.56
High (5-9)	10	11.6	5.44	29.2	16.19
Very High(10+)	4	9.0	1.83	26.5	6.45
Total	32				

[a] "most delinquent" = subjects with a total seriousness score exceeding 15 for two-year follow-up period (range = 16 - 61; mean = 27.7)

had three or more previous occurrence reports filed
on them. Those who had had only one previous
occurrence report filed were assumed to be at an
earlier stage of their delinquency development than
were those who had had two or more previous
occurrence reports. Among the 208 that had had only
one previous occurrence report filed, the recidivism
rate for those who had received service from
community agencies was 57.1%, while the recidivism
rate for those who had received no service was 46.2%
(Table 2). While this difference is not significant
at the .05 level, it is still in the opposite
direction to the hypothesis; thus the second
hypothesis is not supported by these results.

Finally, to test the third hypothesis, the
recidivism rates were examined according to the
intensity of service given to the target children
during the year prior to entry into the study. As
already noted, the recidivism rate for those who had
received no service was 53.6%; for the 76 children
who had received "moderate intensity" service the
rate of recidivism was 63.2%, and for those who had
received "high intensity" service the recidivism
rate was 75.7%. Thus the rate of recidivism
increases with the intensity of service, and the
third hypothesis must be rejected. The association
between the intensity of service given and the
children's anti-social behaviour during the
follow-up period was examined further, by comparing
the level of service intensity with the "total
seriousness scores" of all sbjects, and by comparing
the frequency and severity of delinquent behaviours
of the 32 "most severely delinquent" children with
the intensity of the service they received. The
first analysis (Table 3) shows that the severity of
delinquent offences increases positively and
significantly with the intensity of service
received. The second analysis (Table 4) shows that
among the group of most seriously delinquent
children, those who received intensive service were
no less delinquent -- either in terms of the number
or the severity of offences -- than those who had
received no service at all.

The results indicated that the over-all impact
of the services provided by these fifteen community
agencies -- whether the service was given to the
target child and/or to other members of the family
-- had no salutary effect on the anti-social
behaviours of the target children during the
two-year follow-up period. None of the three
hypotheses were supported. Indeed, the findings

relating to all three hypotheses were in the opposite direction, suggesting that these early interventions may even increase the propensity toward anti-social behaviour on the part of some children.

However, these results should come as no surprise. None of these community agencies were established to deal with the problem of juvenile delinquency; rather, they exist to help children and families with a wide range of social and emotional problems. And as already noted, even those programmes that have been designed specifically to reduce delinquent behaviour in children have failed to do so. Thus, these agencies cannot be faulted for not accomplishing a task for which they were never intended -- a task for which no efficacious method has yet been devised.

IMPLICATIONS FOR POLICY

The results of this study are congruent with the conclusion arrived at by Edwin Schur (1973) when he said:

> ...much of the disenchantment with current delinquency policy arises from the simple fact that it doesn't work (p. 117).

From a thorough review of delinquency prevention and treatment programmes which led him to this conclusion, Schur went on to advocate his policy of "radical non-intervention", about which he states:

> ... thus, the basic injunction for public policy becomes: leave the kids alone wherever possible. This effort partly involves mechanisms to divert children away from the courts but it goes further to include opposing various kinds of intervention by diverse social control and socializing agencies (p. 155).

Although radical non-intervention is a logical policy derived from the present state of knowledge about delinquency prevention and control, unfortunately it is not practicable. And the fact that it is not capable of being implemented, at least at present, highlights the weakness of empirical evidence and rational argument alone as forces for effecting change in policy when the indications from these run contrary to vested interests and popular belief. Radical non-intervention is viewed as heretical by the majority of professionals working in the juvenile justice system and its associated agencies whose livelihood depends upon treating (controlling) delinquent children. But more important, it is antithetical to the growing conservatism in North America, with its strident cries for more stringent "law and order", where public sentiment is unlikely to tolerate a policy that advocates "leaving the kids alone wherever possible".

At the very least, however, there should be a moratorium on any and all programmes intended to prevent juvenile delinquency that are based on the medical model; that is, programmes based on the underlying assumption that the cause of delinquency is something inherent within the child that can be "adjusted" through a process of individual diagnosis and treatment. This assumption underlies virtually all of the treatment given to the children in the study reported; the most commonly used modalities were individual case work, counselling, psychotherapy, and family therapy, in which the primary intent was to change some behavioural pattern of the individual child. This approach to the problem of juvenile delinquency has been found to be futile. Not only is it unlikely to reduce children's anti-social behaviour, but it may even have long-lasting negative effects. In a follow-up study thirty years later of children who had been involved in the previously mentioned Cambridge-Somerville Project, McCord (1978) found that as adults, those who had been in the treatment groups were significantly worse off than those who had been in the control group, on a number of dimensions -- including health, employment and criminal convictions.

A moratorium on all prevention programmes based on the medical model would include cessation of efforts to develop "screening" instruments for the early identification of delinquency. This would reduce the harm done to children in two ways; first, these instruments inevitably produce excessive numbers of false positives (children predicted to become delinquent but who would not) which can result in steering these children unnecessarily into useless prevention programmes; and second, even for those who might be correctly identified, there is no reliable and effective treatment. As Jackson Toby remarked some years ago (1968):

... whereas medical practice aims at precise diagnosis and specific treatment, early identification and intensive treatment of delinquency usually address themselves to an unknown problem with an unproven technique.

Calling for an end to the screening and routing of children into delinquency prevention programmes, however, does not imply that individual, group and family therapies are of little value for all children. On the contrary, countless numbers of children suffer from a variety of emotional, psychological and social problems which can be ameliorated by these modalities. But in a comparative study of delinquent and neurotic children, Bennett (1959) observed that:

... many chronic delinquent children do not fall into the class of case suitable for child guidance or treatment or even for individual psychotherapy (p. 225)

The "chronic delinquents" here are the same as the children with "conduct disorders" identified by Rutter (1965). These children generally:

... come from families where there is discord and quarrelling; where affection is lacking; where discipline is inconsistent, ineffective and either extremely severe or lax; where the family has broken up through divorce or separation; or where the children have had periods of being placed 'in care' at times of family crisis (Rutter, 1975).

A large (but unknown) proportion of children who become chronic official (known to the police) delinquents are of this type; they have been the victims, often since birth, of multiple problems within their families. There is widespread agreement (Jenkins, 1960; Bennett, 1961; Robins, 1966; Rutter, 1975) that the prognosis for these children is poor, regardless of treatment. Neurotic children, on the other hand, generally respond well to treatment. But then, relatively few neurotic children become delinquent. Even though this knowledge has been available for some time now, most children manifesting behavioural disorders continue to be referred to mental health clinics and social agencies in the belief that the disorders can be diagnosed and treated by conventional means. The fact that official statistics show no abatement in the numbers of children coming to the attention of police and courts is hardly surprising.

If the problem of juvenile delinquency is ever to be ameliorated, the focus of attention must shift from the individual child to the social conditions that produce the child. The two institutions having the greatest influence on the socialization of children, of course, are the family and the school. Therefore, one logical approach to the prevention of delinquency is through massive efforts to improve the quality of life in these two social systems. And as already indicated, there is now some considerable knowledge available to give some direction to these efforts.

First, there is voluminous evidence that the children most severely at risk of becoming serious and chronic delinquents (and adult criminals) are those born into chaotic families with parents who are either unwilling or unable to provide adequate and consistent care. Unfortunately, efforts aimed at improving the functioning of these families have so far been largely unsuccessful. "Family life education" and "parent effectiveness training" programmes seldom reach these families; they tend to attract the highly motivated families that would do well anyway. But whether chaotic familes would benefit from such programmes -- even if required by a court -- is doubtful. Here the only recourse may be through schools, by means of family life education (including sex education and the teaching of parenting skills) beginning in early elementary and continuing through secondary school, for all pupils. This might interrupt the recycling of some family problems from one generation to the next. The fundamental issue, however, is a moral dilemma, and is not likely to be resolved until as a society, we give first priority to the right of children to be properly cared for, instead of to the right of parents to possess children. As the issue is defined by Slater and Cowie (1968) following a study of delinquent girls:

> The time is obviously coming when the citizen's right to unlimited parenthood will have to be restricted. In the same way, for the health of the succeeding generation, the right of parents to look

after their child will have to yield in priority to the child's right to be properly looked after.

Until this dilemma is resolved, all available resources should be mobilized and directed toward those problems known to be closely associated with the development of conduct and other disorders in children. These include problems such as family disintegration (separation, divorce), intrafamilial violence (child abuse, spouse abuse), alcoholism and unrestricted birth (unwanted children, teenage mothers, large families), as well as larger social problems that impinge on the family, such as poverty and unemployment.

On most of these problems, we have thus far taken only tentative and hesitant steps. Within the last ten years for example, "child abuse" has become a highly emotional issue, resulting in numerous programmes, while spouse abuse ("battered wives"), a much more prevalent condition, has only very recently been recognized as a problem. Yet there is increasing evidence (Lewis et al., 1979) that children raised in violent familes, where they have either experienced physical abuse or have witnessed their parents abusing each other, are much more likely to become violent delinquents. So the redirection of our energies to the amelioration of some of these family conditions known to generate behavioural disorders in children might eventually contribute to some reduction in children's anti-social behaviour.

The other target of concern is the school system. Much of the work in "screening" for prevention programmes has taken place in the school (Levine and Graziano, 1972) because of its ready accessibility and universal coverage of young children. Indeed, schools have been happy to cooperate with "prevention" programmes and are not at all hesitant to identify children thought to be in need of treatment. The possibility that part of the child's problem might be inherent in the school system itself, has seldom been considered.

However, a recent study of the social organization of secondary schools (Rutter et al., 1979) shows clearly that dimensions of the social structure of the school have direct and significant effects on both academic achievement and the deviant behaviour of pupils. But the dimensions commonly believed to be important, such as classroom size, school size, cost per student, etc., were found to be totally unrelated to either academic achievement or behaviour. The salient dimensions were centred on teacher-pupil relationships and teacher-staff relationships. They included factors such as: "degree of academic emphasis, styles of classroom management, patterns of rewards and punishments, and pupils' opportunities for responsibility and participation" (Rutter, 1980). Since these dimensions of the school's organization are much more accessible and amenable to change than are the problematic dimensions of family life, it would seem that the school system is a logical place to direct intensive efforts for future prevention programmes.

SUMMARY

Some alternative approaches for programmes intended to prevent juvenile delinquency have been suggested; the target for these programmes is not the child, but the two dominant institutions in the life of the child, the family and the school. Whether any of these approaches taken singly or collectively would have any effect on the prevalence of juvenile delinquency is not known. They have not been tried. What is know now, is that traditional approaches, based on the traditional assumption that delinquency is a "disease" and is susceptible to diagnosis and treatment in the individual child, are not only ineffective but may even exacerbate the problem. However, the deeply rooted conviction held by professionals and laymen in the efficacy of this traditional approach, interferes with even considering alternative approaches to prevention. The first and most difficult step required to prepare the way for alternative strategies, is to dispel this myth of "early intervention". Only then, will we be able to plan effectively and to procure the resources required to implement alternative approaches with the necessary commitment and vigour. How to break the power of that myth is of course a task which goes beyond the province of research alone.

NOTES

1. The research was funded by the Welfare Grants Directorate, Health and Welfare Canada

(Project 2555-55-1). A complete report is available from the author.

REFERENCES

Bennett, I. (1960) Delinquent and Neurotic Children. New York: Basic Books.

Berleman, W. C., Seaburg, J. R. and Steinburn, T. W. (1972) "The Delinquency Prevention Experiment of the Seattle Atlantic Street Center", Social Services Review, 46, 323-346.

Byles, J. A. (1979) "The Juvenile Services Project: An Experiment in Delinquency Control", Canadian Journal of Criminology, 21, 155-165.

Caplan, G. (1964) Principles of Preventive Psychiatry. New York: Wiley.

Cloward, R. A. and Ohlin, L. E. (1961) Delinquency and Opportunity: A Theory of Delinquent Gangs. New York: Free Press.

Glueck, S. and Glueck, E. (1950) Unravelling Juvenile Delinquency. Cambridge, Mass.: Harvard University Press.

Glueck, S. and Glueck, E. (1952) Delinquents in the Making. New York: Harper.

Glueck, S. and Glueck, E. (eds.) (1972) Identification of Pre-delinquents. New York: Intercontinental Medical Book Corporation.

Jenkins, R. L. (1960) "Psychiatric Syndromes in Children and Their Relation to Family Background", American Journal of Orthopsychiatry, 36, 450-457.

Lewis, D. O., Shanok, S. S., Pincus, J. H. and Glaser, G. H. (1979) "Violent Juvenile Delinquents; Psychiatric, Neurological, Psychological and Abuse Factors", Journal of Child Psychiatry, 18, 307-319.

Levine, M. and Graziano, A. M. (1972) "Intervention Programs in Elementary Schools" in S. Golann and C. Eisdorfer (eds.), Handbook of Community Mental Health. New York: Appleton Century Crofts.

Lundman, R. J., McFarlane, P. T. and Scarpitti, F. R. (1976) "Delinquency Prevention: A Description and Assessment of Projects Reported in the Professional Literature", Journal of Crime and Delinquency, (July), 297-308.

McCord, J. (1978) "A Thirty Year Follow-up of Treatment Effects", American Psychologist, 33, 284-289.

Merton, R. (1957) Social Theory and Social Structure. Glencoe, Ill.: Free Press.

Nye, F. I. (1958) Family Relationships and Delinquent Behavior. New York: Wiley.

Powers, E. and Witmer, H. (1951) An Experiment in the Prevention of Delinquency: The Cambridge-Somerville Youth Study. Chicago: University of Chicago Press.

Robins, L. N. (1966) Deviant Children Grown Up. Baltimore: Williams and Wilkins.

Rutter, M. (1965) "Classification and Categorization in Child Psychiatry", Journal of Child Psychology and Psychiatry, 6, 71-83.

Rutter, M. (1975) Helping Troubled Children. Harmondsworth: Penguin.

Rutter, M., Maughan, B. and Mortimer, P. (1979) Fifteen Thousand Hours: Secondary Schools and Their Effects on Children. London: Open Books.

Scarpitti, F. T., Murray, E. Dinitz, S. and Reckless, W. C. (1960) "The 'Good' Boys in a High Delinquency Area", American Sociological Review, 25, 555-558.

Schur, E. M. (1973) Radical Non-Intervention: Rethinking the Delinquency Problem. Englewood Cliffs: Prentice-Hall.

Sellin, T. and Wolfgang, M. E. (1964) The Measurement of Delinquency. New York: Wiley.

Shaw, C. and McKay, H. D. (1942) Juvenile Delinquency and Urban Areas. Chicago: University of Chicago Press.

Slater, E. and Cowie, V. (1968) Delinquency in Girls. London: Heinemann.

Solicitor General's Committee (1975) Young Persons in Conflict with the Law. Ottawa: Ministry of the Solicitor General.

Sutherland, E. H. and Cressey, D. S. (1960) Principles of Criminology. New York: J. P. Lippincott.

Toby, J. (1968) "An Evaluation of Early Identification and Intensive Treatment Programs for Predelinquents", in J. R. Stratton and R. M. Terry (eds.), Prevention of Delinquency. New York: Macmillan.

U. S. Interdepartmental Council to Co-ordinate All Federal Juvenile Delinquency Programs (1972) Report. Washington: U.S. Government Printing Office.

Wright, W. E. and Dixon, M. C. (1977) "Community Prevention and Treatment of Juvenile Delinquency: A Review of Evaluation Studies", Journal of Research in Crime and Delinquency, (January), 35-67.

Part II

POLICY AND PRACTICE

(b)   Some Potential Research Contributions.

7

THEORY AND PRACTICE IN JUVENILE JUSTICE: THE PHENOMENOLOGICAL PARADIGM

Stewart Asquith

It goes almost without saying that in the making of decisions about children who commit offences language is of particular importance since what measures are imposed on delinquents and what decisions are made about them are premised upon conceptions of delinquency embodied in the way we talk and indeed write about them. Blankenship (1974) captures the importance of language nicely in suggesting that social control agents:

> ... talk, to each other, to offenders, and to victims, witnesses and interested parties. And they construct documents in which their communication activities are summarised and set in meaningful rela- tionship. The documents are incorporated into the cumulative case records which accompany a deviant person throughout his official career [original emphasis] (p.253).

The relevance of this for social policy in general and criminal policy in particular is that analyses of policy implementation, and indeed policy formulation, have more recently been focused on the different accounts of delinquency displayed through text and discourse and the implications these have for the practical accomplishment of juvenile justice. The theoretical significance, for example of Cicourel's work (1976) was to direct attention to the theories and beliefs about delinquency and delinquency control employed by control agents in the everyday enactment of their official role and to reject analysis of social control which contained, often implicit, a priori assumptions about the decision-making processes involved. For Cicourel the focus of research was to shift from questions about what delinquents are like and what the causes of delinquency are to questions about how delinquents are processed by individuals operating within an organisational and bureaucratic structure and in more general terms to examine delinquency as a socially constructed phenomenon.

Recent studies in a number of fields premised upon a theoretical framework similar to that of Cicourel have examined what have been referred to as the 'ideologies' (Smith, 1981; Hardikker, 1977), 'assumptive worlds' (Young, 1981), 'penal philosophies' (Hogarth, 1971) and 'frames of relevance' (Asquith, 1977) of those responsible for policy implementation and formulation and have been based upon what might loosely be called a phenomenological perspective. The main objectives in this chapter are to explore the methodological and theoretical implications of that perspective for research in the field of juvenile justice and to articulate the relevance it may have for policy analysis. The thrust of the argument will be to explicate the relationship between theory and practice in the context of juvenile justice research and to examine the status of the knowledge gathered on the basis of the phenomenological perspective and the relevance it may have for practical affairs.

In commenting on the significance of knowledge gained through empirical research for social and political life, Bernstein refers to:

> the distinction between theory and practice where 'practice' is understood as the technical application of theoretical knowledge; the distinction between empirical and normative theory where the former is concerned with description and explanation of what is, while the latter deals with the clarification and justification of what ought to be; the distinction between descriptive and prescriptive discourse; the distinction between fact and value (1976, p.173).

A basic premise in our claims is that such distinctions are difficult to sustain and that, in agreement with both Bernstein (1976) and Fay (1975), theory and practice are inextricably linked and furthermore that questions about the status of knowledge are not merely epistemological but are related to questions about power and interest.

Analysis of juvenile justice practice, we believe, can move forward through the precepts of phenomenological theory by articulating the relationship between the practical accomplishment of decision-making by officials to much broader social and sociological concerns.

The chapter is presented in two sections. In the first, we examine the theoretical and methodological assumptions implicit in what may be termed the 'traditional' approach to the study of decision-making in juvenile justice. Our claim is that all social research is premised upon a theory of the social world and that the conception of social reality embodied in traditional research has generally been too restrictive. As a consequence, crucial features of social practices involved in juvenile justice have often been ignored or taken for granted.

In the second, we argue that the phenomenological paradigm offers a more appropriate theoretical framework for analysing decision-making about children since it posits a view of the social world which is premised upon the primacy of the actor in the accomplishment of social practices. A major contribution of this approach to research for policy is that it identifies the significance of control agents as policy makers in the practical accomplishment of and negotiation of juvenile justice through text and discourse. Moreover, and here we also offer criticisms of phenomenologically oriented research which has already been conducted in the field of juvenile justice, the phenomenological paradigm not only offers a means of identifying the different perspectives on the world adopted by social control agents but also points to the need for a sociological analysis of the origins of and legitimacy accorded to these different perspectives.

Two points have to be added at this juncture. The first is that despite what may appear to be a fairly abstract and theoretical discussion, this paper is grounded in a concern for what actually happens to children who commit offences. In that respect, it is hoped that this chapter will be seen as a fitting tribute to the memory of John Spencer who throughout his own career successfully reconciled his academic and more practical involvement in juvenile justice. For our purposes, what we have termed the traditional approach to analyses of delinquency and delinquency control has the potential for perpetuating particular conceptions of delinquency and the practices premised thereon, and for inhibiting critical reflection about the nature of the very phenomenon itself.

The second is that we do not deny that the philosophy of positivism which we argue underlies the traditional paradigm may be appropriate for particular kinds of inquiry. Schutz (1967) himself who did more than most to develop a phenomenological foundation for the social sciences argued that both a positivist and phenomenological approach were necessary to provide a complete picture of human behaviour. Our concern here however is with the theoretical appropriateness of the traditional paradigm to account for an essentially subjective and social activity - the making of decisions about children.

SENTENCING RESEARCH: THE TRADITIONAL PARADIGM

DISPARITY AS A RESEARCH PROBLEM

A common feature of research studies into sentencing is that they may be said to be typical of what Hogarth (1971) refers to as 'black box' or 'legal' models of sentencing research. By this he means that approach to research which is characterised by the collection of information, the 'facts' of the case from official sources, and in which the information provided from the official records and statistics about the offender or the offence (such as the type of offence, seriousness of the offence, past record of the offender and so on) is then correlated with the sentencing decisions actually reached in respect of the cases in question. The sentencing decision is considered in this way to be the dependent variable and the information about the offender or the offence are the independent variables which either singly or in a number of combinations can be said to account for the decision, or pattern of decisions. Such a model of sentencing research may be referred to as the 'black box' model in as much as relatively little is known about the magistrates themselves since it assumes:

> that the only significant variables affecting sentencing decisions are those externally visible 'facts' available from judicial records (Hogarth, 1971, p. 341).

The predominant concern of much sentencing research has been to account for the apparent disparity in sentencing decisions and even a cursory review of the research literature reveals the diversity of factors or 'externally visible "facts"' deployed to explain prima facie inconsistency. The implication has generally been that 'disparity' is not desirable in as much as it is taken to indicate that, in some cases, justice has not been achieved. This however suggests that 'justice' means something along the lines of treating like cases alike and the existence of disparity therefore reflects the fact that like cases have not been treated alike.

But such a principle as 'treat like cases alike' would have been comparatively easier to maintain within a classical framework for sentencing, and as has been pointed out:

> ... the problem of sentencing disparity is closely related to the post-classical emphasis on individualised justice, which has regards to the needs of the individual offender, in contrast to the mechanical juridical emphasis on the nature of the offence (Bottomley, 1973, p. 132).

"Treating like cases alike" actually tells us very little as to the criteria which are to be adopted in deciding the 'likeness' of cases as it is merely a formal, logical imperative for the attainment of justice; it offers no account of 'likeness' which must be explained by reference to the material or substantial element in the notion of justice (Lloyd, 1964; Perelman, 1963). Under classical doctrine, with its emphasis on free will and responsibility, the 'likeness' of cases could be decided by reference to such criteria as the nature of the offence. In that respect, the task of deciding on like sentences for like cases was comparatively straightforward since the criteria for 'likeness' were fairly well circumscribed.

With the development and acceptance of individualised justice, the criteria by which cases can be said to be alike (the material element of justice) become 'need' criteria. That is, important factors as a basis for sentencing decisions are factors relating to the needs of individual offenders and not simply to what Green referred to as legal factors such as the type of offence, seriousness of offence or culpability of the offender (Green, 1961). But there are two problems here which have significance for much sentencing research.

Firstly, the development of individualised justice, of taking the offender's needs into consideration for the purposes of sentencing, has not wholly been at the expense of more traditional objectives in sentencing. Rather, the criminal justice system has become something of a hybrid in that sentencing decisions may well reflect punitive considerations as much as rehabilitative. The history of the development of juvenile justice in terms of the merits of court, tribunal, punishment or treatment has been in this respect a history of compromise (Morris and McIsaac, 1978).

Secondly, that offenders' needs are to be taken into consideration is by no means a straightforward principle because of the difficulty of establishing just what offenders' needs are. Research into the 'causes' of crime or delinquency has been singularly unfruitful in providing objective criteria establishing the causes of delinquency or criminality. Consequently, there are no clear or agreed upon guidelines as to the 'needs' of offenders. Moreover, and certainly related to what has just been said, research into the 'effectiveness' of different types of rehabilitative measures has likewise been somewhat disappointing, adding to the very complexity of the sentencing task.

Thus, there is by no means consensus as to what the objectives or goals of the criminal justice system are, how to achieve these goals and what the needs of offenders are. Consequently, this makes any attempt to compare sentencing decisions and sentencing patterns a rather crude affair (Hogarth, 1971; Bottomley, 1973; Hood, 1962).

As has been noted, much of sentencing research, with notable exceptions, has largely focused on identifying factors which might explain the apparent disparity that appears in sentencing. But because of the difficuty in establishing just what the objectives of the criminal justice system are the notion of disparity then becomes problematic. With the development of individualised justice, and the expansion of the welfare or rehabilitative ethic within the system of criminal justice, the task of sentencing has become more complex. It has thereby also become more difficult to appreciate what the actual bases of sentences are. Consequently, it has become more than problematic simply to assert that

The Phenomenological Paradigm

sentences lack uniformity or consistency, or that
sentencing patterns reveal inequalities, because it
is more difficult to appreciate the factors the
sentencer takes into consideration, the goals he
hopes to achieve, and the reasons for his decision.
Sentences which may, prima facie, indicate a degree
of disparity may in fact be attributed to the unique
circumstances associated with the case; on the other
hand uniformity and consistency of sentencing may
well be due to the ignoring of the unique features
of different cases. The logical implication of the
principle 'Treat like cases alike' is that cases
that are unlike in important respects should be
treated differently. Prima facie disparity or
inconsistency may well reflect the acceptance of the
premises on which individualised justice is based.

The relevance for this chapter of treating the
notion of 'disparity' as problematic, is that the
studies into sentencing research employ different
conceptions of the notion. One of the consequences
of this is that the particular methodologies adopted
by different researchers are determined by the
search for factors to account for 'disparity'.

What is particularly interesting is that many
researchers have in fact claimed that disparity can
only be explained by reference to the human element
though they had neither collected information on the
interpretation of information by individual
magistrates nor on the actual process of the court
hearing and the communication involved. Yet the
conclusion often drawn has been that in the absence
of any identifiable factors, disparity or variation
can be attributed to some indefinable element such
as the 'personality of the judge' even though the
methodologies employed only allowed conclusions
about how individuals make decisions to be made at
the level of oblique inference.

As examples of such studies we would include
Grunhut (1956) who referred to magisterial
preference for particular disposals; Mannheim,
Spencer and Lynch (1957) who identified 'intuitive
assessment' as a prime factor; and Patchett and
McLean (1965) who pointed (like Grunhut) to the
differences in the approaches adopted by
magistrates. In earlier sentencing studies in the
adult court similar conclusions had been reached
where sentencing practice was the focus of inquiry
(see Gauder, 1949; Green, 1961).

In a more up-to-date study of decision-making
in the Scottish Children's Hearings System, Morris
and McIsaac argue that despite the formal commitment

153

to a welfare philosophy, panel members, and others in the system make decisions on the basis of more classical and punitive considerations. Panel members may in fact operate with a disguised form of tariff decision-making where considerations of the offence, the child's involvement in it and so on become relevant criteria on which to base a decision. The problem with this research is that though the authors claim they are concerned with the ideologies of decision-makers and are committed to an interpretive stance, precisely the same criticism can be made of their approach as can be made of the other studies mentioned. That is, most of their evidence about <u>how</u> decisions are made actually relates to <u>what</u> are the personal characteristics of the children involved.

What is obvious from the preceding discussion is that the goals and objectives of systems of juvenile justice are riven with ambiguity and that the administrative and organisational arrangements, in which children who commit offences are dealt with formally, are, in part, the product of attempts to reconcile competing philosophies of delinquency control. The concept of disparity is problematic then insofar as different researchers have located different types of variables to account for different senses of the notion. Disparity is then a concept that was employed by sentencing researchers as a <u>resource</u> in the explanation of sentencing practices.

It is perhaps more than a little invidious to select only a few studies on which to base broad criticisms but those referred to above share a number of features common to sentencing studies of their type in general and it is to a discussion of what we consider to be the major weaknesses of these that we now turn. These are (i) the separation of epistemology and ontology; and (ii) the separation of theory and practice. Though our comments are related to studies in juvenile justice they are derived from more general concerns with what might best be called criminological positivism - that approach to the study of crime and delinquency which operates on a conception of the unity of method in which little distinction is drawn between social and natural sciences.

The Phenomenological Paradigm

(i) The Separation of Epistemology and Ontology

In the simplest of terms our knowledge of the world, and the nature of the world, whether social or physical, are closely associated. How we come to know our world, gather knowledge about it or act in it, is in part at least, determined by what our conception of the nature of that world is. Epistemology and ontology are linked. Any criticism then of the status of the knowledge gained through research, and therefore of its utility, must also make an explicit statement about the ontological assumptions inherent in the research enterprise. The validity of the claims made by traditional sentencing researchers, we argue, must seriously be in doubt because of the nature of the ontological assumptions about social reality often never made explicit in their research. It is not that traditional researchers do not have a theory of the social world but that their theory of the social world, often implicit as it is, is not appropriate to the study of decision-making involving human actors.

Derived as it is from the tenets of criminological positivism the view of the social world espoused by traditional researchers has generally been one of preconstituted facts which are readily identifiable and whose nature is rarely questioned. A preconstituted view of the world allows 'facts' to be objectified, reified and treated as if they are 'out there' and easily discoverable by anyone using the appropriate methodology. For the traditional researcher the implication then is that since his theory of the social world essentially corresponds to that of the natural scientist, social insititutions such as a system of juvenile justice can be studied with essentially the same epistemology and methodology as employed in the natural sciences. What we find then in traditional sentencing research is the paradox that claims have been made about the 'human element' in sentencing (see studies referred to above) on the basis of a research design embodying an essentially positivist conception of epistemology, ontology and methodology. The link between epistemology and ontology is fractured because of the thing-like status accorded to social phenomena – subject and object, knowledge and the object of knowledge, the knower and the known are conceived of as discrete entities in a theory of the social as located in a preconstituted and objectively given world (see

Hindess, 1973). This in itself has a number of implications for the study of juvenile justice which we can best illustrate by reference to the aforementioned studies.

First, research studies have often ignored the influence of the decision-maker himself in determining outcome and the notion of the 'human element' has more often than not attained the status of a residual category employed when the researcher has been unable to offer an acceptable explanation of such occurrences as disparity in sentencing. Inferences about how decisions are made about children within the traditional paradigm have often been based on a priori assumptions made by the researcher about the ways in which information is assimilated, not on empirical investigation of decision-making by individuals. In this way, disagreement about what 'externally visible facts' (Hogarth, 1971) influence decision has generally been between researchers and not those involved in the exercise of decision-making. The relationships drawn between decisions and the facts of a case, in which were often included independent variables drawn from the judge's or magistrate's own background were the product of the theoretical assumptions of the researcher. In this way, a priori assumptions about delinquency, its causes, the needs of delinquents and what to do about delinquents have of necessity to be made by the researcher in the absence of any information about the significance of these issues for the decision-maker. It is for this reason that we suggest that the traditional researcher in juvenile justice has been preoccupied with the 'what' of decisions and not the 'how'.

This brings us neatly to the second implication for research into justice founded upon a theoretical framework in which epistemology and ontology are separated and it is logically related to the first. Because traditional sentencing research has operated on a theory of the social world as being constructed of reified events and facts, the processual nature of decision-making has generally been ignored. In all the works mentioned above (Grunhut, 1956; Patchett and McLean, 1965; Mannheim, Spencer and Lynch, 1957; McIsaac and Morris, 1978), little cognisance has been given to the situated aspect of decision-making. Morris and McIsaac (1978, p. 111) can confidently assert, in the absence of empirical evidence:

> ...the type of tribunal (juvenile court or welfare tribunal) is largely unimportant.

What is crucial is the philosophy underlying that tribunal and the ideology of its practitioners.

By concentrating on the 'facts' of a case, it has been theoretically impossible for such studies to provide any empirical information about the way in which key personnel in the decision-making process conceive of delinquency, its causes and what to do about it and the implications this has for how they interpret information provided through text and discourse. Similarly since the 'facts' of a case could be comprehended from records alone, there was little need to include an analysis of what actually happened in court. Indeed, it has been argued in one study which postulated the human element as a crucial factor in sentencing juveniles that this was unnecessary, and that the methodology adopted had the advantage that the researcher, since he did not attend the hearing of cases, was 'detached' from the courts which he only knew as numbers (Mannheim, Spencer and Lynch, 1957). And in yet another, the researchers presumed that they could in fact assimilate and interpret case information much in the same way as those responsible for making the actual decisions would. In references to the construction of social enquiry reports, Morris and McIsaac (1978, p.105) assert:

> The writers of these reports were usually attempting to persuade the reporters to accept their recommendations for a particular form of action - they were attempting to convey in their report a particular impression. The same impression was probably conveyed to us [our emphasis].

The general point to be made is that, in the absence of empirical data about how magistrates, judges or others responsible for making decisions about children actually go about their task, traditional research studies display a distinct preparedness to impute 'reasonable' motives to individuals (see Blum and McHugh, 1970). Data, in the form of background information about a case, are taken for granted since there is no attempt either to theorise how the data are constructed or how the data themselves are subject to assimilation and interpretation by those involved in the accomplishment of justice for

children. There is in effect in what we have termed
the traditional approach no theory of data but
rather theory and data. That is, there is little
attempt to theorise the construction of the data
themselves or the interpretation of the 'data' by
the subjects of the researchers. What we are
questioning is that theoretical orientation which
reifies facts and events and gives little emphasis
to the fact that the researcher has to include
within his theoretical framework some means of
accounting for the construction of or interpretation
of the facts of a case through text and discourse.
This in itself reflects the problem for the
criminological positivist of moving from 'fact' to
theory, between subject and object.

> The 'subject' and the 'object' from which
> it extracts knowledge may be variously
> conceived but in all cases the structure
> of [such a] conception of knowledge
> establishes some form of fundamental
> opposition between say 'theory' and
> 'fact', 'men' and 'world', subject and
> object (Hindess, 1973, p. 134).

The object of knowledge is what is given and
traditional sentencing studies have in their own way
in the pursuit of knowledge about the
decision-making process concentrated on analysing
the relationship between the 'facts' of a case and
outcome. The 'facts' of a case and indeed what
constitutes delinquency or the needs of children are
taken for granted and are employed as resources in
the research exercise.

(ii) Separation of Theory and Practice

No one could reasonably argue that delinquency
does not pose a problem in practical affairs and it
is not the intention of this chapter to
underestimate the difficulties encountered in
seeking to do something about it. What is being
questioned here however is the status of the
knowledge about attempts at delinquency control
located within the traditional paradigm and the
contribution of such knowledge to policy. One of the
dangers of a theory of the social world (and here we
repeat our claim that the traditional paradigm does
indeed contain an implicit theory of the social
world) in which facts are subject to reification and

in which behaviour is explained generally in terms of antecedents is that little cognisance is taken of the different constructions imposed on phenomena and the negotiation of legitimacy of world views. As Rock (1973) argues in relation to deviant behaviour a formal policy statement is needed precisely because of the pluralism of views about the nature of delinquency and what to do about it. (We return later in this chapter to discuss the significance of potentially divergent views of delinquency within a system of juvenile justice). But by operating on a conception of the social world in which facts are objectively given, researchers in the traditional paradigm argue that they are able to conduct research with objectivity and complete ethical neutrality. However, a danger must surely be that claims to ethical neutrality and objectivity conceal the fact that despite attempts to be objective and ethically neutral in methodological terms, in theoretical terms, the research is in fact premised upon a particular conception of the social world. It is no coincidence that criminological and penological research which developed historically with a strong positivist influence have often been criticised for being conservative, in the sense of supporting a particular form of social, political and economic structure, despite the claims of researchers that the canons of the scientific enterprise were being adhered to. Fay (1975, p. 65) argues that, despite attempts to remove personal bias and prejudice:

> ...the positivist model does rest on a certain conception of politics, man and society and that, indeed, it is in terms of this conception that what is to count as evidence, truth, a descriptive term and so on is determined.

We are not suggesting that those who have worked, and indeed still do, within the traditional paradigm are overtly supporting a particular conception of social reality. Rather, the traditional paradigm in itself embodies a theory of the social world and attempts to be objective or morally neutral have to be appraised in that context. The theories and formulations derived from such an approach are not completely separate from practical life; theory and practice in juvenile justice are not separate in the sense that the researcher merely provides technical information for the purpose of policy formulation.

Even in positivist epistemology, practice and theory are inextricably linked and it has been argued that what we have termed the traditional paradigm derived as it is from a positivist stance, is particularly appropriate for practical concerns, such as delinquency and crime, because it is in its very conception geared to the task of control (Fay, 1975). Put in terms of the reference to Bernstein earlier in this chapter, the traditional paradigm, even where claims to objectivity and ethical neutrality are espoused for the methods employed in empirical research, accommodates theoretical statements about what is _and_ what ought to be. That is, the traditional paradigm _is_ involved in moral and political discourse, and the practical and the theoretical are not discrete enterprises.

In summary then, knowledge gleaned through research into juvenile justice located within the traditional paradigm must be seriously questioned for a number of reasons. First, since the facts of a case are treated as given, much of what is actually involved in the process of decision-making in systems of juvenile justice is taken for granted. This must surely be particularly significant given the lack of definitive statement about delinquency or need available in commonsense knowledge and embodied in legislative statements. Second, such knowledge is premised upon an approach which does not in fact provide technical morally neutral information but which is premised upon particular conceptions of the nature of the social world. Third, these conceptions of the social world are predominantly those of the researcher, not of the subjects of this research. Fourth, theory and practice are conceived of as being discrete, and as we shall see in the next section this had important implications for analyses of policy implementation and creation.

THE PHENOMENOLOGICAL PARADIGM

A fundamental objective in phenomenological sociology is to study the everyday world of the layman and not just the scientist as problematic and worthy of empirical investigation. In seeking to articulate the conditions that underlie understanding and knowledge in all their modes it is not exclusively concerned with methodological questions pertaining to the scientific, whether of the natural or social sciences. It is concerned with the knowledge men have of the world and its relationship to practical interests. Indeed the distinction between lay and scientific, commonsense and theory, is one that the phenomenological sociologists (under the influence of Alfred Schutz) and the phenomenological psychologists (under the the influence of George Kelly) would find difficult to sustain. For both Schutz (1967) and Kelly (1970) men are scientists or theorists and it is no coincidence that in an appraisal of this perspective in relation to policy analysis Young and Mills (1978) review both the theoretical and methodological postulates of both Schutz and Kelly. Our task is somewhat similar in that what we seek to do in this section of the paper is to examine what are taken to be central elements in the phenomenological paradigm and to examine their relevance to analyses of the practical accomplishment of juvenile justice. Since ultimately the object of inquiry is juvenile justice practice, the objective of any research enterprise in this context is to present as accurate a picture as possible of what is actually involved in the practical accomplishment of decisions about young offenders. The basic premise underlying this chapter is that the knowledge about decision-making offered by those operating within the traditional paradigm is inadequate because it presents a distorted view of practice by ignoring crucial features in the juvenile justice process.

Four elements in phenomenological theory are to be discussed. These are:

(i) Intentionality;

(ii) Multiple realities;

(iii) Intersubjectivity; and

(iv) Language.

All of these are of course related and they are to be considered in terms of their contribution to analyses of practice in juvenile justice.

(i) Intentionality

In contrast to the traditional paradigm, there are not objectively given 'facts' independent of theorisation and conceptualisation since the social

world is continually subject to processes of
interpretation and re-interpretation. Our knowledge
of the social world is inextricably linked to what
are our conceptions of the world or parts of it. In
terms of the notion of intentionality, epistemology
and ontology are linked since consciousness is
always consciousness of something. There are no
'facts' independent of the constructions of actors,
whether they be researchers, scientists or lay men.
What is important is not the procuring of a
definitive statement as to what social reality is
but how it is construed for the purpose of practical
life. This has a number of implications for analyses
of practical juvenile justice.

Reports or accounts of the world, for example,
in the area of concern in this chapter, social
enquiry reports, case records, verbal communications
and such, have to be understood in reference to a)
the processes by which they were constructed and b)
the interpretation imposed upon them by those to
whom such accounts are available. In the
accomplishment of juvenile justice, as Cicourel
(1976) argues, the focus of empirical inquiry has to
be the lay theories of delinquency employed by key
personnel in the social control network. The reasons
for focusing attention, as suggested earlier in this
paper, on text and discourse is that theories of
delinquency are embodied in the very way we talk and
write about delinquents and consequently how we deal
with them. In one sense then, theory and practice
are not distinct in that practical activities are
governed by the assumptions and beliefs in the stock
of knowledge available to the actor. The 'facts'
about delinquency displayed through text and
discourse cannot be treated as objectively given as
in the traditional paradigm. Rather than being
conceived of as 'resources' for the researcher to
incorporate into his research design and theory of
the social world, they are themselves 'topics' of
enquiry (see Smith, 1981). At this juncture, the
distinction between the traditional and
phenomenological paradigms can be illustrated by the
diametrically opposed philosophies of meaning
presented by Wittgenstein - the correspondence or
picture theory of meaning (in which the meaning of a
word or sentence can be verified by checking it
against the real world) and the theory of meaning as
use (see Blum and McHugh, 1970). And in fact many of
the analyses of deviance conducted by
ethnomethodologists have been located within a
conceptual framework derived from Wittgensteinian

philosophy (McHugh, 1970; Douglas, 1970) as have been less sociological inquiries into the process of justice (Pitkin, 1972; Bruckner, 1978).

The general point, however, being made here is that analyses of sentencing or decision-making in juvenile justice, and indeed in criminal justice in general, which ignore how actors (for our purpose magistrates, social workers, probation officers, police and so on), construe the world, ignore crucial elements of the assimilation, interpretation and construction of accounts of delinquent behaviour. In juvenile justice, the implication then from this perspective is that the object of inquiry is not the objective facts of delinquency but is more appropriately conceived as the processes and practices by which the concept of delinquency is objectified. That is, how 'subjective meanings become objective facticities' (Berger and Luckman, 1967 p. 30) or achieve fact-like status.

The systems of belief or assumptions employed by actors in accomplishing social practices have been characterised in a number of ways by different authors. Thus we find studies of the 'ideologies' of social workers and probation officers (Smith, 1977; Cicourel, 1976; Hardiker, 1977); of magistrates (Lemon, 1974); the 'penal philosophies' of magistrates (Hogarth, 1971); the 'assumptive worlds' of political actors (Young, 1981); the 'working ideologies' and 'frames of relevance' of Panel members (Morris and McIsaac, 1978; Asquith, 1977). Insofar as these refer to the significance of the values and assumptions espoused by the actor, in this case, about delinquency, we shall refer to these collectively as ideologies. Though the term 'ideology' has become somewhat bastardised as of late, we shall follow Smith's definition as:

> a configuration of relatively abstract ideas and attitudes in which the elements are bound together by a relatively high degree of inter-relatedness or functional interdependence (1976, p. 50).

Moreover, he adds that an ideology may be a) formal, as an abstract system of ideas, or b) informal, as an operational philosophy which organisational members employ in determining action and decision-making. Although the empirical focus of these studies is different, all assert the primacy of the actor's construction of social reality in the modification and implementation of the formal goals

163

and practices of an institution or policy through the practical accomplishment of this institutional role. A number of implications derive from this.

First, social policy as realised in practice may well take a form different from that intended by the spirit of the formal ideology embodied in the policy statement. There may in effect be what Stoll (1968) refers to as 'strain' between the objectives of the formal ideology on which the policy is based and the objectives set by and adopted through the informal working ideologies of those responsible for its implementation. This is particularly so in the context of juvenile justice where the current prevalence of a welfare philosophy has meant that legislation and policy have necessarily been somewhat vague. The difficulty in defining and identifying children's 'needs' is reflected in the legislative statements which have generally taken the form of delegating responsibility for the identification, assessment and meeting of a child's needs to specific agencies; hence the significance of text and discourse as the product of ideologies of those involved in the social control network.

Secondly, since the formal ideology embodied within policy statements may well be subject to mediation through the informal working ideologies of individual actors, it is possible to conceive of those who have formally been given the task of implementing policy as involved in policy formulation. As a result of the strain between 'formal' and 'informal' ideology, the individual actor, particularly within a system of juvenile justice, is given wide discretion. In this way, he is able not only to determine the criteria to be employed in making a decision for any particular case but is also able more generally to determine the overall profile of the policy statement. He is in effect given sufficient discretion both to formulate and to implement his own conception of delinquency and its control.

(ii) Multiple realities

Logically related to (i) is the precept that there is no one definitive view of social reality but a diversity of views which have to be recognised in the implementation of policy. In juvenile justice any analysis of decision-making has to accommodate a study of the ideologies employed by different agents (social workers, judges, magistrates, and so on) and the possibility of competing ideologies manifested within any single organisational and bureaucratic structure. In relation to juvenile justice in Scotland, for example, Smith (1977) and Parsloe (1975) have shown the existence of different ideologies within professions such as social work and we ourselves have considered the implication of differing ideologies of delinquency control between the various professions involved and the ideologies of those lay members of the community ultimately responsible for making decisions (Panel members in Scotland and juvenile magistrates in England). In the final analysis, the reaching of a decision is the product of negotiation between potentially competing ideologies of delinquency control maintained by key personnel by which they construct, interpret and assimilate information about the children who appear before them. As Smith (1980) argues, more empirical information is needed about the decision-making process because only in this way can more knowledge be gathered about the nature of the social and bureaucratic structure within which the decisions are made. By this we take him to mean the relationships between the different agencies involved and the legitimacy and credibility accorded to particular views of social reality embodied within text and discourse.

Moreover, the recognition of the possibility of a multiplicity of views of delinquency control within any system of juvenile justice necessarily demands that the perceptions of parents and children of their involvement in the formal processes of social control be taken into consideration. This is particularly so since, in theory at least, many systems of justice for children have become less formal and less ritualistic in the attempt to invite their greater participation. Yet there is little empirical data about the assumptions about delinquency control employed by those who are immediately affected by any decision actually reached, the implications this may have for the decision-making process as a whole and the status and credibility accorded to parents' and children's views by those who adminsister justice. Some preliminary work has been initiated in this area (Morris and Giller, 1977; Petch, 1977; Lissenberg, 1980).

The danger of an approach to analysing the making of decisions on the basis of treating the 'externally visible facts' of a case as independent variables which are then related to outcome (the decision) is that much of what actually happens is either ignored or interpreted in terms of the a priori assumptions made by the researcher. In particular, the selective and interpretive activity of control agents and the negotiation of justice between potentially different ideologies are taken for granted. The suggestion made here is that more empirical information is required about aspects of juvenile justice which could not be theoretically accommodated within the traditional paradigm, but which are surely crucially significant in the translation of social policy into practice.

(iii) Intersubjectivity

Again, the discussion of the notion of intersubjectivity will be closely related to what has been said about ideologies and multiple realities. Earlier we argued that more empirical information is required about the ideologies of control agents. A criticism has been made of the phenomenological paradigm to the effect that research into ideologies logically results in a position of ideological relativism or anarchism, i.e. individuals see the world differently and there are as many views of the world as there are individuals in it. Hindess, for example, in criticising early work on juvenile justice conducted from a phenomenological perspective argued that Cicourel (1976) and Douglas (1970) were guilty of:

> ...a complete relativism and ... a necessary agnosticism instead of a serious concern with objective knowledge (Cicourel, 1976, p. xvi).

That is, he is concerned at the lack of objectivity in the claims to knowledge by Cicourel and Douglas and in the lack of universal or general statements about the world. The problem to which Hindess refers is the possibility that if there are as many views of the world as there are people in it, then there is no possibility of objective knowledge since knowledge is purely relative and dependent upon the beliefs of each individual actor. With reference to research in social work and juvenile justice based on a phenomenological approach, for example, it could be argued that all that is being presented are the views of significant individuals within the social control network. However, there is more to the phenomenological enterprise than that and though we cannot in the scope of this paper fully explore this debate, the criticism of complete relativism can, we believe, be rejected in such a way as to make a meaningful contribution to future research into juvenile justice.

Of the studies mentioned above which have sought to examine the ideologies of those responsible for the formulation or implementation of policy, surprisingly few ideological positions employed by actors have been identified. Now it could be argued that this was a direct result of the restrictive categories and conceptual schemata employed by the researcher. However, such a criticism has to be made in acknowledgment of the properties of an 'ideology' in the sense employed in this chapter.

To make sense of the social world we have to be able to ascribe meaning to it and in this respect an ideology provides recipes for acting in the world of practical affairs. However, the world, or construction of it, is not simply the world of an actor but is a world that is shared with others through the rules employed to constitute truly social action and social practices. The concern of the phenomenological researcher is to articulate the basic rules or procedures which allow for interaction and communication. Social practices are shared in the sense that their accomplishment depends on a framework of rules and procedures which serve to constitute action as social and allows others to identify it as such. There can be no private social world much for the same reason that Wittgenstein could argue that there is no private language. Social reality and social practices are intersubjectively experienced and though there may well be multiple constructions of social reality for the practical purpose of acting in the world assumptions about its nature are necessarily shared. Though there may be a number of ideologies for example about delinquency control, assumptions about what delinquency is and what to do about it will be shared by those who adhere to a particular ideology. There are a number of questions prompted by this which should well merit further examination in juvenile justice.

First, given that there may well be a number of shared positions on justice for children, how is it that particular ideologies come to be incorporated into either formal policy statements or the informal practices of those responsible for policy implementation. Second, how is it that certain positions come to predominate in any particular system of juvenile justice. In this respect, empirical attention has to be focused on the procedures by which individuals are accepted or rejected as candidates for key posts in juvenile justice. The point of this exercise would be to identify the ideological assumptions which the individual would be expected to share and which are built into the very process of selection. Smith (1977) and May and Smith (1970), for example, have already done some work with reference to Scottish juvenile justice in which they have argued that the process by which panel members are selected is governed by predominantly social work typifications and stereotypes about delinquency and control. Third, and obviously closely related, is the question of the origins of ideologies or put more simply, how it is that people come to share ideologies. This question could be tackled on a number of levels but at this juncture we would merely suggest that the ideological assumptions embodied in the training procedures for professionals, such as social workers, probation officers and the police or even for lay men involved such as juvenile magistrates, panel members and so on would be an appropriate object of empirical inquiry.

This is not to suggest that actual practice is no longer the focus of concern; rather the general point is being made that information about delinquents, in the form of case records or verbal communications will be the product of and subject to differing interpretations which are premised upon the ideological positions inherent in the training and selection programmes of the respective agents and agencies. As a rather simple illustration, one need only consider the rather different interpretations imposed on delinquency statistics in particular and crime statistics in general by different agencies, for example, the police and social workers. On a more theoretical level, Cicourel (1976), Kitsuse and Cicourel (1963) and Hindess (1973) have all examined statistics as indexical of the processes of their production and not just as indicators of the distribution of 'delinquency' in society.

The Phenomenological Paradigm

(iv) Language

From what has gone before the importance of language for analyses of decision-making should by now be apparent and only a few brief comments are to be added here. In locating 'ideologies' as appropriate empirical objects of research language is obviously significant as a major medium through which they can be identified. It is through language that social realities, meanings and knowledge are intersubjectively constituted and communicated, and it is through language that behaviour becomes normatively bound and conventionally guided and that we impose structure and order in the world. Earlier we suggested that linguistic philosophy and phenomenological sociology share fundamental precepts, in particular, the coherence of linguistically, intersubjectively valid ways of seeing the world. The importance of text and discourse is that it is indexical of a particular concept of the social world, which is not objectively knowable but can only be appreciated through the concepts we employ in making sense of the world and in acting upon it. In this way, epistemology and ontology are linked to the language we use. Moreover, language is practically oriented and any analysis of language or of the way in which concepts are used is necessarily about praxis, a point that is developed in more detail elsewhere (Smith, 1981). To consider how a word or concept such as delinquency is used, and to appreciate the processes by which it is objectified is ultimately to consider the practical concerns and interests of the actor. And with specific reference to the relationship between moral definitions and delinquent behaviour, even with the common currency of a treatment or welfare philosophy, Warren and Johnson (1972, p. 69) assert that the study of deviant behaviour from the phenomenological perspective is:

> simply the observation of the meanings of morality and immorality as acted out in everyday life. It concerns how moral rules are constructed, how they are maintained and how infractions are handled.

Similarly, language is contextually and situationally employed. Thus, Cicourel (1976) directs researchers to the logic-in-use employed in the practical activities of control agents locating the 'theories', 'knowledge' and language within the situational constraints surrounding juvenile justice practice. Young also argues:

> ... the assumptive world is a perception of the world; ultimately it can only be studied within that world. The primary mode of research on assumptive worlds in the action setting must therefore be to encourage (political) actors to give accounts of their behaviour in the action context; the student of assumptive worlds must study the praxiology of policymaking (1977, p. 17).

In summary then the phenomenological paradigm demands that empirical research should replace the making of a priori assumptions about the processes by which decisions about children who commit offences are arrived at. Theoretically, the researcher has to locate the 'facts' of a case or the 'facts' of delinquency within the practical concerns of the decision-maker, report writer and so on. The emphasis on text and discourse is ultimately a concern to articulate the rules which constitute practice in juvenile justice, hence the analysis by such writers as Blankenship (1974) of case records. Practice cannot be gauged simply from an appreciation of the intentions embodied in formal policy as the practical accomplishment of juvenile justice may well be determined by different goals and objectives maintained by those responsible for the implementation of policy and a process of negotiation between potentially conflicting ideological positions. Despite the identification by a number of researchers of competing ideologies within systems of juvenile justice, it is a simple fact that decisions are reached, hearings are held and the system rarely, if ever, breaks down. What the phenomenological perspective directs the researcher to is an empirical investigation of the unexplicated features which allow the very business of decision-making to take place. The theoretical stance is one in which practice is seen as the accomplishment of human agency and not simply the product of 'externally visible facts'. Fay in rejecting the theory of social reality enshrined in what we have called the traditional paradigm, states:

> ... men are not generally schizoid in their thought such that they view social

life in one way when they wish to study it
and in a quite different way when they
come to question as to how the knowledge
they have gained is relevant to the
practical problems which confront them
(1975, p. 12).

Ideologies of Delinquency and Social Structure

We have already argued that the moral
definitions of delinquency employed by social
control agents form an appropriate object of
empirical inquiry of the practical accomplishment of
justice and that through analyses of text and
discourse the nature of the social structure within
which decisions are made can best be appreciated.
Thus far, social structure has been defined as the
organisational and bureaucratic structure of formal
systems. In this last section however the definition
is to be broadened in that we wish to offer some
comments as to how analyses of practice in juvenile
justice may be articulated to much broader social
and societal concerns. Recent researchers working
within the phenomenological paradigm (Cicourel,
1976; Douglas, 1970; Smith, 1977) have satisfied
themselves with examining the ideological positions
maintained by actors and the implications these have
for the administration of juvenile justice. Indeed,
a criticism of phenomenological, and in particular
ethnomethodological, analyses has been precisely
that they have focused almost exclusively on small
scale micro-sociological concerns and have contented
themselves with 'snapshots' of social situations.
Though we are perhaps unable to present a fully
developed theoretical position, it is our intention
to comment on the ways in which the phenomenological
paradigm can indeed contribute to a broader
sociological analysis of practice in juvenile
justice. In particular, we are concerned to develop
a theoretical analysis of delinquency control which
is critical in the sense of appraising the very
social institution of juvenile justice and the
definition of social reality enshrined therein. Here
we agree with Rock (1973) in his assertion that:

A sociologist who organised his study at
the level of commonsense thought alone,
would be able to contribute little, if

anything, to understanding about social processes.

Our ultimate concern is with practice, the application of knowledge to practical affairs, in that only when the bases of social and political institutions are subjected to critical appraisal will there be greater opportunity for investigating the phenomenon in question. To this end, it is worth pointing out that there are a number of parallel lines of thought between those who see in linguistic analysis the seeds of a more radical form of critique of social order. (See for example Pitkin (1972) and Giddens (1976) and the phenomenological sociologists who see in their own approach a similar potential, in particular Rock (1973).) Our argument is that the micro-sociological concerns of writers such as Cicourel (1976), Douglas (1970) and Smith (1977) can be theoretically articulated to macro-sociological interests through means of analysis derived from phenomenological theory itself. This is not to suggest that such studies are not important but rather that the identification of conceptions of aspects of social reality is a necessary stage in the development of a critique of the legitimacy of particular world views. McBarnett's criticism that phenomenologically oriented studies of criminal justice 'get lost in micro-sociological description and indignant demystification' (1978) need not necessarily hold.

Two fairly obvious points can be made. First, in terms of individual actors there is a distinct lack of consensus as to what delinquency is and how best to deal with it. The implications of this for practice have already been alluded to. Second, in terms of formal policy statements definitions of delinquency and practices premised thereon are continually subject to review with consequent implications for the organisation and administration of juvenile justice. One need only think of the most recent proposals for change in juvenile justice in Northern Ireland (Black Report, 1979) which postulate a conception of juvenile delinquency as rational responsible behaviour meriting punishment – a view which is diametrically opposed to the treatment philosophy which forms the present currency for juvenile justice. A criticism that could be made then of studies of practice divorced from a broader sociological analysis is that, given the diversity of potentially 'available ideologies' of delinquency, they largely ignore the question of

why and how at particular points in time certain
conceptions of delinquency are granted more
legitimacy than others. Ideologies of delinquency,
as already stated, are shared by groups of
individuals and have social structural origins.
Illustrating the social origins of bodies of
knowledge, Berger and Luckmann argue:

> Reality is socially defined. But the
> definitions are always embodied, that is,
> concrete individuals serve as definers of
> reality ... Put a little crudely, it is
> essential to keep pushing questions about
> the historically available conceptual-
> isations of reality from the abstract
> 'what?' to the sociologically concrete
> 'says who?' (1967, p. 134).

Bodies of knowledge, for our purposes theories of
delinquency, are socially, historically located and
linked to specific interests. Since a number of
bodies of knowledge or theoretical positions may be
socially distributed, conflict between competing
claims can only be resolved by the ascription of
legitimacy to specific forms. Such conflict involves
a problem of power in deciding which definition of
reality will be 'made to stick' (Berger and
Luckmann) a point similarly made by Giddens in
claiming that 'frames of meaning' are unbalanced
insofar as they are related to power through, for
example, the possession of relevant types of
knowledge. What then stands for social reality, the
'official' line on delinquency for example, is only
understandable in terms of the relationship between
knowledge, legitimacy and power. This has a number
of implications for analyses of practice within a
particular form of social institution.

Specific forms of knowledge come to dominate
official thinking and in relation to delinquency,
systems of juvenile justice must be seen as only one
means by which conceptions of social reality and the
structure of social relationships are maintained and
transmitted. Accordingly, for critical purposes,
they have to be analysed in relation to other forms
of social institutions and their social structural
bases. It is a truism in criminal justice that in
western industrialised societies criminal behaviour
is taken to be mainly a lower socio-economic
phenomenon - that those who get caught up in the
formal processes of social control are generally
those who are working class, poor, live in deprived

areas, unemployed and so on. Through being based upon a particular conception of social reality then, institutions, such as a system of juvenile justice, can be construed as perpetuating the dominant conception of social order, of the world 'as we know it' and play a crucial function in the process of legitimation or what Berger and Luckmann (1967) refer to as 'universe maintenance'. In juvenile justice, despite the continual review of formal policy statements and continual modifications to the systems of control, the structural bases of bodies of knowledge are rarely challenged. Whether in the form of a punishment or a treatment oriented philosophy, delinquency is conceived of as essentially an individualistic, working class phenomenon and delinquency control is likewise conceived of as essentially a problem dealing with individuals.

Earlier, we suggested that the acquisition of ideological positions on delinquency control through training and selection form an appropriate object of empirical inquiry. This can be taken one step further by again explicating the relationship between selection and training, for example, of magistrates, panel members, social workers, and so on, to conceptions of social reality. Only certain individuals can be given the responsibility for making decisions about children - those who possess the 'relevant' knowledge. Current thinking, though there are indications of a totally opposite approach emerging, is that delinquency control is best and more justly achieved through a welfare oriented philosophy in which treatment, welfare, therapy or care are to be offered to the delinquent child. With the expansion of the welfare philosophy in delinquency in the post war period, there has been a corresponding growth in the professional agencies servicing juvenile justice systems. Berger and Luckmann (1967, p.130) state:

> Therapy entails the application of conceptual machinery to ensure that actual or potential deviants stay within the institutionalised definitions of reality ... Since therapy must concern itself with deviations from the 'official' definitions of reality, it must develop a conceptual machinery to account for such deviations and to maintain the realities thus challenged. This requires a body of knowledge that include a theory of

deviance, a diagnostic apparatus, and a conceptual system for the 'cure of souls'.

Now a similar statement could be made about punishment by reference to the maxim that what we do about delinquency depends on how we conceive of it. But there are particular dangers associated with therapy and specifically the fact that delinquency control has come to be seen as the province of specialised experts who, on account of their expertise, skills or knowledge are granted the responsibility for determining what should happen to delinquents. Pearson (1975) states the relationship between conceptions of the social world and a welfare philosophy thus:

> Under the conditions of a reified social reality the technical competence and moral veracity of the welfare professional become merged; deviance appears to have its rightful place in the domain of technical accomplishment (p. 68).

Even where laymen are involved in the administration of juvenile justice it has been suggested that through the typification and stereotypes of delinquency embodied in the very processes of selection and training, the ideology espoused by such persons may well reflect the dominant professional ideology (Smith, 1977). As Berger and Luckmann suggested, questions about what is the right decision about the delinquent child are legally related to who makes that decision. Only those who share in the dominant ideology, at least in part, can be expected to participate in the actual accomplishment of justice. The implication of Pearson's argument is that the welfare treatment approach is conservative in promoting and perpetuating but one view of the social and moral order and of social relationships; that professional agencies have attained a position of power in determining who is delinquent, what is and how to deal with it. The knowledge of the decision-maker is imbued with power insofar as it is up to him to decide what is relevant information for the purpose of decision-making, and inasmuch as he has been selected for his role on the basis of a legitimate ideology. The danger of an approach to delinquency control in which specialised knowledge is located within a system manned predominantly by experts and in which the problem of delinquency is conceived of as a technical problem is that the accomplishment of juvenile justice is removed further from moral discourse. Moreover, criticisms as to the lack of adequate legal and procedural safeguards in a treatment based system of social control fail to appreciate that, in its very theoretical conception, such an approach serves to promote a definition of social reality which is in fact rooted in a social structure that in itself may well display injustice and contribute to the very phenomenon itself.

The legitimation of a body of knowledge is a process through which those who share in that knowledge are granted power in the sense that the definitions of social reality embodied therein come to dominate in social practices through which alternative constructions of the social world are rejected. Text and discourse about delinquents then are indexical of specific views of the world and the writing of reports about delinquents or the making of decisions about them has to be seen in terms of a specific body of knowledge and the interests it serves.

For these reasons, we argue that the phenomenological paradigm requires that we examine the social and structural origins of theories about delinquency and that, in particular, analyses of decision-making, of practice within juvenile justice systems have to be related to the functions these may serve in maintaining a certain form of social structure which by its very nature contributes to the phenomenon they seek to eradicate - delinquency. Just as we would argue that it is impossible to conceive of individuals or their ideologies outwith a social context, so we argue that analyses of practice in juvenile justice, if they are to be truly critical, must illuminate the social structural origins of the processes by which theories of delinquency receive legitimation and by which specific groups of individuals attain a position of power. That is, though what constitutes just practice for delinquents is essentially a moral question, the issue of which moral definitions come to dominate and receive institutional expression or specific points in time is essentially a sociological one (see Ossowska, 1971). Again at the risk of labouring the point despite the perhaps fairly astract nature of the preceding discussion the concern is to promote a theoretical stance which allows for a possibly radical reappraisal of the premises upon which many of our cherished and long established social and political institutions and the practices adopted therein are based. It is a theoretical position that is generally ultimately about the quality of social and political life but which is in the context of this chapter directly focused on the nature of the experiences of social reality available to a specific section of society – those who have historically been most likely to get caught up in formal processes of social control.

Phenomenological theory can contribute to analyses of practice in juvenile justice in two main ways. First, the theories of delinquency espoused by control agents are identified as appropriate objects of empirical investigation in the study of the decision-making process. The 'facts' of a case and accounts of it presented through text and discourse are to be treated as topics for inquiry rather than as resources taken for granted in the a priori assumptions of the researcher. Second, questions about the origins of the ideologies of control agents and the legitimacy accorded to specific positions may be articulated to analyses of the relationship between power, knowledge and social structure. The making of decisions about delinquents can be construed as premised upon a particular conception of social reality and social relationships. Only when the nature of the ideologies maintained by control agents and the interests they serve are identified will approaches to delinquency control be open to critical appraisal. Concern with the theoretical conceptions of delinquency embodied within formal responses to control and with the conceptions of delinquency maintained by control agents and manifested in the practical accomplishment of juvenile justice is ultimately a concern for what happens to children. The pursuit of justice for children demands more than incremental and gradual modification of existing systems, and phenomenological theory, we believe, points to the need for further analysis of the very processes by which delinquency is socially constructed.

REFERENCES

Asquith, S. (1977) "Relevance and Lay Participation in Juvenile Justice", British Journal of Law and Society, 4, 61-76.

Bernstein, R. (1976) The Restructuring of Social and Political Theory. London: Methuen.

Berger, P. and Luckmann, T. (1971) The Social Construction of Reality. Harmondsworth: Penguin University Books.

Black Report (1979) Report of the Children and Young Persons Review Group (Northern Ireland). Belfast: HMSO.

Blankenship, R. (1974) "Case Records - Towards a Sociolinguistic Perspective on Deviance Labelling", Social Research, 58, 253-261.

Blum, A. and McHugh, P. (1970) "On the Failure of Positivism", in Douglas, J. (ed.) Understanding Everyday Life. London: Routledge and Kegan Paul.

Bottomley, K. (1973) Decisions in the Penal Process. Oxford: Martin Robertson.

Buckner, H. T. (1978) "Transformations of Reality in the Legal Process", in Luckmann, T. (ed.) Phenomenology and Sociology. Harmondsworth: Penguin Modern Sociology Readings.

Cicourel, A. (1976) The Social Organisation of Juvenile Justice. New York: Wiley.

Douglas, J. (1970) Deviance and Respectability: The Social Construction of Moral Meanings. London: Basic Books.

Fay, B. (1975) Social Theory and Political Practice. London: Allen and Unwin.

Gaudet, F. (1949) "The Sentencing Behavior of the Judge", in Brandon, V. and Katash, S. (eds.) Encyclopaedia of Criminology. New York.

Giddens, A. (1976) New Rules of Sociological Method. London: Hutchinson.

Green, E. (1961) Judicial Attitudes. London: Macmillan.

Grunhut, M. (1956) Competence and Constitution of the Juvenile Court. Oxford.

Hardiker, P. (1977) "Social Work Ideologies in the Probation Service", British Journal of Social Work, 7, 131-154.

Hindess, B. (1973) The Uses of Official Statistics in Sociology. London: Macmillan.

Hogarth, J. (1971) Sentencing as a Human Process. Toronto: University of Toronto Press.

Hood, R. (1962) Sentencing in Magistrates Courts. London: Stevens.

Kelly, G. (1970) "A Brief Introduction to Personal Construct Theory", in Kelly, G. Perspectives in Personal Construct Theory. New York: Academic Press.

Lissenberg, E. (1978) "The School's Influence on the Image and Attitude Building Process with Relation to Crime and the Administration of

Criminal Justice", unpublished paper, Universiteit van Amsterdam.

Lloyd, D. (1964) The Idea of Law. Harmondsworth: Pelican.

Mannheim, H., Spencer, J. C. and Lynch, G. (1957) "Magisterial Policy", in Baldwin, J. and Bottomley, K. (eds.) Criminal Justice. Oxford: Martin Robertson.

May, D. and Smith, G. (1970) "Policy Interpretation and the Children's Panels: A Case Study in Social Administration", Applied Social Studies, 2, 91-98.

McHugh, P. (1970) "A Common Sense Conception of Deviance", in Douglas, J. (ed.) op. cit.

Morris, A. and McIsaac, M. (1978) Juvenile Justice. London: Heinemann.

Ossowska, M. (1971) Social Determinants of Moral Ideas. London: Routledge and Kegan Paul.

Parsloe, P. (1976) "Social Work and the Justice Model", British Journal of Social Work, 6.

Patchett, A. W. and McLean, J. D. (1965) "Decision-making in Juvenile Cases", Criminal Law Review, 699-710.

Pearson, G. (1975) The Deviant Imagination. London: Macmillan.

Perelman, C. (1963) The Idea of Justice and the Problem of Argument. London: Routledge and Kegan Paul.

Petch, A. (1977) Consumer Reaction in the Social Services. University of Stirling: Diploma Dissertation.

Pitkin, H. F. (1972) Wittgenstein and Justice. Berkeley: University of California Press.

Rock, P. (1973) Deviant Behaviour. London: Hutchinson.

Schutz, A. (1967) The Phenomenology of the Social World. Evanston: Northwestern University Press.

Smith, G. (1977) "The Place of Professional Ideology in the Analysis of Social Policy: Some Theoretical Conclusions from a Pilot Study of the Children's Panels", Sociological Review, 25, 843-865.

Smith, G. (1980) Social Need. London: Routledge and Kegan Paul.

Smith, G. (1981) "Discretionary Decision-making in Social Work", in Adler, M. and Asquith, S. (eds.) Discretion and Welfare. London: Heinemann.

Stoll, C. S. (1968) "Images of Man and Social Control", Social Forces, 47, 119-127.

Warren, C. A. B. and Johnson, J. M. (1972) "A

Critique of Labelling Theory from the Phenomenological Perspective", in Scott, R. and Douglas, I. (eds.), Theoretical Perspectives on Deviance. New York: Basic Books.

Young, K. (1977) "Values in the Policy Process", Policy and Politics, 5, 1-22.

Young, K. (1981) "Discretion as an Implementation Problem", in Adler, M. and Asquith, S. op. cit.

Young, K. and Mills, L. (1978) "Understanding the 'assumptive worlds' of Governmental Actors: Issues and Approaches". Report to the SSRC Panel on Central/Local Government Relations.

8

ORIENTATIONS TO THE MEANING OF HELP: RESEARCH IMPLICATIONS

Ben Shapiro

INTRODUCTION

How do we think about "help"? What does it mean to the help-giver and to the help-receiver? How does this meaning influence behaviour as we seek and use help, or as we offer and deliver help? How does this meaning develop and change in response to the experience of participating in a helping process in a particular situation and in a particular setting? To what extent is this meaning unique and idiosyncratic, and to what extent is it shared with others on the basis of position in a social structure or as a result of having a particular cultural, social, or ideological orientation? What are its essential characteristics? What are its consequences and its implications for the formulation of social policies and the design of social programmes?

Bruce and Spencer, in their analysis of the Scottish Children's panels for the care of children in trouble or in need, used dramaturgical categories to discuss the "scene", the "dramatis personae" and their ideas, and the essential elements of the "performance". Therefore, it would be appropriate to examine:

> whether the children's hearing is to be perceived as a minor court of law, or a tribunal, or a welfare agency. The training of panel members, which in most areas was undertaken by university teachers in the field of psychology and sociology, laid stress on the role of the hearing as a decision making body in the field of social welfare. The administrators, and many of the Reporters,

>drew on the image of a tribunal when planning the procedures and practices to be adopted by the hearings. To the general public, however, and to most of the families appearing at hearings for the first time, it was just another juvenile court (Bruce and Spencer, 1976, p. 108).

This "grey area" as the authors describe it affects the "intelligibility" of the system, and much of their report is devoted to suggestions for modifications in order to clarify the "meaning" of the "performance" for its participants and for the general public. A policy debate not fully resolved about whether there should be a shift from a "traditional crime-punishment" approach to a "welfare" or "educative" approach continued to be reflected in some of the ambiguities of the new system although the responsibility had in fact shifted to an integrated social service delivery system. The persistence of the traditional perception, despite the official shift, indicates the power of a deeply-rooted frame of reference for all actors and its consequences for the functioning of the system.

In his classic analysis of blood donorship, Titmuss discuss the deeply-rooted significance of human blood in human culture.

>Symbolically and functionally, blood is deeply embedded in religious doctrine; in the psychology of human relationships; and in the theories and concepts of race, kinship, ancestor worship and the family (1970, p. 16).

He goes on to suggest that the "gift of blood" can be conceptualized as a form of giving which expresses altruistic motivations, and indeed that:

>the ways in which society organizes and structures its social institutions - and particularly its health and welfare systems - can encourage or discourage the altruistic in man... It is indeed little understood how modern society, technical, professional, large-scale organized society, allows few opportunities for ordinary people to articulate giving in morally practical terms outside their own network of family and personal relationships (p. 225).

The problem presented here is that of extending a familial frame of reference to a much broader range of applications. Blood and altruism, both essentially associated with the concept of kinship, can be made the subject and object of a gift between strangers perhaps at the opposite end of a spectrum of relationship-defined meanings (Mauss, 1954; Watson, 1980). Can strangers become in a sense "blood brothers or sisters"? Titmuss suggests that a society which values human freedom will formulate social policies which provide opportunities for gifts of precisely this kind.

The first example represents an attempt to redefine meaning, which runs the risk of presenting mixed meaning messages, and introducing confusion in the minds of those who are involved in a variety of roles. The dramaturgical metaphor helps to highlight the problem. In the second example we have an attempt to transfer meaning from one context (the familial) to another (the relationship among strangers) and thereby to create new meaning and to counteract the alienating tendencies of modernization.

In both examples more attention is paid to the intents, and their effects, of the policy-makers than to the actual meaning-orientations and perceptions brought to the helping interaction by the participants in the interaction. But the connection between these is implied.

Recent theoretical, methodological and empirical work has devoted attention to the relationship between social interaction, helping interaction as a special case of social interaction, value orientations, ideology, and social structure (Heyman and Shaw, 1978; Levinger and Raush, 1977; Lowe, 1969; Shapiro, 1975). Differentials of power, status, and orientation between help-giver and help-seeker, have been considered as possible explanations of failures of access and accessibility, for breakdowns in the helping process, and for ineffectual helping efforts (Maluccio, 1979; Mayer and Timms, 1972; Rees, 1975). Attempts have been made to bridge the gap by developing "client-centred" theories of practice to re-orient the professional practitioner (Rogers, 1971), use of paraprofessionals and indigenous personnel who purport to be more like the population they serve (Austin, 1977; Budner et. al., 1973; Sobey, 1970), by encouraging and development of self-help efforts by groups with special needs and problems (Katz and Bender, 1976; Killilea, 1976; Leiberman et. al., 1979), and, ultimately by recognizing and stimulating the "natural helping" efforts among people in their daily interactions (Collins and Pancoast, 1976; Gottlieb, 1978).

Any attempt to define match (between help-giver and help-receiver) in terms of similarity, whether of demographic characteristics, personality, or social-cultural-ideological orientations has proved to be problematic (Carson and Heine, 1962; Dougherty, 1976; More, 1977). Alternative explanations in terms of balance or exchange come closer to recognition of the complexity involved (Heider, 1958; Homans, 1961).

The concern underlying all of the examples and studies cited above is to find ways of improving the flow of help and of improving the structures within which this flow takes place. They reflect a growing understanding that in addition to these social structures there are "social structures of the mind" which must also be understood (Foa and Foa, 1974). Meanings of help may influence behaviour on the helping interaction; meanings of helping structures may influence the functioning of those structures.

A STUDY OF HELPING IN ISRAEL

PURPOSE

The study to be reported in this chapter was undertaken in 1979-80 in Israel and was concerned with what people mean when they think about "help", how this affects the ways in which they seek and use helping relationships and what implications this has for the organized helping services and professions.[1]

The findings reported here have been selected for the purposes of this chapter and reflect in particular the structure of meaning in the context of a range of helping formats, settings, and roles. It will be evident from the description of the instrument and of the sample that other findings are not included. It should also be recognized that these findings are the results of beginning explorations and must be regarded as tentative, and for the purposes of formulating hypotheses for more systematic investigation in the future.

The Meaning of Help

CONCEPTUAL FRAMEWORK

(a) Role-Relations as Frames of Reference

This work proceeds from the premise that people can, and often do, compare interactions in different role-relations, as a strategy for giving meaning to new interactions on the basis of interactions in role-relations which are familiar from personal or vicarious experience, or as part of a more generalized repertoire of conceptions shared with others. These "familiar" conceptions are used as frames of reference in forming expectations of the other, for interpreting behaviour, and for guiding one's own behaviour.

Meaning may be attached in a general way by indicating, for example, that a particular helping interaction resembles the kind of help given by a parent to a child. It may, however, be more specific by adding particular attributes: the interaction resembles a parent's help to a child in that it is given unconditionally, or that it is accompanied by a particular effect. Persons may tend to think stereotypically about helping, always using the same frame of reference, while others may make more differentiated use of frames of reference, related to need or problem, personal situation, setting, availability of helping resources, and other factors. The use of frames of reference may be socially patterned by position in the social structure, or variations in cultural orientations.

Various lists of role-relations have been used in the literature in order to study the process of role differentiation, perceived role differentiation, the use of role relations as a basis for studying the structure of thinking about social interaction, the study of personal networks and helping networks, and the study of the actual use of different role-relations for helping purposes (Eisenstadt, 1956; Rieger-Shlonsky, 1969; Rosenberg, 1978; Shils, 1957).

(b) Dimensions of Helping

In a preliminary study undertaken in Toronto, [2] three groups of help-givers (voluntary blood donors, cabin counsellors in a children's camp, and professional social workers in a variety of settings) and three groups of help-receivers (residents in a maternity home for pregnant adolescents, elderly persons served by four community-based centres for senior citizens, and recent immigrants from Israel, the Caribbean, and the Indian sub-continent) were given lists of role-relations, and asked to compare them in terms of the similarity or difference of help given. Since this study had the additional objective of developing instruments for the study of meaning, there were differences in the lists of role-relations used, in the task required of the respondent in reference to such a list, and in the analytical techniques. A form of multi-dimensional scaling was used to discover the structure or dimensionality underlying the series of stimuli (i.e. the role-relationship frames of reference) presented to the respondent (Shepard et. al., 1972; Wish, 1976).

In summary, all six groups of respondents were found to share a similar dimension as their first, or dominant dimension. This dimension was labelled a relational, or structural dimension. That is, respondents tended to cluster role-relations in such a way that reflected a tendency to differentiate role-relations on the basis of the social structure of the participants in the relationship and to use this differentiation as a way of differentiating between kinds of help.

Other dimensions that could be identified but weighted less than the structural dimension were labelled a substantive or content dimension (grouping role-relations in terms of characteristics of the help sought or given, such as personal-impersonal, general-specific, informal-formal, close-distant, etc.) and a context or situation dimension (reflecting the particular need/problem situation of the help-seeker or the particular time-space context of the helping).

(c) Paradigms of Helping

With reference to the relational or structural dimension identified above, three particular clusters of role-relations were differentiated and identified as "paradigms of helping". These were:

1. A kin paradigm

2. A peer paradigm

3. A patron paradigm

This finding tended to support a hypothetical formulation advanced in an earlier paper, suggesting a set of paradigms that might be considered basic or "primordial" (Shapiro, 1977). The formulation was based on the observation that the four basic types of role-relations in the family - two of them "horizontal" (mates and siblings) and two of them "vertical" (parent-child and child-parent) - taken together provide a familial or kin paradigm, but also provide prototypes for the other two paradigms: the horizontal types for the peer paradigm, and the vertical types for the patron paradigm.

(d) Summary of Preliminary Work

1. Role-relations (e.g. parent-child, mates, siblings, friends etc.) were conceptualized as frames of reference for attributing meaning to helping relationships

2. Multi-dimensional scaling of comparisons of these role-relations by six samples of respondents in the Toronto study revealed three major dimensions in the respondents' thinking about help: the relational-structural, the substantive-content, and the context-situation dimensions. For all six samples, the first of these was the dominant dimension used

3. With reference to this first, relational-structural dimension, three clusters of role-relations were observed and labelled as paradigms: the kin, peer and patron paradigms

4. These findings of the Toronto study tended to confirm earlier theoretical formulations predicting the emergence of paradigms of this kind.

(e) The Current Study

The current study in Israel provided an opportunity to study the use of these paradigms (and their constitutent clusters of role-relations) in the context of their use by help-givers and

help-receivers in four settings and three helping
formats. The framework for the current study is
therefore based on the set of paradigms derived from
the Toronto study and related theoretical material.
   The framework is summarized in Figure A. The
three sectors of the circle represent the three
major paradigms, originally hypothesized and
supported empirically as aspects of the first
dimension used by the six groups of Canadian
respondents. The particular role-relation items used
in the interview to indicate "meaning" - related
variables are listed by sector in Figure A. While no
multi-dimensional scaling analysis was conducted
with particular reference to the 54 respondents in
this study, an analysis of all the respondents in
the Israel study, including help-givers and
help-receivers for whom there was no opposite
number, gives general support to this
conceptualization. Indeed, the most frequent
clusters of items for all 112 respondents in the
larger study were as follows:

Parent-child/siblings/mates	29.3%
Friends/neighbours/persons	8.1%
Teacher-pupil/clerk-client/ doctor-patient	20.3%

Other clusters of three or more items were less
frequent.
   The itemized list of role-relations used for
different purposes in the interview was as follows:

Kin	(Parent-child (Between siblings (Between mates
Peers	(Between friends (Between neighbours (Between school or work colleagues (Between soldiers (Between persons [3]
Patrons	(Teacher-pupil (Clerk-client (Doctor-patient (Patron-protege
(Not classified)	Charity [4]

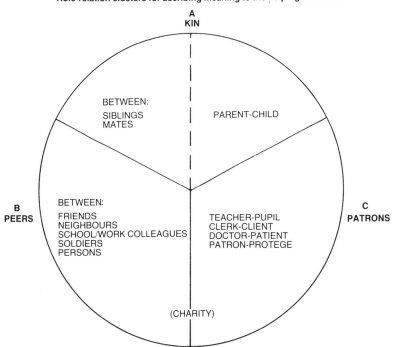

Figure 1.
Role-relation clusters for ascribing meaning to the helping interaction

THE DESIGN AND METHOD

Respondents were categorised as either "help-givers" (G) or "help-receivers" (R) and were drawn from the following settings:

I. Development Town "Aleph", had a changing population (about 2,000) including migrants from the large cities seeking challenging new experiences or jobs and housing. The respondents in this setting were involved in a programme to provide newcomers to the town with "foster families" to assist in their orientation and absorption to their new community. For purposes of this study, the helping format was conceptualized as a form of "natural helping", although initiated and organized under the auspices of the Absorption Service of the Town Council. Help-givers were local residents and received no training, supervision, or compensation.

II. Development Town "Beth", had a relatively stable population (about 7,500) which had migrated from North African countries in the 1950s and 1960s, having a traditional orientation to religion, and to family life. The help-givers in this setting were involved in a programme to train para-professional community workers, for direct service or for work as community-level generalists. Trainees were local residents who participated in a supervised practicum during the training period - and had prospects for local employment following the completion of their training.

III. Jerusalem Neighbourhood "Gimel", was an urban neighbourhood with a mixed population with regard to socio-economic status, cultural and ethnic background, recency of migration to Israel, and educational experience. The help-givers in this setting were employed by a neighbourhood community centre as para-professionals in a variety of roles vis-a-vis neighbourhood residents and members of the setting, including a programme to assist parents to support their school-age children's learning efforts. The help-givers were residents of Jerusalem, but not necessarily in this neighbourhood.

IV. Jerusalem Neighbourhood "Daleth", was a new urban neighbourhood with a population of recent immigrants to the country from Europe and the Middle East. The help-givers were professional social workers offering service to residents of the neighbourhood. Additional respondents for this "professional helping format" were drawn from Beth and Gimel.

For the purposes of the analysis reported here, data from help-givers and help-receivers in these settings were included only when data were available for both the help-giver and the help-receiver with whom he/she was involved in a helping relationship. Based on this criterion, 27 dyads were considered (i.e. 54 individuals: 27 Gs and 27 Rs) as follows:

Setting I - 6 dyads

Setting II - 12 dyads

Setting III - 5 dyads

Setting IV - 4 dyads

All Settings- 27 dyads

The interview followed a structured schedule and included the following areas:
(a) Personal and social characteristics of the respondent, including personal networks
(b) Perceptions of the need/problem situation being considered in the current helping, and profile of the help being given/received
(c) History and current status of the helping relationship
(d) Helping meanings as conveyed by reference to the list of 13 role-relations in order to characterize helping in general, and the current helping; and by reference to a list of 27 bipolar descriptors of helping
(e) The helping network recruited by both help-giver and help-receiver in relation to the current need/problem

Table 1. Demographic Characteristics of Respondents

Demographic Characteristics	NATURAL "Aleph"		PARA-PROFESSIONAL "Beth"		"Gimel"		PROFESSIONAL "Daleth"	
(N)	G (6)	R (6)	G (12)	R (12)	G (5)	R (5)	G (4)	R (4)
Average Age	30.2	24.8	29.2	39.3	34.8	35.0	38.3	30.3
Average Years of Education	11.5	11.2	10.4	7.1	12.2	10.4	15.8	9.3
Females (as % of N)	33	17	100	100	100	100	50	50
Married (as % of N)	100	100	83	100	80	80	25	25
Asia/Africa Born (as % of N)	50	17	92	75	0	60	25	50
Religious/traditional (as % of N)	50	50	92	100	80	100	75	50

(f) Evaluations of the helping process and helping relationship

The same interview was used with both G and R with minor adjustments in wording to focus on the shared current process.

A comparison of the demographic composition of the respondents in the four settings (see Table 1) suggests important social and cultural differences which must be taken into account in addition to differences among the settings (rural-urban, small-large community, recently developed-established community, homogeneous-mixed, etc.), and differences with respect to the helping format in which respondents were involved (natural, para-professional, and professional).

In particular, it should be noted that the help-receiver "newcomers" to Aleph were the youngest of the respondents, that they included the highest proportion of males, and that they were mainly Israeli-born. The respondents from Beth were the least educated (particularly the Rs), and included the highest proportion of Asian-African born and religious or traditional respondents.

The following analyses were undertaken for the 54 respondents who were involved in helping dyads:

(a) Personal network patterns
(b) Paradigms used in thinking about help in general
(c) Frames of reference used in characterizing the current help
(d) Descriptors of current help
(e) Evaluation of the current helping as a dependent variable.

FINDINGS

Many of the assumptions required for a rigorous statistical analysis of the data were absent. The findings must therefore be considered at this stage to be preliminary and impressionistic, and suggestive of further hypotheses.

(a) Personal Network Patterns

Respondents were asked to list up to ten persons not living in their household "whom you

Table 2. Personal Network Patterns

(N) Network Pattern	NATURAL "Aleph"		PARA-PROFESSIONAL "Beth"		"Gimel"		PROFESSIONAL "Daleth"	
	G (6)	R (6)	G (12)	R (12)	G (5)	R (5)	G (4)	R (4)
A (kin)	0%	50%	8%	33%	40%	20%	0%	25%
B (peer)	67%	33%	50%	8%	60%	60%	50%	75%
A + B (both)	33%	17%	42%	59%	0%	0%	50%	0%
No clear pattern	0%	0%	0%	0%	0%	20%	0%	0%

consider to be close to you (you like them very much etc.)" and to indicate their relationship to those listed, using categories in the list of role-relations if possible. There was very infrequent use of "patron" role-relations. Most respondents tended to be clearly using kin or peers or both categories together in describing their personal networks (see Table 2).

It will be noted that the proportion of "kin-specialists" was highest among the help-receiver "newcomers" to Aleph, who were in fact most likely to be separated from their immediate and extended families. This may be taken as an index of their newness in the new environment and retention of ties external to this new environment. Those most likely to be "peer-specialists" were the help-givers in all settings, although the help-receivers in the professional format were most peer-oriented. In Beth which was a relatively stable, homogeneous community both Gs and Rs were frequent users of both A and B relationships in their personal networks. Indeed, they made frequent reference to relatives as friends, and may in fact have been close to merging the two categories, as if the community were regarded by them in "tribal" terms. (In fact clan lines were, to some extent, preserved as a relevant frame of reference in certain communities which were settled at the same time by immigrants from the same region).

(b) Paradigms Used in Thinking about Help in General

The findings reported above with respect to "personal network patterns" refer to the actual relationship patterns of respondents. The assumption is that thinking about relationships and about helping relationships in particular takes place in the context of these actual relationship patterns described as personal networks. The respondents' thinking about help is dealt with at two levels: "thinking about help in general", and "characterizing the current helping". The first of these is a more abstract, generalized phenomenon which provides a cognitive context for the second, although it may itself be influenced both by prior helping experiences, and by more general conceptions current in the respondent's social environment. As a generalized conception of helping, the paradigm is taken as an indicator of the respondent's expectations with regard to the current helping - or

Table 3. Paradigms Used in Thinking about Help in General

| | NATURAL "Aleph" | | PARA-PROFESSIONAL "Beth" | | "Gimel" | | PROFESSIONAL "Daleth" | |
	G (6)	R (6)	G (12)	R (12)	G (5)	R (5)	G (4)	R (4)
(N) Paradigms								
A (kin)	32	0	25	8	40	20	0	25
B (peer)	17	0	8	0	0	0	50	25
C (patron)	0	0	8	0	0	40	25	0
A + B	0	0	0	8	0	0	0	25
A x B	0	0	17	17	20	20	50	0
A x C	17	0	0	43	20	0	25	0
B x C	17	50	25	0	0	0	0	0
A x B x C	0	0	0	8	20	20	0	0
(A + B) x C	0	50	17	0	0	0	0	0
A x (B + C)	0	0	0	8	0	0	0	0
No clear paradigm	17		0	8	0	0	25	25

any prospective helping interaction.
Respondents were asked to consider the list of
13 role-relations:

> Here are some typical kinds of
> help-givers. Group the 13 types on the
> cards according to the degree of
> similarity of the help given. You are
> requested to form - according to your own
> way of thinking - at least two separate
> groups and not more than six such groups.

The data were analyzed on the basis of being
able to identify three or more items associated with
a paradigm before determining that a grouping
reflected that paradigm. If two paradigms were
grouped together, and therefore considered to be
similar, they were represented, for example, thus: A
+ B. If two paradigms were used, but grouped
separately, indicating that they were differentiated
by respondents, they were represented thus: A x B.
Table 3 summarizes the analysis.
It will be noted that A (kin) is a frequently
used paradigm, both on its own, and as
differentiated from B (peers), and from C (patrons).
In this respect, the help-receivers of Aleph were
different, in that they tended to focus on a
differentiation between B and C (or between A + B
and C). The receivers of paraprofessional help also
made frequent use of C as a paradigm for thinking
about helping. In particular, the receivers of
paraprofessional help in Gimel used the C (patron)
paradigm alone 40% of the time (no other receivers
used this paradigm alone) and together with A and B
another 20% of the time. Unlike the paraprofessional
receivers of Beth, who associated C with the A (kin)
paradigm, these urban receivers seemed oriented to
professional modalities of helping, although they
were engaged currently in a paraprofessional format.
The receivers of professional help did not use C in
this study. Within each setting, there were
differences between givers and receivers of help,
which suggests that a dyad-by-dyad analysis
(reported below) should be undertaken.
In addition to the differences noted above, it
is possible to add that both Gs and Rs in the
paraprofessional situations tended to be similar to
one another in terms of the number of paradigms they
used, "natural" Rs tended to use more paradigms than
the Gs, while the "professional" Gs tended to use
more than their clients. This may be a reflection of

Table 4. Frames of Reference Used in Characterizing the Current Help [a]

		NATURAL "Aleph"		PARA-PROFESSIONAL "Beth"		"Gimel"		PROFESSIONAL "Daleth"	
		G (6)	R (6)	G (12)	R (12)	G (5)	R (5)	G (4)	R (4)
(N)									
Frames of Reference									
Kin	Parent-child	3.8	5.3	5.2	4.8	2.2	5.8	7.0	5.0
	Between siblings	2.8	3.2	3.2	4.6	4.6	6.4	4.5	2.8
	Between mates	3.5	3.8	6.3	5.5	7.0	6.8	7.0	5.0
Peers	Between friends	1.2	1.5	1.7	3.3	2.0	3.2	2.5	2.0
	Between neighbours	4.5	2.2	3.8	5.0	2.8	5.8	7.0	2.8
	Between colleagues	4.0	3.8	5.5	5.7	3.2	3.5	5.5	2.8
	Between soldiers	4.5	5.3	5.6	6.0	5.0	7.0	5.5	4.0
	Between persons	2.0	2.7	2.4	3.3	1.4	2.0	1.0	2.8
Patrons	Teacher-pupil	4.5	4.3	5.0	3.8	2.4	3.6	5.5	3.5
	Clerk-client	7.0	7.0	6.8	5.8	6.0	5.2	7.0	5.5
	Doctor-Patient	5.5	6.3	5.7	4.8	6.6	6.2	5.0	2.8
	Patron-protege	6.2	3.7	6.0	4.6	5.8	6.2	7.0	3.8
Charity		6.7	7.0	6.9	6.3	6.0	5.6	7.0	4.5
Summary	A (kin)	3.4	4.1	4.9	5.0	4.6	6.3	6.2	4.3
	B (peer)	3.2	3.1	3.8	4.7	2.9	4.3	4.3	2.9
	C (patron)	5.8	5.3	5.9	4.8	5.2	5.3	6.1	3.9
	Charity	6.7	7.0	6.9	6.3	6.0	5.6	7.0	4.5

a Mean Scores are used, based on a 7-point scale (1 = very similar; 7 = very different levels of sophistication in thinking about helping which may be associated with other socio-cultural factors.

(c) Frames of Reference Used in Characterizing the Current Help

Respondents were asked to "indicate the degree to which the help received or given actually is similar to or different from the types of helping you saw on the cards" (i.e. the 13 types enumerated above). The measure labelled here as "Frames of Reference" is taken as an indicator of the respondent's perception of the current helping, and therefore different from "paradigms", which indicate expectations.

Again, it will be clear from Table 4 that the peer paradigm was most frequently used, followed by the kin paradigm, and then the patron paradigm and the "charity" item. Generally speaking, within the peer paradigm, the "between friends" and "between persons" frames of reference were preferred, within the kin paradigm the "between siblings" frame of reference was preferred, and within the patron paradigm the "teacher-pupil" frame of reference was preferred.

In comparing settings, respondents in Aleph rated both kin and peer paradigms more highly than respondents in the other settings, and this was particularly true for the kin paradigm. In comparing givers and receivers of help, receivers rated the peer paradigm more highly than givers, but the reverse was true for the other paradigms.

Within settings, the greatest differences between Gs and Rs appeared among participants in the professional helping format: their perceptions of the current helping were furthest apart. The help-givers were thinking in terms of "help between persons" (like their counterparts in the other helping formats); the help-receivers were thinking in terms of "help between siblings", "between neighbours", and "between school or work colleagues" as well - and, unlike any of the other groups of respondents, in terms of doctor-patient helping. This broader band of peer-oriented frame of reference creates an interesting disparity which bears closer examination.

(d) Descriptors of the Current Helping

Table 5. Descriptors of the Current Helping

Descriptors [a] + / −	NATURAL "Aleph" G (6)	R (6)	PARA-PROFESSIONAL "Beth" G (12)	R (12)	"Gimel" G (5)	R (5)	PROFESSIONAL "Daleth" G (4)	R (4)
Skilled / Unskilled	−	−	+	+	+	+	+	+
Family-like / Business-like	+	+	+	+	−	−	−	−
Ongoing / Transitory	+	+	−	−	+	+	+	o
Freely chosen / Of necessity	+	+	+	+	+	+	+	−
Altruistic / Self-interested	+	+	+	−	−	−	+	+
In-depth / Superficial	+	+	+	−	+	+	+	−
Not Controlling / Controlling	+	+	−	−	+	−	+	−
2-way / 1-way	+	+	o	−	−	+	+	−
Unofficial / Official	+	+	o	−	+	−	+	−
Open / Discreet	+	+	−	−	−	+	+	−
Permissive / Demanding	+	−	+	+	−	+	−	−
Between persons who are:								
Similar / Dissimilar	+	+	−	−	−	−	+	+

a Based on a 7-point scale, '+' reflects a mean score of 1-3; 'o' a mean score of [...] a mean score of 5-7.

Respondents were asked to indicate "to what extent the following pairs of definitions characterize the help given/received", using a list of 27 pairs of bipolar adjectives. All respondents characterized the current help as equal, close, co-operative, personal, constructive, voluntary, given as a right, trustworthy, sensitive, understanding, useful, hopeful, honourable, important, and encouraging independence. With respect to the remaining 12 pairs of adjectives there were, however, differences among groups. The findings are presented in dichotomous form in Table 5.

On first inspection, it will be evident that there was greatest agreement between Gs and Rs in the natural helping format and least agreement in the professional helping format.

With respect to the descriptors themselves, those in the natural helping format differed from all the others in that the current helping was viewed as unskilled rather than skilled; in common with the other development town respondents "family-like" as opposed to "business-like"; and in common with those in the professional helping format "between similar persons" as opposed to "between different persons". This last comparison is somewhat surprising and does not represent a marked difference; but it indicates a "strangeness" which is contrary to the intentions of the initiators of the para-professional helping format. The Beth paraprofessional Gs and Rs also stand out in their description of the helping as "transitory" and "controlling" reflecting the fact that this was a practicum in connection with their training programme. Apart from the temporary nature of the practicum, the training may have influenced trainees to identify more strongly with the "power of the professional" than with the aspirations of their clients.

A further analysis was undertaken to examine the relationship between frames of reference employed by respondents in describing the current helping and the descriptors used by the same respondents, without regard to setting, helping format, or helping role.

Those who characterized the helping using primarily kin-type (A) frames of reference used the following descriptors: Equal, Ongoing, Two-way, Altruistic, Freely chosen. Those who used peer frames of reference (B) used the following: In-depth, Unofficial, Encouraging independence,

Table 6. Evaluations of the Current Helping and Dyadic Similarity

Evaluation of helping		Both G & R positive (N = 11)	G & R differ (N = 10)	Both G & R negative (N = 6)
Network patterns of Both G & R	(A	36	20	33
	(B	64	50	50
Helping paradigms of Both G & R	(A	45	30	83
	(B	18	30	17
	(C	9	50	0
Frames of reference of Both G & R	(A	9	0	17
	(B	36	40	33
	(C	0	0	17

Percentages do not total 100 because A, B and C clusters may occur alone, or in conjunction with one another, or not at all.

Two-way, Altruistic. Those who used patron frames of reference (C) used the following: Unequal, Superficial, Official, Transitory, Skilled, One-way. This listing does not include a number of descriptors shared by these groups. It is intended to highlight difference in perceptions of the helping process, and to provide additional interpretations of the meaning of the kin, peer, and patron orientations when used in describing the current helping.

(e) Evaluation of the Current Helping as a Dependent Variable

Respondents were asked to evaluate the current helping using five criteria:

1. Degree of similarity between the help requested and the help given
2. Degree of understanding shown by the other in the helping relationship
3. Degree of empathy shown by self to other
4. Degree of empathy shown by other to self
5. Degree of match as seen by the other

Each criterion was rated on a 5-point scale. For the purposes of this analysis a mean score for the 5 scales was computed for each respondent, and respondents were classified as "positive" or "negative" in their evaluations in terms of whether they were above or below the grand mean for all respondents.

To test the hypothesis that satisfaction with the helping relationships is most directly related to the degree of similarity of orientations of the giver and receiver in each dyad, with respect to the meaning of help, an analysis was undertaken, and summarized in Table 6.

Givers and receivers were compared in Tables 2 – 5 on the basis of responses for givers and receivers aggregated separately. In Table 6, their responses were first compared, dyad by dyad, and only then aggregated. It will be seen that, when personal networks were similar, they were likely to be peer-oriented, without regard to their evaluations of the dyad. When generalized paradigms were similar, they were likely to be kin-oriented and evaluations of these kin-specializing dyads were likely to be similar as well, particularly in a negative direction. When generalized paradigms were

Table 7. Personal Network Patterns and Helping Paradigms

	NATURAL "Aleph"		PARA-PROFESSIONAL "Beth"		"Gimel"		PROFESSIONAL "Daleth"	
	G (6)	R (6)	G (12)	R (12)	G (5)	R (5)	G (4)	R (4)
Personal network patterns	B	A	B	A+B	B	B	B	B
Helping Paradigms	A	BxC	AxBxC	AxC	A	C	AxB	AxB

A = kin; B = peers; C = patrons; + Associated paradigms; x Differentiated paradigms similar and patron-oriented,however, the evaluations of the members of the dyad were likely to differ. When frames of reference were similar, they were likely to be peer-oriented, without regard to evaluations, as was the case with the personal network measure.

In summary, similarity with respect to personal network patterns and use of frames of reference tended to be peer-oriented, but not associated with similarity or direction of evaluation of the current helping. On the other hand, most similarity was found among dyads who used kin-oriented paradigms of helping and arrived at similarly negative evaluations of the helping. On the other hand, most similarity was found among dyads who used kin-oriented paradigms of helping and arrived at simlilarly negative evaluations of the helping. It appears that kin-orientations aroused expectations about the quality of a relationship which were more difficult to satisfy than relationships defined in other ways.

DISCUSSION

(a) Personal Network Patterns and Helping Paradigms

The measures developed for each of these concepts were different and provided different data which were analyzed differently. There has been no rigorous attempt to test the validity or reliability of these measures. Personal networks represent sets of relationships reported by respondents as significant to them. Paradigms, as used here, refer to their generalized ways of thinking about help, using role-relations as the components of these paradigms, and/or interepreted as <u>expectations</u> as they related to the current helping and/or other prospective helping interactions in which they might become involved, while frames of reference using the same role-relation items for characterizing the current helping are interpreted as <u>perceptions</u> of the actual helping.

The fact that respondents and groups of respondents frequently turn out to be differently oriented on different measures (see Table 7) suggests that different phenomena are indeed reflected.

(b) Kin, Peers, and Patrons

i) The "kin" orientation appears as a personal network specialization among the help-receivers in Aleph and in Beth. In the former case, they are newcomers, involved in a "neighbour-to-neighbour" adoption programme and appear to have retained network ties that are external to the host community during this adoption period. In the latter case, many of these kinship ties are within the community in which the respondents have been residing for a number of years and are combined in personal networks within peer ties; in fact, the distinction is at times blurred.

As a paradigm for helping, the kin orientation appears more frequently and not necessarily among the same groups of respondents as above; help-givers in two settings use it alone (Aleph and Gimel), or differentiated from peers (professionals) or from both peers and patrons (Beth). Help-receivers use it in combination with peers (professional dyads) or differentiated from patrons (Beth). The kinship orientation to helping goes beyond personal network behaviour; it orients persons to <u>expectations</u> that helping will be of a particular character, <u>resembling</u> helping that goes on between members of a family and whatever that connotes for those who think in this way.

ii) The "peer" orientation is a more pervasive type of personal network, with the exceptions noted above. As a paradigm it expresses expectations amongst the help-givers of Beth and the professional help-givers, and the help-receivers in the latter instance, and in Aleph. It always appears together with one or the other paradigm.

While the friend and person-to-person frames of reference are considered to be associated with the peer orientation, they are found among the preferred descriptions of the current helping by all groups of respondents - indeed as their most preferred perceptions of the current helping. They are, however, more selective of other peer-oriented frames of reference (see Table 4).

iii) It has already been pointed out that the "patron" orientation is virtually absent from the personal networks of the respondents. It does appear as a paradigm among the receivers in Aleph and Gimel and among both Gs and Rs of Beth. These respondents include in their definition of helping a conception that helping can go on between persons of unequal status.

The fact that there were individual respondents and groups of respondents who did not employ identifiable patterns of meaning in the sense used in this study may be interpreted as: an artifact of the measures used; a reflection of their inability to conceptualize in the ways required by the instruments; a reflection of the unstable nature of their symbolic environments; or as a result of their use of different types of cognitive categories for thinking about help.

(c) Natural Helping, Para-professional Helping and Professional Helping

The intention in Aleph was to mobilize old-timers in a voluntary, _natural_, capacity vis-a-vis newcomer neighbours to assist in their absorption into the town. The help-givers were involved in peer-oriented personal networks; the newcomers in kin-oriented networks. By contrast, the help-givers thought about help with kin-oriented paradigms, and their receivers with peer-oriented paradigms. Each perceived the helping with frames of reference consistent with these paradigms. This reciprocal response of each group to the other is striking in its symmetry, yet problematic in that each group "missed" the other; they were not on common ground in their definition of the helping relationship. They were also disparate in their evaluation of the helping. A programme of "natural helping", a neighbour-to-neighbour process of unskilled helping, might be defined as family-like or as peer-like. But these definitions are different. The first would presumably require an intensity of relationship which, apparently, the old-timers expected to offer: a kind of surrogate family. The newcomers, still rooted in their family ties elsewhere, were more tentative and did not expect to make that kind of investment; the peer orientation was more suitable for them. This was a "temporary community" at this stage of their involvement and this perception fashioned and shaped their expectations accordingly.

The para-professionals in Beth were residents of the town who were recruited and trained for this purpose. The para-professionals in Gimel were not residents of the urban neighbourhood in which they served, and had varying amounts and kinds of training and preparation. Both Gs and Rs in both settings were peer-oriented in their personal networks (with an admixture of kin ties for the Rs in Beth).

Expectations were defined in terms that differentiated the kin paradigm from the patron paradigm in the case of Beth, for both Gs and Rs. Expectations were similar but perceptions differed. The trainees were committed to an orientation in common with their "clients" but were behaving as if this were not the case. This is not an uncommon effect of the process of recruiting (or co-opting) indigenous resources and using them as extensions of the formal (professional) service delivery system.

In the case of Gimel, Gs expectations were defined in terms of the kin paradigm, and Rs in terms of the patron paradigm: their expectations differed because they came out of different milieux and life experiences. But they were apparently able to arrive at similar definitions of the situation, which captured the intent of the para-professional format.

For the participants in the professional dyads (Daleth), there were common types of personal network (peer). However, although both Gs and Rs used kin and peer paradigms, the former differentiated these, and the latter did not. The former did not exhibit a pattern for characterizing the current helping and there was wide variation among individuals. The receivers used both peer and patron role relations as frames of reference. Their use of patron items was the most extensive of all groups of respondents, a not unexpected response to helping from professional helpers. However, they omitted any reference to kin-oriented role-relations, revealing a disparity both between Gs and Rs and between expectations and perceptions of what actually happened. It is perhaps not surprising that, of all the respondents, the receivers of professional helping expressed least satisfaction with the helping.

(d) Settings and Cultures

Variations among the four settings may be associated with cultural factors reflected to some extent in Table 1. For example, in Beth, with a high proportion of respondents born in North Africa, below-average levels of education and a generally traditional attitude to religion, and residence for a period in excess of 10 years on the average, one might expect to find a stable, traditional orientation to interpersonal relationships and to the meaning of help. By contrast, one would expect that the more recently settled, more secular, Israel-born population of Aleph would be more modernized, but somewhat less crystallized in their views of helping. The urban residents of Gimel and Daleth were more heterogeneous and less likely to exhibit common patterns of orientation.

However, the assumption that people bring relatively stable frameworks of meaning into social relationships must be questioned (Shapiro, 1978). The degree of stability or turbulence in the "symbolic environment" within which the helping interaction takes place might be an important variable to take into account. Thus, the co-existence in Beth of a noted faith healer together with an elaborate apparatus of personal service and income support programmes, the tendency in that environment to politicize religious affiliations and to use political-religious affiliations as a key to access to programmes and services, tended to complicate and confound the "symbolic environment". The relative isolation of this community, in time and space, from the roots and supports for its belief systems, constitutes a threat to the continuity of traditional orientations.

The expression of these processes in terms of culturally patterned meaning-related expectations and perceptions becomes more problematic than might appear on the surface, and this is reflected in the data.

CONCLUSION

This study was not designed to establish whether the "meaning" of help used by persons engaged in helping interactions is the most important variable influencing their behaviour or attitudes toward the helping relationship. Nor was it designed to discover whether there might be other ways of conceptualizing and operationalizing "meaning" as related to helping. Given the scope of the study, however, some confirmation was obtained that:

(a) People can and do associate helping in general, and in particular situations, with one or more familiar sets of role-relations;

(b) Clusters or "paradigms" can be identified and labelled as "kin", "peer" and "patron" and these are used in different combinations by different respondents;

(c) Personal network patterns (i.e. actual social structures) do not necessarily correspond to meaning patterns (i.e. "social structures of the mind"), whether defined as expectation-meanings or perception-meanings;

(d) Help-givers do not necessarily think the same way as their corresponding help-receivers, and there may be some relationship between these differences in expectation and perception with regard to the meaning of the helping interaction between them, and differences in their satisfaction with that process;

(e) While meaning patterns do not show evidence of strong patterns of association with helping role (giver-receiver), helping format (natural, para-professional, professional), helping setting (characterized in social and cultural terms), or indeed with specific demographic characteristics of the respondents - when these are treated in aggregated form - the findings suggest that meaning patterns may be associated with many of these types of variables.

Because this analysis is based upon a small sample of respondents (N=54) selected on the basis of their accessibility and interest to the researcher, rather than on the basis of their representativeness of a defined population, it should not be regarded as generalizable in any way. Nor can causal inferences or associations among variables be established. It is exploratory in the sense that it begins to apply the concept of meaning, and methods of measuring meaning, developed by Foa, Wish and others in the context of relationships generally, to the specific context of helping roles and relationships. The fact that "people can and do associate helping in general, and in particular situations, with one or more familiar sets of role relations" suggests at least two lines of future research.

The first of these lines of future research involves greater precision in measurement and a more rigorous application of the canons of research methodology in order to discover associations among demographic variables, situational variables, helping formats, helping roles, and meaning-related categories. The second, however, involves qualitative research in order to achieve "intimate familiarity" with the helping interaction of the type advocated by Sotland (1976) with an expectation that the richness and complexity of this phenomenon can be further explored and explicated.

IMPLICATIONS

The Titmuss analysis of blood donorship referred to at the outset draws heavily on kinship-related associations for evolving deeply rooted, primordial forms of social meaning. Bruce and Spencer show the influence of prevailing, and conflicting, ideologies of help upon the ways in which the helping process is perceived. In his study of the client-worker interaction "face-to-face", Rees describes the "world of experience" that each brings to bear on the interaction in terms of widely held ideological conceptions of moral character (Rees, 1978). He advocates experimentation with new forms of organization, based on more flexible assumptions about professional and client roles.

Within the framework of the conceptual categories used in the present study, it is possible to speculate about alternative strategies for the design of social programmes. The first of these involves the creation of social structures for helping purposes which evoke and create socially desirable meanings. Titmuss suggests that voluntary blood donorship may be seen as a strategy for strengthening the fabric of society and perhaps indicates a readiness to participate in other forms of mutual help and transfer of resources. Rees also advocates variations in social structure, this time on a face-to-face basis in the hope of generating feelings of acceptance, trust, and mutual understanding and hence more effective helping. This represents perhaps an attempt to convert a stranger relationship in the patron paradigm to one more easily understood as an instrumental form of peer relationship in which there is not necessarily an identity of roles, but rather a mutually accepted reciprocity of roles.

Strategies which are based upon the identification of existing social structures, in the form of personal networks, the strengthening and mobilization of these structures for helping purposes, also imply that, by so doing, relationship norms of kinship, peership and patronship will function appropriately and enhance the policy-maker's programme objectives and policy goals (Collins and Pancoast, 1976; McKinlay, 1973; Ruveni, 1975; Speck and Attneave, 1973).

Recent efforts on the part of policy decision-makers in North America to shift responsibility for helping away from government and the formal service delivery system to the voluntary efforts of relatives, friends and neighbours represent a paradigm shift which, on the surface, would appear to be a re-affirmation of the value of natural helping networks. When, however, it represents the appropriation of a kin-peer paradigm as a rationalization for the abdication of public responsibility for meeting human needs which cannot otherwise be met, it becomes clear that meanings have their uses and their potential misuses.

There is, therefore, no guarantee that social structures will produce either the desired or the desirable impact upon our thinking. Bruce and Spencer make a significant point in emphasizing that the intent of "performance" is not necessarily matched by its perception. The implication is that more direct attention must be paid to: analyzing the "social structures of the mind"; ways of designing and presenting help in order to match or specifically influence helpful meanings; and ways of evaluating its meaning-related impact.

Beyond structural strategies, therefore, are more detailed strategies related to the content and process of helping and to the definitions of roles, formats, and settings. The meaning-messages they convey must be attended to and consciously, purposefully, and sensitively managed. This requires attention at the broadest level of social policy formulation and programme development, and at the day-to-day level of face-to-face helping interaction. This requires attention in the education and preparation of professionals and managers, and in the recruitment and assignment of everyone connected at every level of the helping process.

Will it be helpful for helping to be seen as similar, for example, to that of a parent to a child and in what respects? What has to be done and said so that it will indeed be seen in that way? For whom will this be appropriate and useful, and in relation to what types of situations? With respect to what other role-relations can questions of this kind be meaningfully asked? With respect to what frames of reference other than the role-relations type can they be asked?

Ultimately, conceptions of helping are not the exclusive province of theories of society and of scientific practice, nor are they the exclusive province of practical politicians and policy-makers. The purpose in asking questions of this kind is to locate and to sustain the real links between helping and human culture.

NOTES

1. This research project was conducted under a Research Grant from the Social Sciences and Humanities Research Council of Canada No. 410-78-0185.

2. This study was conducted under the auspices of the Helping Networks research programme of the Faculty of Social Work, University of Toronto. A report is in preparation. The assistance of Anke Oostendorp is gratefully acknowledged. In addition, the co-operation of colleagues Caryl Abrahams-Maclachlan, Esther Blum, Ernie Lightman, Albert Rose, Benjamin Schlesinger, and their respective research groups of MSW students is gratefully acknowledged.

3. The "Between persons" item was included as a generalized reference to the Peer Paradigm in order to provide respondents with a general opportunity to use this paradigm without having to list all the possible role-relations that might be appropriate. In fact, this item was heavily used, often in conjunction with one or more of the specific peer-related items. Its use was problematic in that it is at a different level of abstraction from the other items, with the exception of the last.

4. The "Charity" item was included because of the frequent use of this concept as a frame of reference. Respondents tended to use this term in different ways. The Hebrew word for charity is tzedakah, derived from a root meaning "justice". For many of the respondents, help described in this way was a matter of distributive justice, given and received as a matter of right, and with dignity. For many of the respondents, charity meant

213

non-egalitarian and stigmatized helping. While these findings are of interest in themselves, the wide divergence in meaning suggested that for many of the analyses, this item should be excluded.

REFERENCES

Austin, M. S. (1977) Professionals and paraprofessionals. New York: Human Sciences Press.

Bruce, N. and Spencer, J. (1976) Face to Face with Families: A Report on the Children's Panels in Scotland. Loanhead: Macdonald.

Budner, S. Chazin, R. M. and Young, H. (1973) "The Indigenous Nonprofessional in a Multi-Service Centre", Social Casework, 54, 354-359.

Carson, R. C. and Heine, R. W. (1962) "Similarity and Success in Therapeutic Dyads", Journal of Consulting Psychology, 26, 38-43.

Chin, R. (1976) "The Utility of Models of the Environments of Systems for Practitioners" in Bennis, W. G. et al., The Planning of Change (3rd edition). New York: Holt, Rinehart and Winston.

Collins, A. H. and Pancoast, D. L. (1976) Natural Helping Networks: A Strategy for Prevention. Washington: National Association of Social Workers.

Dougherty, F. E. (1976) "Patient-therapist Matching for Prediction of Optimal and Minimal Therapeutic Outcome", Journal of Consulting and Clinical Psychology, 44, 889-97.

Eisenstadt, S. N. (1956) "Ritualised Personal Relations: Blood Brotherhood, Best Friends, Compadre, etc.: Some Comparative Hypotheses and Suggestions", Man, 56.

Emery, F. E. and Trist, E. L. (1975) Towards a Social Ecology: Contextual Appreciations of the Future in the Present. New York: Plenum/Rosetta.

Foa, U. G. and Foa, E. B. (1974) Societal Structures of the Mind. Springfield: Thomas.

Gottlieb, B. H. (1978) "The Development of a Classification Scheme of Informal Helping Behaviours", Canadian Journal of Behavioural Science, 10, 105-115.

Grosser, C. et al. (eds.) (1969) Non-Professionals in the Human Services. San Francisco: Jossey-Bass.

Heider, F. (1958) The Psychology of Interpersonal Relations. New York: Wiley.

Heyman, B. and Shaw, M. (1978) "Constructs of Relationship", Journal for the Theory of Social Behaviour, 8.

Homans, G. C. (1961) Social Behaviour: Its Elementary Forms. New York: Harcourt, Brace and World.

Hunt, D. E. (1971) Matching Models in Education: The Co-ordination of Teaching Methods with Student Characteristics. Toronto: Ontario Institute for Studies in Education.

Katz, A. H. and Bender, E. I. (1976) The Strength in Us: Self-Help Groups in the Modern World. New York: New Viewpoints.

Killilea, M. (1976) "Mutual Help Organisations: Interpretatons in the Literature", in G. Caplan and M. Killilea, Support Systems and Mutual Help: Multidisciplinary Explorations. New York: Grune and Stratton.

Leiberman, M. A., Borman, L. D. et al. (1979) Self-Help Groups for Coping with Crisis: Origins, Members, Processes, and Impact. San Francisco: Jossey-Bass.

Levinger, G. and Raush, H. L. (eds.) (1977) Close Relationships: Perspectives on the Meaning of Intimacy. Amherst: University of Massachusetts Press.

Lowe, C. M. (1969) Value Orientations in Counselling and Psychotherapy: The Meanings of Mental Health. San Francisco: Chandler.

McKinlay, J. B. (1973) "Social Networks, Lay Consultations and Help-Seeking Behaviour", Social Forces, 51, 275-92.

Maluccio, A. (1979) Learning from Clients: Interpersonal Helping As Viewed by Clients and Social Workers. New York: Free Press.

Mauss, M. (1954) The Gift. London: Routledge and Kegan Paul.

Mayer, J. E. and Timms, N. (1972) The Client Speaks: Working Class Impressions of Casework. New York: Atherton.

Moore, E. E. (1977) Matching in Helping Relationships. Unpublished doctoral dissertation, University of Toronto.

Rees, S. (1975) "How Misunderstanding Occurs", in R. Bailey and M. Brake (eds.), Radical Social Work. London: Edward Arnold.

Rees, S. (1978) Social Work Face to Face. London: Edward Arnold.

Rieger-Shlonsky, H. (1969) "The Conceptualisation of the Roles of a Relative, a Friend, and a Neighbour", Human Relations, 22, 355-69.

Rogers, C. (1969) "Characteristics of a Helping Relationship", in D. L. Avila, A. W. Combs and W. W. Purkey (eds.), The Helping Relationship Sourcebook. Boston: Allyn and Bacon.

Rosenberg, J. (1978) "Discovering Natural Types of Orientation: An Application of Cluster Analysis", Social Service Review, 52, 85-106.

Rosenfeld, J. M. (1964) "Strangeness between Helper and Client - A Possible Explanation of Non-use of Available Professional Help", Social Service Review, 38, 17.

Ruveni, U. (1975) "Network Intervention with a Family in Crisis", Family Process, 14, 193-204.

Shapiro, B. Z. (1975) "Encountering the Politicized Client", The Social Worker, 43, 171-176.

Shapiro, B. Z. (1977) "Mutual Helping - A Neglected Theme in Social Work Practice Theory", Canadian Journal of Social Work Education, 3, 33-44.

Shapiro, B. Z. (1978) Mutual Helpers, Volunteers and Professionals: A Study of the Israeli Experience. Toronto: Occasional Paper No. 1, Faculty of Social Work, University of Toronto.

Shepard, R. N., Romney, A. K. and Nerlove, S. B. (1972) Multi-Dimensional Scaling: Theory and Applications in the Behavioural Sciences. New York: Seminar Press.

Shils, E. (1957) "Primordial, Personal, Sacred and Civil Ties", British Journal of Sociology, 8, 130-145.

Shulman, N. (1977) "Role Differentiation in Urban Networks", in C. Beattie and S. Crysdale (eds.), Sociology Canada: Readings. Toronto: Butterworth.

Silverman, P. R. (1969) The Client Who Drops Out: A Study of Spoiled Helping Relationships. Unpublished doctoral dissertation, Brandeis University.

Sobey, F. (1970) The Nonprofessional Revolution in Mental Health. New York: Columbia.

Sotland, J. D. (1976) Social Life: The Qualitative Study of Human Interaction in Natural Settings. New York: Wiley.

Speck, R. V. and Attneave, G. L. (1973) Family Networks. New York: Vintage.

Tessler, R. C. and Polansky, N. A. (1975) "Perceived Similarity: A Paradox in Interviewing", Social Work, 20, 359-63.

Titmuss, R. M. (1970) The Gift Relationship: From Human Blood to Social Policy. London: Allen and Unwin.

Watson, D. (1980) Caring for Strangers. London:

Routledge and Kegan Paul.

Weiss, R. S. (1973) "Helping Relationships: Relationships of Clients with Physicians, Social Workers, Priests and Others", Social Problems, 20, 319-28.

Wellman, B. (1980) A Guide to Network Analysis: A Working Paper. Toronto: Structural Analysis Programme, University of Toronto.

Wish, M. (1976) "Comparisons among Multi-Dimensional Structures of Interpersonal Relations", Multivariate Behavioural Research, 11, 297-324.

Wish, M., Deutsch, M. and Kaplan, S. J. (1976) "Perceived Dimensions of Interpersonal Relations", Journal of Personality and Social Psychology, 33, 409-20.

Wolf, E. R. (1968) "Kinship, Friendship and Patron-Client Relations in Complex Societies" in M. Banton (ed.), The Social Anthropology of Complex Societies. London: Tavistock.

9

SOCIAL WORK, POLICY, GOVERNMENT AND RESEARCH: A MILDLY OPTIMISTIC VIEW

Gilbert Smith

One of the more intriguing features of the social science community is the consistency with which it is inclined to disregard its own findings. While we organize much of our University teaching around one hour long lecture periods, we know that most people concentrate for only about twenty minutes at a time. While we continue to select students for scarce University places on the basis of public examination results at secondary school level, we know that such results are rather poor predictors of final degree levels. While the social composition of our own faculties often under-represents blacks, women and working class groups, we can explain and criticise similar features of other professions and institutions. Likewise, while most social scientists engaged in policy related research behave most of the time as though their findings might influence subsequent government decisions, our understanding of the policy process casts serious doubt upon such optimism.

In this paper I shall try to take seriously some observations that have been made about the nature of social research and social policy making and I shall advance a somewhat pessimistic view of the relationship between the two. I shall suggest (and this is by no means new) that an optimistic perspective on the relationship between social research and decision making at government level is largely unjustified. There is little evidence to support it and significant features of both the structure of decision making in government and current trends in social policy research augur against it. However, I shall end on an optimistic note for I shall suggest that the justification for policy related studies does not and should not, in any case, lie in the criterion of 'usefulness'. The current 'cult of utility' as it has been called has its dangers as well as its attractions. Ironically, I shall suggest, attempts to be useful may well turn out to be counter productive. The real justification for policy related research lies elsewhere.

Although much of the debate is relevant to policy formation in general, throughout this chapter I shall have social policies particularly in mind and, most particularly, social work policies.

TWO VIEWS: OPTIMISTIC AND PESSIMISTIC

As I have said, most social scientists undertaking policy related research behave as though there is at least the potential for the results of the research to influence decisions made about the design and implementation of relevant policy. As Rein (1976) has pointed out the advocates of this optimistic view are then preoccupied with ways in which this role can be made more effective.[1] A pessimistic view, on the other hand, expects no such influence. Indeed the advocates of this position see the optimists as being dangerously naive in encouraging policy researchers to believe that they have an influence far greater than that which they really have. Pessimists either confess that apart from their own curiosity, or some other personal motivation, they can hardly justify their own activities (simply; 'It's nice work if you can get it'.) or else (as I shall do) they search elsewhere for a rationale. Let us look at the presumptions upon which the two 'ideal type' views are based.

First, optimists have a particular view of the nature of the social problems that social services are purportedly designed to solve. They tend to see them, substantially if not entirely, as a matter of ignorance. There is the feeling that social problems are like diseases in medicine. They persist because we do not know what causes them and thus cannot devise an effective cure. Poverty, alcoholism, violence in the family, child neglect, homelessness, marital breakdown and crime for example, are thus subjects for investigation with a view to displaying the true nature of the problem. There is faith that in revealing the character and extent of such problems, better policies for their solution will ensue. This point is linked to a second presumption of the optimistic view. Optimists accept that a substantial measure of agreement both on underlying values and on specific service objectives unites the researcher and policy maker. Thus both are functioning with the same framework of ideas as T.H. Marshall (much quoted) has agreed, 'Without a foundation of new consensus, no general social welfare policy would be possible' (Marshall, 1972). Social research is taken to be a part of this consensus. The benign functionalism which characterises much history of the welfare state is taken also as the basis for the relationship between decision making and research. It is true, as Rein (1976) notes, that optimists do sometimes attempt to induce what Thomas Kuhn calls a paradigm change. However, the point of particular relevance here is that when this occurs optimists expect the framework of ideas within which research and decision making operate to change together. Thus, except in the short term, the consensus would remain undisturbed.

Thirdly, optimists take policy making to be a relatively rational process. The debate between rationalist and incrementalist models of decision making is well known.[2] In the context of the present discussion the important fact is that the 'rational' model is more comprehensive than disjointed incrementalism in its search for objectives, selection of alternatives and evaluation of effectiveness. Decision making is thus seen to be heavily dependent upon routine intelligence and original research and so wide open to the influence of social scientists capable of generating such information. The evaluative stage of the policy process is the stage at which optimists particularly aspire to seeing their findings have significant effect. For if new policies are adopted on the basis of these evaluations and these new policies are themselves subsequently evaluated, then the optimist sees policy research as having established a permanent niche in the decision making structure.

Fourthly, and closely associated with the first three points, optimists believe that research findings simplify policy making and decision taking. There is the presumption that ignorance is trouble rather than bliss and that the policy maker will therefore inevitably welcome the light that social research is bound to shed upon the task of devising new and more effective policies.

Fifthly, optimists presume that policy making is primarily a 'top down' process. Optimists share the conventional distinction between policy making on the one hand and policy implementation on the other. Furthermore they presume that it is influence of the policy maker which is crucial and they are therefore most particularly concerned to gain acceptance of research findings at central government level. For example, the topic of the place of research in the civil service is given more prominence within the optimistic camp than, say, the problems of gaining acceptance of research amongst the front line officials of social security offices or nursing auxiliaries in psychogeriatric hospital wards.

Finally, there is a presumption that is never made very clear but nevertheless permeates the optimistic view. It is that the interchange between research and government policy takes place in an age of growth. Townsend pointed out in the early 1970s (Townsend, 1975) that certain social problems accompany social growth. Although living standards on average rise, inequalities in living standards also develop. There is an increase in poverty as defined in relative terms. Investment in the social services is inclined to lag behind investment in other sectors of the economy. Yet if what we are interested in is the impact of research upon Government policy to deal with such problems a growth economy does give optimists some grounds for their optimism. It is reasonable to expect that funds will be available for policy related research both within government departments and within institutions sponsored by the research councils and other bodies. It is also reasonable to assume that as services expand (albeit not always in line with the most rapidly growing sectors of the economy) new policy options will be under active consideration with a view to initiating new kinds of services. Within the climate of expansion the research community itself will be expanding too. New teams of research workers will be open to suggestions from government about the 'useful' directions in which their research could grow. Evaluations are welcomed since the policy maker has little to lose from their findings. They can be used as the basis for attracting further resources either to launch alternative strategies or to expand the service if it has proved a success. Above all the practitioner and the policy maker gain a degree of prestige by being able to point to the association of a new initiative with systematic research.

Pessimists point out that without being clear about what they are doing, optimists have for too long assumed that the relationship between social research and policy making that pertained in an age

221

of growth, was endemic to the structural relationship between social research and government. Now, in the 1980s, that services are shrinking and policy making becomes a very different kind of activity pessimists point to the fragility of what were thought to be firm relationships.

Let us therefore now turn to a pessimistic view of the influence that social research has upon government. For it differs from the optimistic view on all counts.

First, pessimists see current social problems not so much as matters of ignorance (although few would claim that questions of knowledge have no part to play) as matters of political will. Extensive research has been conducted already, it is agreed, upon society's major ills. What is now required is action in the face of these vested interests which stand to lose out because of the costs involved in effective solutions. The analogy with medicine is misleading and if optimists persist in using it pessimists point out that advances in the nation's health have been far greater as a result of public health legislation and rising nutritional standards than as a consequence of 'scientific discoveries'. The pessimistic view has little faith in the power of knowledge per se. It may be a necessary condition for solving some problems but it is far from a sufficient one.

Secondly pessimists differ from optimists in that rather than detecting an underlying value consensus they view policy debate as a matter of constant conflict in competition between competing paradigms. Though far from presuming a shared view on the forms of social order that are seen as ideal, a pessimistic view on the role of research in government policy making presumes rather that much research will be dismissed by government because it fails to conform to an appropriate paradigm. [3] At the very least the pessimistic view sees little reason for believing a priori that research which casts itself as relevant for government decision making will be seen as such by policy makers themselves.

Thirdly, the pessimistic view has little faith in the rational character of policy decisions. A systematic review of evidence and logical relationships between stages in the argument may well characterise scientific reasoning itself. But if policy making were such a reasoned activity pessimists point out that there would be no need for policy makers at all. The entire process could be left to expert social scientists.

Fourthly, the pessimist has little faith in the ability of social scientists to simplify the policy makers' task. Most often, in practice, it is pointed out, research only shows how complicated the issues really are - generalizations are hedged with reservations. The advantages of one policy are weighed against its previously unrecognised disadvantages. The unanticipated consequences of policy decisions are embarrassingly displayed. In short research is actually inclined to complicate the practice of decision making. There is an important sense in which ignorance is bliss. Most policy makers wish to appear to have made a sound decision regardless of whether or not by some scientific criteria the decision was or was not sound. Pessimists do not see why they should be welcomed if all they do most of the time is to show that the policy was wrong.

Fifthly, pessimists point to the fact that conventional 'top down' models of the policy process have severe weaknesses. They are largely drawn from images of bureaucracy in which the lines of authority and responsibility on the organizational charts are confused with real organizational relationships. In practice, many students of organization argue, changes and working routines are initiated by 'front line' (or 'coal face' or 'grass roots') officials or professionals. These routines then filter 'up' the organization and thus constitute operational policy which is subsequently and post hoc, as it were, justified and codified by more general policy statements. For example, the Children and Young Persons Act 1963 which gave to the officials of Children's Departments the power to dispense materials to families in order to prevent children coming into care, is often quoted as an instance on which legislation and 'policy' followed professional practice. [4] Even when policy temporally precedes practice it is the cumulation of practice decisions which actually constitutes that policy and thus determines the nature and, to a degree, the scope of provision. Such observations as these the pessimists view as further evidence of the limited impact of research on decisions made centrally within government.

Finally, pessimists point to the fact that the problems policy makers now confront are those of contraction, not growth. The question is not what new initiatives to launch but what existing services to cut. This significant change in the whole climate

of policy making has important implications for the
relationship between policy making and research. For
a start research may be funded at a significantly
lower level. 'In house' government research teams
are disbanded (or 'bedded out' in civilservicese) if
not abolished. Government funds for sponsored
research are squeezed and in spite of an increasing
focus upon policy relevant research the funds of the
Social Science Research Council are progressively
cut. Pessimists see all this as a clear sign that in
the eyes of government even policy related social
research is little more than a dispensable luxury.
Of course the trend is understandable. In a rapdly
growing economy budgets for service provision and
budgets for research are not seen to be in direct
competition with each other (even although there is
a sense in which they really are). However when
funds are scarce the decision taker is very
conscious of the fact that research is not only
failing to aid decision making but is also absorbing
funds which might avoid at least in part painful
decisions being taken if they were not being devoted
to research.

In a climate in which services are contracting
(or at least not expanding at nearly the rate to
which the providers and recipients of services have
become accustomed) the policy maker also has an
entirely different approach to evaluation. When
services are expanding the message is, 'We are
trying something new and exciting and we genuinely
wish to know whether or not it has proved to be a
good idea'. If it is shown to be successful the
policy maker seeks considerable publicity for the
enterprise through the initiation of research
activity and through the publication of favourable
results. But when services are contracting the
message is, 'We know that by cutting what we believe
to be a beneficial service we are doing the wrong
thing. We do not need research to tell us that.'
Moreover even where policy makers would welcome
research guidance on which option to cut, they are
unlikely to press for research partly because it
would probably highlight the serious consequences of
reduced services. Although in many ways the
decisions involve similar considerations in practice
the pessimist points to the fact that policy makers
treat a decision about what new service to launch to
be a very different kind of decision from a decision
about what existing service to abandon. And this
difference highlights the very slight influence

exercised by social research upon the machinery of government.

TWO VIEWS: AN ASSESSMENT

There are several ways in which we could attempt an assessment of the strength of these two views. The most obvious tactic would be to attempt to identify within the recent (say post war) history of social policy, the impact of social research as opposed to other variables. The task would be a formidable one and certainly beyond the scope of this present paper. And in any case there would be some very difficult methodological problems to solve. For as Heine von Alemann (1976) points out, what one is really attempting to do in seeking to answer such a question is to evaluate evaluations. And the problems of straightforward evaluations are difficult enough. The controls required in comparative analysis or in 'before and after' studies are never as exact in social science as those enjoyed in the clinical trial or within experimental science. Criteria for evaluation are often ambiguous. The problems of measurement are formidable. Above all the absence of a discrete programme with specified objectives or goals as a target for evaluation is invariably a major difficulty. All of these complexities are magnified in the activity of what we might call evaluation once removed. To take just one example von Alemann shows how difficult it is even to define minimum criteria for organizational effectiveness for social research.

Nevertheless if social research were a significant influence upon government decision making we would expect this influence to feature in most histories of the development of social policy. As Fraser (1973, p. 127) notes in his standard history of the British Welfare State:

> Booth virtually had to invent his own social classifications and had to pioneer methods of social investigation: these achievements alone ensured him an important place in the history of social science. For contemporaries he provided the real statistics of poverty which were essential if sensible solutions were to be found ....

But Fraser is extremely cautious about assigning too

great a significance to the impact of social
research alone. He adds:

> Booth and Rowntree gave to the growing
> public concern over poverty the
> statistical evidence on which to build the
> case for state aid .... The case for
> greater state intervention with the
> problems of poverty was now put; the
> execution of new policies lay in the
> political arena.

There are few examples as dramatic as the work
of Booth or Rowntree in more recent history. Perhaps
one contender might be the work involved in the so
called 'rediscovery of poverty' but many would read
Townsend's Poverty in the United Kingdom (Townsend,
1979) as a monumental witness to the failure of
social research to make any significant effect upon
policies designed to deal with one of the key
problems of our society. If Townsend's central
argument is that decisions about the poor must be
based upon decisions about the rich then this is
decidedly not the course which subsequent
·governments have pursued.
  Bulmer (1982) gives numerous examples of the
relationship between social policy and social
research and discusses two case studies in
particular detail; research on urban deprivation and
on physical disability. Although he points to the
considerable potential of social research to
influence policy in a variety of ways he is unable
to produce a case for the sustained actual impact of
social research upon government policy in any very
direct way. Even an examination of the impact of
research on Government Commissions or Committees of
Enquiry indicates only a rather tenuous relationship
between social research and the contents of a
report. And, of course, the relationship between a
report and any action on the part of Government is
equally tenuous. At best, Bulmer concludes, the
evidence might support the 'enlightenment model'.[6]
That is:

> They [government officials] seem to employ
> it [social research] more to orient
> themselves to problems than to find
> solutions to discrete policy problems.
> Research provides the intellectual
> background of concepts, orientations and
> empirical generalizations that inform

> policy. It is used to orient
> decision-makers to problems, ... to get
> new ideas .... Much of this use is not
> direct (Bulmer, 1982, p. 48).

The evidence certainly does <u>not</u> support the
'engineering model' in which:

> Social scinece provides the evidence and
> conclusions to help solve a policy
> problem. The social scientist is a
> technician who commands the knowledge to
> make the necessary investigation and
> interpret the results (ibid., p. 42).

A second way of trying to adjudge the relative
merits of an optimistic as opposed to a pessimistic
view of the contribution of research to policy is to
examine the actual role of the research social
scientist within government. Certainly in the
context of research relevant to social work policies
such an examination offers only limited ground for
optimism. For when we ask, 'Given the position of
the researcher, is it sensible even to expect the
influence to be significant?' we can see that there
are a priori, important organizational reasons for
anticipating only limited influence.

One point to make in this context is to draw
the distinction - crucial to the whole structure and
function of the British civil service but not always
fully appreciated by those dealing with government
agencies from the outside - between advisors and
administrators. In significant respects researchers
employed within government are similar to those
working from non-government and 'Quango' bases. They
are all essentially advisors. And advice does not
have to be taken. Of course there are differences
between government and non-government researchers in
that, amongst other things, advisors employed
directly by an organization have direct access to
inside data, probably a close sympathy with the
terms of the original policy problem and are in a
better position to judge those points in the
decision making process at which research results
are likely to have greatest impact. Nevertheless
resarch workers occupying, as they do, an advisory
position within government departments exercise
functions which are quite different from the career
civil servants in administrative grades who hold
direct executive responsibility to Ministers for the
operation of their departments' policies. And since

administrators can, and frequently do, rightly claim
that they must take account of a wide range of
political, economic and other factors extending
beyond the scientific rationality of research
results, and since this process entails judgements
which the researcher has no part in questioning,
ultimately the power differential between researcher
and executor of political policies (the so called
'administrator') is substantial.

Moreover, in the field of social work and other
policy areas which involve major professional groups
for their implementation (the medical profession is
perhaps the major parallel example) the social
scientist is often an advisor at one remove; that is
an advisor to an advisor. For in policy fields such
as social work, health, education and criminal
justice administrators and Ministers draw upon the
advice not only of social scientists but also of
psychologists, statisticians, economists, doctors,
social workers, architects and others. Within the
Department of Health and Social Security (DHSS) and
the Scottish Office the group of professional social
workers - the Social Work Service (SWS) and the
professional arm of the Social Work Services Group
(SWSG) respectively, - is very much both larger and,
in its senior personnel, more senior than the group
of social researchers to be found in these
departments. These professional advisors are charged
with providing an advisory and consultancy service
both to Ministers, sometimes directly but more
usually through administrators, and to local
authorities, although with considerable political
caution in the case of the latter given the
political independence of local from central
government. The SWS and SWSG are also in practice
partly responsible for effecting those functions of
inspection which central government exercise over
local authorities in respect of legislation in the
social work field.

The specific organizational location of social
research in relation to professional advice within
government differs between different sectors of
government. Large research units such as the Home
Office Research Unit (HORU) have grouped researchers
together. The Central Resarch Unit (CRU) in the
Scottish Office did the same although some teams
(such as a group within the SWSG have been
'outposted' to work day-to-day within particular
departments. Other researchers have been linked to
statistical and to computing services. Under some
more recent arrangements teams of resarchers in DHSS

have been 'bedded out' with policy divisions and branches. But whatever the organisation chart may say most researchers in government are involved day-to-day in the triangular relationship of research – professional advice – executive function. This means that frequently, in order to gain impact, social research must be effective, <u>through</u> the social work advice – that is at one remove from the policy process within the department or at two removes if what we are really seeking is impact upon Ministerial thinking.

To put the point more generally, the notion of government or external research having a direct influence upon state social work policies (for example) loses the sense of the complex and multifarious relationships, checks and balances which are typical of the political pluralism of British Government. Rather social research is but one, and often not very significant or powerful factor, in a whole sea of advice, information, judgements, data, prejudices and existing policies which influence the emergence (rather than 'production') of what we loosely term 'social policy'.

I have mentioned that research is seldom the most powerful of factors in developing policies. The point is again reinforced by comparing the position of research advisors not only with professional advisors but also with statisticians and economists. Both of these latter groups have much more established positions within government than social researchers. There are many more of them, they have better career prospects (with more senior positions open to them) and, above all, have a function which is clearly recognised and <u>apparently</u> understood by administrators and politicians in a way that the potential services of sociologists, political scientists and social administrationists are not. Their relative immobility within the civil service and the longer time span of their operations further distances these latter groups of social scientists from the culture and traditional modes of operation of the administrative grades. The impact of what is considered to be the 'right and proper way of doing things' should not be underestimated within the British civil service. It <u>is</u> an inherently 'conservative' institution, and this is a source of some of its most important strengths as well as some of its alleged weaknesses. Thus traditional and cultural variables are not of insignificant consequence in grasping the influence that any group is likely to exercise. The values of continuity, stability, incremental change, consensus politics and the importance of the presentational imagery are, apparently, viewed as consistent with a substantial economic and statistical advice service in ways that are not consistent with what are regarded as the confrontational myth-busting and generally more 'radical' stances of some of the newer social sciences.

Now these comments are rather general and are perhaps based as much upon a sense of the way in which the civil service operates as upon any specific research on the impact of research investigations. In any case our tradition of 'closed government' (in spite of various recent attempts to encourage 'open government' in Britain) protects an Official Secrets Act which makes it very difficult to publish details of the actual micro-processes of decision making within government departments. The point is that there is enough in these comments to justify a rather pessimistic response in answer to the question, 'Given the position of research within the institutions of government, is it sensible even to expect social science to influence social (work) policies?'

At the time of writing, in Britain at least, if not in North America and much of Western Europe also, a rather pessimistic approach to the issues that I am addressing in this paper is fostered by the attitude of the current Government towards the Universities in general, the social sciences in particular and especially the Social Science Research Council (SSRC). First we have the reported but thwarted attempt of the Secretary of State for Education and Science, Sir Keith Joseph, to abolish or at least radically reduce the size of the SSRC. For the most part in this essay I am trying to consider the implications and nature of the relationship between social work policy and related research rather than argue the rightness or wrongness of this relationship (although I readily admit that my use of the terms 'optimistic' and 'pessimistic' speedily display my vested interest as a social scientist). Nevertheless, it is somewhat exasperating for social scientists who have been heavily criticised by their more esoteric colleagues for even attempting to make their research relevant to government policies, now to find these attempts meeting with little positive response from government. Three contemporary points are relevant to the issues being discussed here.

First, some government Ministers and department officials appear to define "useful" so narrowly as to be almost the same as "consistent with current government policy". Given this approach the only place assigned to social research is that of confirming existing policies and prejudices. Research with implications for change or consistent with opposition policies is perceived as unnecessarily disruptive. Thus, almost by definition, social research can make little contribution to the policies of the current government. A second point of some irritation is the point that government's failure to use social research does not mean that it could not have been used. To take a now historical example, it has often been observed that the reorganization of social work that followed the Seebohm and Kilbrandon Reports in the late 1960s and early 1970s was based upon very little research evidence. It is certainly true that very little original research into the problems under consideration at that time was deliberately commissioned. But it is also true that little of the research which was then available and might have been helpful was consulted in a way which seriously involved it in the policy process. And there are many current examples of bodies of research which are, apparently, simply ignored. For instance we know that "short sharp shocks" do not reduce real juvenile delinquency levels. Social scientists have long been suggesting that aspects of the adversarial character of divorce legislation exacerbate rather than ameliorate some features of the marital relationship. Urban sociologists and criminologists have much to tell us about community relationships, race relations and policing policies in the inner cities, most of which has been seriously neglected by politicians who then establish intensive enquiries of various kinds when trouble brews. The point is that the failure to use social research within the policy process should not be equated with the uselessness of this research. Were resources equivalent to those invested in conducting good research also invested in making use of it, then we would not enter, as we so often do, the vicious circle in which failure to use is taken to imply uselessness and to justify subsequent failure to commission and consequent subsequent failure to use.

The third point is related to a third source of irritation. Much social research does not have the impact upon social policy that it should have because it is not funded adequately. Of course one would hardly expect a social scientist to do other than argue that social science research should be more generously funded. I am not simply making that point. I am drawing attention to the fact that the current government's attitude towards social science research in Britain indicates clearly that it expects it, in general, and the SSRC in particular to take more than an 'across the board' share of reductions in funds and certainly more than that recommended by the Advisory Board for the Research Councils or that recommended by the independent review of Lord Rothschild, established by the Secretary of State himself. Thus at a time when governments in many western industrial societies are facing major and in many cases quite new social problems, in Britain at least the resources devoted to studying these problems are being seriously reduced. Thus social scientists are further handicapped in their ability to make the case for the utility and policy relevance of their work. Perhaps the real surprise is that any social scientists at all can cling to an optimistic view.

In this section, then, I have suggested that there are good grounds for adopting a rather pessimistic view of the relationships between social research and government decisions. I have advanced three reasons for adopting this position. First, historically, social research has not been shown to have a very significant impact upon government social policy. Although the potential has been described, convincing accounts of the realization of this potential are more difficult to come by. Second, the place of social scientists within the institutions of government, suggests that we are sensible to be cautious in ever expecting social research to have any major impact. Third, current government attitudes towards social science and social research give little encouragement to the optimistic position.

Nevertheless, as I indicated at the start of this essay, many social scientists do persist in conducting resarch with aspirations to policy influence and government departments do employ social scientists and do continue to sponsor and fund research initiatives. It would certainly be facile to conclude that policies are entirely immune from research influence. Therefore, in the final section of the essay, I propose to introduce a somewhat more optimistic tone in offering some answers to the questions 'Why, then, does government do anything to foster research?' and 'Why, then, should policy related research be conducted at all?'

SOME CHORDS OF OPTIMISM

Let us first address the question of why it is that government continues to sponsor social research, in a variety of ways (both 'in house' and commissioned) at all. A social scientist convinced of the strength of what I have termed the pessimistic position is likely to offer one or more of what some would regard as rather cynical answers: that research is merely a part of the appearance of rationality; that research is merely an adjunct to an action programme that has been decided upon already; that research is a way of postponing action; that research is used to confirm prejudice; that it disarms critics of established policy; or that the structure of government sponsorship ensures, anyway, that little genuinely critical research is conducted. I wish to suggest that if there is truth in these comments they nevertheless contain seeds of optimism from the point of view of the policy oriented social scientist.

I have already commented upon the importance of "the way things are done" within the civil service. Undoubtedly an important component of government decision making, whatever else it may or may not have in common with the processes of social research, is that its mode should at least give the appearance of coherent rationality. I have already referred above to the debate within social science between those who view decision making as inherently rational and those who see it as a form of 'Scientific Confusion'. The point here is that few would deny that whatever his or her actual practices, the decision maker apparently feels constrained to present action as if it were rational and social research as a part of this rationality. The 'onus of justification' lies with those who would adopt any non-rational procedure and since rational modes of decision making entail the review of a range of policy options, collection of data, evaluation and so on, this gives the resarcher at least a toe hold on decision making. There is at least a chance of being able to 'call the bluff' on the policy process and insist on the relevance of research results.

A second reason for government persisting with social research is that it is often an adjunct to an action programme. The Community Development Projects are one of the best known examples of research launched in this vein but temporary employment schemes for unemployed youth, alternatives to inpatient care for the elderly mentally infirm and the development of foster homes for severely mentally handicapped children are further examples of policy initiatives launched in conjunction with research 'monitoring' exercises. Sometimes, clearly, rather weak policies are pursued with the defence that matters can always be revised once the results of the 'evaluation' or 'monitoring' exercises are known. Yet here again, although initiated for what the social scientist might regard as the wrong reasons, social research does have a toe hold upon subsequent policy making and if continuance of the policy realy does depend upon a 'favourable' research report, the influence of research may be considerable.

Alternatively research is sometimes used to justify delayed action. Within the system of British Government the establishment of a Royal Commission or Departmental Committee of Enquiry is a classic and well known gambit for avoiding having to take action, at least until 'the problem has gone away'. The initiation of major research programmes is sometimes also used in this way (although less frequently than simply an 'enquiry'). It is true that since the very purpose of the exercise is to de-fuse the situation it is likely that by the time the research is complete the issue may no longer be crucial. But is is additionally true that the publication of the research results may also place the research team in an influential position in their ability to raise again for discussion, issues which some policy makers at least had hoped to remove from the agenda of debate.

The suggestions that research is merely used within social policy to disarm critics, to confirm existing prejudices, and is in any case only commissioned in terms which ensure 'favourable' results are closely related points. Few processes engender a sense of pessimism amongst social scientists as readily as that of encouraging the feeling that their research is being manipulated. Yet the response here is similar to that which I have already made to the observation that resarch is used within an irrational process of decision making. At least these various activities entail an acknowledgement that research is a legitimate and important part of the policy process and cannot legitimately simply be ignored.

There are then, some grounds for 'optimism' even in the face of somewhat pessimistic interpretations of why government agencies continue to foster social research. But social scientists need not rely upon these crumbs of comfort alone. There are good grounds for continuing effort in the field of policy related research even in the light of the overwhelming strengths of the general pessimistic view. Oddly, the strongest justification for policy related research may be largely outside of what is generally termed the 'policy process'.

First, a good deal of policy relevant research is worth conducting for the same reason that mountains are worth climbing; simply because they are there. The pursuit of truth and scholarship are not justifications for social research which are widely, at least publicly, invoked nowadays. Indeed Members of parliament and the like intent on scrutinizing the use of public funds are likely to hold 'abstruse' and apparently 'useless' topics of research up for public ridicule. But as has often been noted in discussions of the customer-contractor principle in research the distinction between 'pure' and 'applied' research is unclear and apparently 'irrelevant' research today may well be highly 'relevant' tomorrow. Thus policy researchers should still remain optimistic in the sense in which I am using it in this essay, even without the immediate prospect of direct policy influence.

Second, even if research never apparently has direct policy influence it is widely recognised that it may nevertheless, indirectly influence the 'stock of ideas', or 'the climate of knowledge', within which policy debate is conducted. Indeed very few investigations in social science are precise or definitive enough to be implemented directly and immediately and this is one of the reasons for the difficulty, to which I have already referred, of assessing the impact of social research upon government. The optimist must cling to the view that an element of faith is rightly a part of the motive for conducting social research.

Thirdly, government is not the only legitimate target for policy relevant research. As Townsend (1972) amongst others has observed, a policy problem has often acted as the spur to research which has then made a significant contribution to theories, methods or substantive findings in other areas of social science. For example, much of the interactionist literature in sociology sprang from a clearly policy relevant tradition of social problems research. Similarly, aspects of the methodology of participant observation and other techniques of qualitative research were developed by social scientists with an acute awareness of the significance of their work in a policy context. Recent debates on the methodological problems of using official statistics have been sired by work on criminological data and the social problem of suicide.

And finally, political officials and bureaucrats are not the only legitimate targets for policy relevant research. As I have already noted in passing, in this essay, much policy is heavily dependent for its implementation upon doctors, nurses, social workers and other professionals operating in the 'front line' of service agencies. While a pessimistic view on the likely impact of research on policy may be justfied if the targets are those groups primarily involved in policy formation, a more optimistic view may be justified if the research is directed towards groups with greater influence on the process of policy implementation. Some researchers have even taken the view that the research is likely to gain maximum impact by informing service recipients - claimants, clients, patients and others - about the nature of the services and the issues of policy involved. Such an approach takes seriously the pluralistic character of the process of policy formation and implementation and views research as a significant factor in effecting the outcomes of social policy.

SUMMARY

In this essay I have set out two views, an optimistic one and a pessimistic one, on the likelihood of research related to government policies having a significant impact upon decisions in the social policy field. I have given my reasons for agreeing with those who generally find the arguments for a pessimistic view to be more persuasive. I then addressed the questions of why, therefore, government should continue to sponsor research if it was largely uninfluenced by its results and why social scientists should continue to conduct policy related research when it seemed to achieve so little.

I tried to conclude on something of an optimistic note. If we are looking for a direct, immediate and readily apparent impact of specific pieces of research upon particular policy decisions, then we are trying for the moon. However government does, apparently, feel constrained to sponsor, conduct and be seen to be using social research and in a variety of ways this offers the social scientist a toe hold on the policy process. It is in the areas of the climate of opinion, the agenda for debate, the available stock of ideas and the attitudes of professionals and recipients of services, that the impact of research is most likely to be apparent. In fact if we are seeking a justification for 'useful' research, we find it by abandoning the narrow 'cult of utility' in favour of more subtle and indirect forms of social influence.

NOTES

1. The discussion here draws upon Rein's essay but differs on several points. In particular I see a <u>pessimistic</u> rather than a <u>sceptical</u> position as being the opposite of an optimistic view.

2. Elsewhere I have argued that this debate is actually an artificial one since both models have errors in common which are far more significant than their differences. See Smith and May (1980).

3. Of course the debate is not simply one of consensus versus conflict models. Much discussion within social policy and administration has been concerned with various pluralist and neo-Marxist alternatives to the traditional functionalist view. See, for example, Mishra (1977), Taylor-Gooby and Dale (1981) and Room (1979).

4. The discussion is clearly linked to the debate about the place of 'discretion' in welfare. See Adler and Asquith (eds.) (1981).

5. There is a parallel in the emergence of the sociology of sociology as a specialist area of research within sociology.

6. Bulmer draws upon Janowitz (1972).

REFERENCES

Adler, M. and Asquith, S. (eds.) (1981) Discretion and Welfare. London: Heinemann.

Bulmer, M. (1982) The Uses of Social Research. London: Allen and Unwin.

Fraser, D. (1973) The Evolution of the British Welfare State. London: Macmillan.

Janowitz, M. (1972) Sociological Models and Social Policy. Morristown, New Jersey: General Learning Systems.

Marshall, T.H. (1972) "Value Problems in Welfare Capitalism", Journal of Social Policy, 1, 20.

Mishra, R. (1977) Society and Social Policy: Theoretical Perspectives on Welfare. London: Macmillan.

Rein, M. (1976) "Values, Social Scinece and Social Policy", chapter 3 of Social Science and Public Policy. Harmondsworth: Penguin.

Room, G. (1979) The Sociology of Welfare: Social Policy Stratification and Political Order. Oxford: Martin Robertson.

Smith, G. and May, D. (1980) "The Artificial Debate between Rationalist and Incrementalist Models of Decision Making", Policy and Politics, 8.

Taylor-Gooby, P. and Dale, J. (1981) Social Theory and Social Welfare. London: Edward Arnold.

Townsend, P. (1975) "The Problems of Social Growth", chapter 24 of Sociology and Social Policy. Harmondsworth: Penguin.

Townsend, P. (1979) Poverty in the United Kingdom. Harmondsworth: Penguin.

von Alemann, H. (1976) "Problems in the Evaluation of Social Science Research Organisations", in E. Crawford and N. Percy (eds.) Demands for Social Knowledge: The Role of Research Organisations. London: Sage.

Part III

CONCLUSIONS

10

POLICY, PRACTICE AND RESEARCH: AN OVERVIEW

Alex Robertson and John Gandy

The claim that social services can be improved
through the application of relevant research has an
obvious attraction for the planners and managers of
those services. And whilst definitions as to what
actually constitutes 'research' have often tended to
be rather ambiguous, it is widely argued (and
accepted) that the information gained from
properly-conducted studies can help to make social
policies both more effective in attaining the
objectives they were designed to meet, and more
efficient in their deployment of human and financial
resources for the achievement of those
objectives.[1] The acceptance of such assumptions
has of course been evidenced in several attempts
over recent years to structure the policy-making
process in Western political systems. In chapter 3
of the present volume, for example, Hans Mohr
observes that over the last three decades a large
part of the "answer" to social problems has
increasingly been sought in "technological"
approaches.
     The considerable increase which has occurred
over the last 15 - 20 years in the amount of
research commissioned by policy-makers, and the
growth in the number of research units devoted to
monitoring social policies and their effects,
together with reliance on systems analysis,
operational research, programme-planning-budgeting
systems, technological forecasting and 'futures'
research all reflect the rationalist notion that
knowledge can be harnessed for the amelioration of
human problems (see, for example, Williams, 1971;
Berry, 1974; M. Thompson, 1975, chapters 1 and 5).
     But despite this investment in research, and
the generally greater technical sophistication of
researchers themselves, it has to be acknowledged

that the impact of research on both policy-decisions and practice has at best been disappointing. In this volume, Jack Byles argues that substantial sums of money continue to be invested in programmes for the "treatment" or "prevention" of delinquency, despite the considerable body of evidence which suggests that such approaches, and the concepts on which they are based, are both invalid and ineffectual. Mohr expresses more general misgivings about the validity and likely effectiveness of attempts to keep the law in harmony with changing human aspirations and social forms through the use of "rational" analysis and conscious "reform" of legal arrangements. Other authors reviewing the literature on research utilisation (Rosenblatt, 1968; Caplan et al., 1975; Knorr, 1977; Rothman, 1979; Rubin & Rosenblatt, 1979; and Weiss, 1980) have also been led to the conclusion that research has had only a limited direct impact on policy-making.

To cite a well-known concrete instance, the Planning-Programming-Budgeting System (PPBS) developed by economists at the RAND corporation in the mid-1960s was based on the assumption that rigorous analysis could produce a flow of information which would substantially improve the base of knowledge on which decisions might be made. The promise contained in such claims led President Johnson to introduce a system of planning, programming and budgeting throughout the agencies of the U.S. Federal Government in 1965. With respect to the social policies handled by such agencies as the Department of Health, Education and Welfare and the Office of Economic Opportunity, a fundamental tenet of this system was of course the notion that evaluative studies would enable one to assess the impact and efficiency of particular programmes, with a view to further improving their performance (see, for example, Williams and Evans, 1969; Haveman, 1970; Rivlin, 1970; Denniston et al., 1978; Seidman, 1978). PPBS, in other words, was seen as capable of 'objectifying' the policy-making process.

The outcome of this ambitious experiment is now a matter of history. PPBS was formally abandoned by the U.S. Federal Government in 1971; and whilst the lessons drawn from that experience have varied - from the radically pessimistic conclusions of writers like Victor Thompson (1969; 1976, Chapter 3) and Wildavsky (1970) who argue that the belief that decisions can be made more rational and systematic is a chimera, to the suggestion that people should identify and accept its limitations and attempt to work within them towards the goal of rational planning (see, for example, Rivlin, 1970; White, 1978) - it seems generally accepted that a system such as PPBS cannot produce the kind of information that is needed to clarify political choices on many crucial topics (see, for example, Gorham, 1967; Wildavsky, 1968; Richardson, 1972; Booth, 1981).

Other, equally discouraging, examples are not hard to find. In Canada, for example, there has been a reluctance among all levels of government to support special programmes for one-parent families, despite the considerable amount of research evidence that clearly establishes their special needs as a group (National Council of Welfare, 1976, 1979). In Great Britain, the experimental series of Community Development Projects, with their built-in research programmes, have had a negligible effect on subsequent policy and practice. And finally, the Seebohm Committee's sponsorship of research (HMSO, 1968) gave an important stimulus to the creation of research units in social services/work departments throughout Great Britain; and writers such as Foren and Brown (op. cit., chapter 6) have suggested how, in principle, the work of such units might contribute to planning and decision-making in departments responsible for the delivery of human services. Subsequent experience, however, has led many local-authority researchers to take a rather more sceptical view of their role, and Booth (1979) argues that research rarely produces definite conclusions which can be acted upon by the policy-maker, who almost always has to take account of a wider range of factors than research can usually encompass.

This chapter will seek to examine what the present authors see as the more important reasons for the apparent lack of influence of research upon policy, and attempt to draw some conclusions concerning the kinds of contribution which research is capable of making to future policies. This will be done through the examination of issues raised, either directly or by implication, in other contributions to this volume. Our discussion will be organised around four major and connected themes which appear to us to underlie many of the difficulties in creating an effective role for research in policy-making. The first three of these concern: a) the kinds of policy-relevant research that have, to date, been undertaken by social scientists, and the (actual or potential) contribution to policy-making of such research; b) the differing frames of reference adopted by researchers and policy-makers in approaching and evaluating the research task; and c) the constraints placed upon relationships between researchers and policy-makers by the institutional settings within which they usually have to relate to each other. The chapter will close with d) a consideration of the relationship between policy and practice; and the implications this has for the implementation of research findings.

POLICY AND POLICY-RELEVANT RESEARCH

From the instrumental perspective of the policy-maker, the research undertaken by social scientists within the social policy area may usefully be classified into the two broad types of "descriptive" and "evaluative" studies with the latter of these being capable of further division into two sub-types. Descriptive research broadly corresponds to what Bulmer (1978, p. 39) terms 'intelligence' activity, or 'predominantly fact gathering'. As the term 'descriptive' implies, the purpose of such research is to present an accurate 'factual' picture of the world as the researcher finds it (and insofar as the inevitable selection of variables for study and the inadequacies of data-gathering technologies will permit), on the assumption that policy-makers may then respond, by devising appropriate policies or programmes, to the 'reality' uncovered by the investigator. Good examples would be the Government Information Services which exist on both sides of the Atlantic, producing the census and other types of statistical reports referred to by Bulmer (op. cit.).

At the level of commonsense, such data would be useful for identifying 'needs' within given populations; but their usefulness to the policy-maker beyond that point becomes somewhat problematic. Perhaps the most crucial factor determining the utility of descriptive research is the extent to which the data produced by descriptive studies can be related to a theoretical framework which may point to specific solutions. The best example of such a link between descriptive data and a tested, policy-relevant, theoretical model is probably provided by epidemiological research in medicine. The identification of particular individuals (or of the proportions of a given population) suffering from conditions - such as tuberculosis or other infectious diseases - whose aetiology and treatment can be accounted for within a theoretical framework, can fairly easily be related to the development of specific policies or programmes of intervention to deal effectively with the problem. (By contrast, epidemiological data on conditions such as cancer and 'life-style' related diseases, concerning which knowledge is rather less secure, give rise to much less specific indicators for intervention.)

In the social-services field, of course, there is virtually no area where knowledge is so systematic and consolidated as is by and large the case in medicine. The use of findings from research in this area - concerning, for instance, the numbers of elderly people living on their own, or the proportions of families existing below a certain level of income - as a vehicle for the guidance and development of policy therefore ultimately depends on the use of intuition or personal predilection on the part of the policy-maker. The impact of such findings on policy is accordingly likely to derive more from the creation of a feeling that 'something must be done' - with such monitoring exercises indicating the magnitude, rate of increase, etc. of a 'problem' - than from a clear knowledge, to which the data themselves can be related, of what is likely to be the (most) effective way of dealing with the issue. In certain notable instances researchers may, by judicious presentation of their data, draw attention to a discrepancy between the situation uncovered by their findings and the situation which they feel <u>should</u> exist. Examples of this approach would be contained in the work of researchers such as Peter Townsend (1962), whose descriptions of the circumstances existing in old people's homes in the 1960s generated widespread feelings of moral outrage, which had a direct and fairly immediate effect on the development of policies for the elderly. Additional examples may be found in the reports produced by organisations like the Child Poverty Action Group or the Canadian Council on Social Development. And as Roy Parker points out in chapter 1 of the present volume, descriptive studies which draw attention to cross-national differences in modes or levels of provision can be a useful source of pressure for change and of ideas for alternative patterns of service delivery. With reference to our earlier discussion, however, the important point to note is that these policies were not based on theoretical models which pointed to strategies that would be likely to alleviate such problems; but rather on feelings of public disquiet and the (entirely laudable) desire to introduce some kind of action to remedy such failings.

The second - evaluative - mode of research has been widely presented (particularly by North American authors) as holding out the greatest promise for enlarging the social-science contribution to policy-making. And following a familiar distinction, evaluative research can be sub-divided into two constitutent types, which are normally labelled 'process' and 'outcome' evaluations.

xOutcome' evaluations attempt to assess the effects produced by policies or programmes, and the extent to which such results measure up to programme 'goals' (however these may be defined). As such, they perhaps come closest to the scientific ideal of verification - and it is probably this fact which best explains their still-burgeoning popularity. There is now a very extensive literature on evaluation research; and whilst Rossi's (op. cit.) review of evaluation activities in US Federal Government agencies leads him to rather depressing conclusions about the overall quality of that corpus of research, some very ingenious developmental work has, for example, been completed at Carleton University's Centre for Social Welfare Studies, in an attempt to refine and expand research methodologies in this area (see, for example, Carleton University Centre for Social Welfare Studies, 1977; Cook, Cook and Mark, 1977; Rutman, 1977a, 1977b; Rutman and de Jong, 1977).

A fundamental problem with many outcome evaluations is that they are unable to specify with any precision which, and to what extent, particular factors within the policy, treatment-method or regime, etc. assessed by the research, have contributed to the results (normally defined in terms of the stated 'objectives' of the programme under scrutiny) the programme has achieved. Thus, in assessing the relative effectiveness of different types of residential regime for dealing with disturbed children, it may be difficult to establish - beyond the global and aggregative fact that programme A produces better results than programmes B, C and D - whether the greater success of that programme is attributable to its formal 'therapeutic' content, or to alternative factors such as the quality of informal relationships between staff and children, or the proximity of the programme in question to better leisure-facilities. This is in part at least a methodological problem, which may be overcome by the development of instruments like Moos's (1974; see also Heal, Sinclair and Troop, 1973) measures of social environment, which enable one to obtain a (crude) quantitative estimate of process variables like social 'climate'. But a large area of potentially-relevant factors still seem likely to remain untouched by and impervious to the development of measures such as these.

In large degree, however, this is also a problem of epistemology. In terms of the natural-scientific ideal, investigation moves through three discrete stages. At the stage of induction, a general hypothesis is formulated in order to explain certain apparently regular connections between observed phenomena (at which stage, of course, the findings of descriptive studies may be useful as the basis for one's hypothesis). Second is the stage of deduction, when the scientist examines and elaborates the relationships between the various assumptions implied in his explanatory theory, in order to work out and specify in a set of hypotheses, the consequences which would logically follow if his theory is correct. At the final stage - of verification - these hypotheses are tested in controlled circumstances, in order to assess the overall validity of the theory (or more correctly, to demonstrate that it is not false).

If outcome evaluations are intended to approximate to the verification stage in the ideal scientific world, then it is important to note that, in evaluations of particular social services, what is being tested is less a theory (although theories or hypotheses of various sorts may be implied in aspects of the programmes under study) than a practical arrangement, in which assumptions as to what is likely to be an effective course of action in dealing with a problem are blended with a number of practical and administrative factors and arrangements relating, for example, to things such as the types of staff whom trade-union regulations will permit to work in certain capacities; the enthusiasms and personal strengths and weaknesses of those staff; and a variety of extraneous and unpredictable contextual factors, such as particular aspects of the neighbourhood within which the programme is operating. The elements under scrutiny in evaluative research are accordingly far removed from the discrete entities observed, manipulated and tested by the natural scientist. These problems are further compounded by the difficulties of design and methodology which confront researchers in this area, to mean that the findings of evaluative research can be at best approximate (see, for example, Rossi, op. cit.).

As against this, however, one might reasonably argue that research and the knowledge gained from it are cumulative. In other words, effective recommendations for policy will emerge when a corpus of research findings is available, to suggest where regularities exist in particular kinds of programmes, and the circumstances under which variations will occur. This would seem to be a particularly important consideration in the social sciences, where one is dealing with phenomena which are related to each other in complex ways, and where variations peculiar to a particular situation may have a significant bearing on the findings one elicits from that situation; and where one is in any case normally dealing with trends that are tested against the probabilistic criteria of statistics, rather than of their (dichotomous) truth or falsity. Such an argument does of course run counter to the assumptions of the "customer-contractor" principle, with its belief that a single piece of contracted research can produce the answer to a given problem. It would also imply that government departments and other funding agencies should be willing to regard research as a long-term investment, with somewhat unpredictable returns, rather than seeing it as producing concrete and relatively speedy answers to immediate problems.

An ambitious variant of the "cumulative" approach was pursued by the California Youth Authority, in their sequential series of evaluations of the factors which contributed to various treatment-effects in residential establishments for delinquent children (Warren, 1969). Rather more modestly, the recently-initiated series of "Research Highlights", bulletins issued under the joint aegis of the University of Aberdeen, the Scottish Office's Social Work Services Group, and the Scottish Branch of the Social Services Research Group, are attempting to review and draw together research findings on important topics in the social work services, in a form which will be helpful to managers and practitioners in those services

(Research Highlights, 1981a; 1981b; 1982a; 1982b).
But to return to the original point, a major problem of outcome evaluations is that of identifying the particular factors which contribute to any results pinpointed by an investigation. It is in filling this hiatus that process evaluations may perhaps serve their most useful purpose. From a methodological point of view, process evaluations are rather less glamorous exercises than evaluations of outcome; and it is possibly for this reason that few investigations of this type seem to be undertaken or reported in the literature. The purpose of process research is to identify – normally through the use of 'soft' methodologies like participant observation – what seem to be the most important elements contributing to the outcomes of any given programme, and the way these elements relate to each other within the policy or treatment-programme itself (see, for example, Sinclair, 1971). This kind of research is therefore reliant on description and inference from observation, in order to build up a sensitive composite picture of the functioning of a programme. Asquith makes a point very similar to this in his appeal for more phenomenological approaches in research on juvenile justice, to balance the "black box" models which have tended to predominate in research in this area to date. In the absence of effective theoretical frameworks to make total sense of social programmes, this kind of essentially empirical analysis can obviously be a valuable means of identifying similarities and differences between the features of various approaches, what arrangements might be transferable between programmes, and the extent to which such modifications seem likely to improve the success of the programmes concerned.
In principle, therefore, different kinds of research might be seen as capable of making different kinds of appropriate instrumental contributions to the policy-making process. In practice, however, the magnitude of the contribution made is likely to be more limited. This may in part be attributed to technical complications of the kind just outlined, which relate to the nature of the research enterprise in social science. Further difficulties would, however, seem to derive from the character of the relationships that normally exist between policy-makers and researchers themselves. And such difficulties can, in the opinion of the present authors, be attributed to two basic factors.

First are the differing perceptions these two groups hold of the research process, and the expectations of research to which these varying perceptions have given rise. Second is the fact that relationships between policy-makers and researchers must take place within departmental and decision-making structures which assume or ascribe particular types of role to the two sets of participants. We intend to deal with these issues in turn.

POLICY-MAKERS AND RESEARCHERS: DIFFERING FRAMES OF REFERENCE

One of the primary themes identified in several of the contributions to this volume has been that the different values, attitudes and expectations of the producers (researchers) and users (elected officials, administrators and practitioners) of research are major determinants of the general impact of research on policy and practice. Indeed, Davis and Salasin (1978, pp. 99-100) have been prompted to suggest that policy-makers and scientists live in "two worlds". Thus, in the present volume Byles (chapter 6) and Willett (chapter 5) both describe research that is undertaken in the belief that the dispassionate presentation of critical (factual) material will help to change policies, and contrast this with the tendency of those responsible for policy to suppress or ignore "inconvenient" findings. Similarly, in his discussion of "Knowledge and City Planning" Norman Dennis points to the ability of Environmental Health Officers to use the same factual data to arrive at entirely contradictory conclusions at different times, largely depending upon the practical (or political) need to produce a particular judgment based on those data.

Olive Stevenson (in chapter 2 of this volume) and others (Mayntz, 1977; Sharpe, 1977; Rein & Tannenbaum, 1979) point to the central role values occupy in decisions affecting social policy and practice, and to the inappropriateness of the "value-neutral" stance assumed by many social-science researchers. In this connection Rein and Schon (1977, p. 248) have observed that:

> Problem specification is not purely a trial and error process. We often have strong value preferences; and these shape not only the way in which problems are

set, but what we are prepared to accept as fact.

Both the researcher and the policy-maker tend to start with rather unrealistic expectations as to what social scientists can contribute to policy-decisions (Bulmer, 1978). Nonetheless, the differing values of the researcher and the user of research not only influence their respective definitions of the problem and their interpretations of any "facts" uncovered, but are also most important in any recommendations they may make as to what are appropriate courses of action. The different and often conflicting value orientations of these two sets of actors may result in fundamental disagreements of perceptions and approach to problems which may militate against the effective use of research in policy-making (Weiss, 1977). An example of basic value differences between social researchers on the one hand, and policy-makers and practitioners on the other, is their orientation to decision-making. Social scientists see decisions about policy and practice as rational, deliberate and linear while policymakers see them as part of a political process where research is considered along with extra-rational and non-quantifiable factors such as political demands, intuition and experience. On the basis of his examination of 575 instances of the use of social science information by upper level government officials in the United States, Caplan concluded that:

> the major problems that hamper utilization are non-technical - that is, the level of knowledge utilization is not so much the result of a slow flow of relevant and valid knowledge from knowledge producers to policy makers but is more due to factors involving values, ideology and decision-making styles (1973, p. 195).

A lack of communication between researchers and users of research has been identified by Lindblom and Cohen as a second major factor that inhibits the use of research.

> In ... policy making many suppliers and users of research are dissatisfied, the former because they are not listened to, the latter because they do not hear much

they want to listen to (1977, p. 1).

The reasons for the lack of communication are both cognitive and structural, and reflect differences in the education, skills and ideology of the two primary sets of actors. One barrier to communication, as pointed out by Rothman (1979), is the difference in function that exists between the two groups. The primary function of the social scientist is "comprehending" society, while that of the practitioner is "changing" society. Consequently the users of research expect investigators to provide clear and unambiguous answers to the kinds of questions posed. At best, this is frequently extremely difficult, because imperfections in the concepts and methods with which social scientists must work tend to undermine the possibility of their providing "hard and solid bases for decisions" (Knorr, 1977, p. 179). Weiss (1978) advances the proposition that "the less able policy makers are to crystallize their informational needs, the less likely they are to use information effectively." Such a situation frequently occurs in policy decisions concerning programmes and services with ambiguous or conflicting goals. Examples may be found in evaluations of the results produced by programmes designed to change behaviour and in issues on which the community is clearly divided such as sex education for adolescents, abortion, affirmative action, or capital punishment.

In contrast to researchers, who regard research as an end in itself, policy-makers and administrators are evaluated on their ability to act effectively in dealing with problems and research is therefore seen by them as a means to an end. Thus the test of the value of research for policy-makers and practitioners is whether the findings are normative, prescriptive and, above all, that the consequences are not problematic whereas researchers assess the value of research using norms and criteria from the academic community. The different perspectives on what constitutes good research create tension and mistrust and misperceptions of the respective roles and functions of users and suppliers of sound research (Rothman 1979).

This point is developed further by Littrel (1976) in his useful discussion of the 'defeasibility' of information. Littrell points out that, in identifying the special conditions under which belief in and action upon knowledge are to be limited or suspended ('defeasing'), social scientists normally employ a principle of methodological adequacy, whereas policy-makers tend to employ a principle of 'utility'. Gilbert Smith makes essentially the same point in his observation on the power differential created between researchers and administrators by the fact that administrators can claim that they must take account of a wide range of factors beyond research.

> In a loose sense, the principle of utility requires that knowledge be useful if it is to be believed in and acted upon. In a more restricted sense, the principle of utility demands that useful knowledge benefit a greater public good (p. 8).

The former sense of utility justifies the politician's limiting his acceptance of social-science knowledge if he believes that such knowledge cannot be put to some practical use. The latter (stronger) sense of utility creates special circumstances that may enable a policy-maker to justify to himself the 'defeasance' of social science data. Littrell therefore concludes that, although policy-makers may well accept the data themselves to be valid, they may be able to justify a refusal to accept or use them because the data are irrelevant to the (politically more important) principle of 'utility'.

Users of research complain that the suppliers often provide them with knowledge that is not useful – and even irrelevant – while suppliers complain that the requests of users are so general and vague that they are not reasonable and must be reformulated. In view of the widespread nature of such complaints, it seems surprising that so little effort is made to involve users in the specification of the research problem. Wilson, an academic with considerable experience in the preparation of research reports for the United States government, comments that:

> Good social science research, especially including evaluated experiments, requires the collaborative effort of the head of an agency, key subordinates, the affected operating personnel and outside analysts and evaluators (Wilson, 1978, p. 91).

A similar position is taken by Davis and Salasin (1978) and Rothman (1979), who regard consultation with users in planning research as one way of increasing its relevance for the policy or practice issues that are addressed in the research. The reasons for the general absence of collaboration between the suppliers and users of research probably differ according to the nature of the issue and the institutional setting. Experience does however suggest that the following perceptions are commonly held by researchers and that these tend to reduce the extent to which they collaborate with policy-makers. Policy-makers and practitioners are seen as users or consumers of, rather than participants in, research. Users or consumers commission research because they lack the knowledge and skill to participate in the rigorous and systematic analysis that research entails. Research involves a technology and expertise that precludes the involvement of non-experts in the conceptualisation and design of research. Users have a vested interest in the outcome of research and their participation will introduce a bias in the research process.

The lack of user participation in research may result in researchers' ignoring the political considerations which underlie policy formulation. Booth analysed the experience of governments in the United States and Great Britain with research designed to improve the efficiency of social welfare programmes. He found that social researchers designed and conducted efficiency and cost effectiveness studies that policy-makers could not use because of political considerations. Thus, he suggests that a more appropriate role for research in the social services is to provide policy-makers with the information that would help them do their jobs better. The information that policy-makers need is:

> ... that which helps to reveal or
> illuminate the real nature of the
> political choices which they face, which
> means information attuned to the language
> of priorities rather than efficiency
> (Booth, 1981, p. 12).

Researchers have traditionally taken the position that if there is no evidence that their research can be tied directly to an action-orientated decision, then the research itself has not been utilised (Rich, 1977). This position has tended to obscure the uses that have been made of research and the indirect impact it may often have on policy and practice. Weiss (1977b) identifies the following uses of research by upper-level bureaucrats in her study of the usefulness of research to officials in governmental mental health agencies in the United States. Among the uses she identifies are: General guidance in establishing needs and developing strategies; Continuing education; To challenge and clarify the thinking of officials; and To support a position and to promote their case.

A study of seven service-orientated U.S. government agencies resulted in similar findings, with the author cautioning that it is important for social scientists to rethink their "pre-occupation with action implications in the application of scientific knowledge to ... policy making" (Rich, 1970, p. 209). One result of this pre-occupation has been to overlook other functions that knowledge serves, such as organisational learning and planning and influencing the way in which problems are defined and specified at the level of individual administration. The use of research in policy formulation and implementation does not follow the pattern of use of research in the natural sciences or engineering but this should not be "equated with the thesis that social research has little or no impact on the policy making process" (Knorr, 1977, p. 179).

Social scientists who have studied the problems of the utilisation of research in policy formulation and programme development have found that policy-makers do use research - though in different, and no less important, ways than was envisaged in the "Social Engineering" or socio-technological model of problem-solving. On the basis of her review of a number of cases and surveys, Weiss (1977, p. 534) for example, concludes that although research findings are seldom used directly to determine the over-all shape or particular details of policies and programmes, research is used:

> ... to help them (policy-makers and administrators) think about the issues and define the problematics of a situation, to gain new ideas and new perspectives. They use research to help formulate problems and to set the agenda for future policy actions. And much of this use is ... a result of long term percolation of social science concepts, theories, and findings

into the climate of informed opinion
(Weiss, 1977, p. 534).

Town reviewed two action research projects in
Britain and found the contribution of research to
evaluation to be unimpressive. Likewise he sees the
major contributions of research to policy
formulation as those of developing ideas, testing
assumptions and formulating hypotheses to the ends
of providing "a clearer understanding of alternative
goals, redefinition of concepts and reformulating
policy measures (1978, p. 185).

This perception of the role of research in
policy-making rejects the "social engineering" model
in favour of the "enlightenment" model (Weiss,
1977). It rests on the proposition that the most
important role for research in policy-making is to
provide an intellectual setting of concepts,
propositions, orientations and empirical generalisations that will expand the policy-maker's frame
of reference and thus influence policy decisions. In
chapter 9 of this book, for example, Gilbert Smith
argues that we should abandon a narrow "cult of
utility" in favour of the idea that research
exercises more subtle and indirect forms of
influence within policy making.

But we would also argue that, although research
on the utilisation of research in policy-making
provides strong support for the notion that research
has an indirect impact on policy deliberations, both
policy makers and researchers must continue their
efforts to achieve direct and instrumental use of
research in decision-making about policy and
practice. To accept "enlightenment" as the major
role of researchers is a pragmatic response to a
difficult situation. It is, however, a response that
will find support among those who take the limited
view that for social scientists the production of
knowledge is an end in itself. But unless ways are
found to increase the utilisation of research there
will be little or no pressure on policy makers to
devise new and innovative responses to issues of
policy or practice.

POLICY-MAKERS, RESEARCHERS AND THE ORGANISATIONAL CONTEXT OF DECISIONS

a) The "discrete functions" model

In common with other forms of public-sector planning, planners in the social services have to harness, steer, and create a manageable relationshp between the twin steeds of rationality and (democratic) political control. In the traditional attempt to structure that relationship - variously termed the "decisionistic" (Habermas, 1971), the "democratic rationalist" (Hammond and Mumpower, 1979), or as we shall call it, the "discrete functions" model - there is a clear division of function between policy-makers and researchers, the former group specifying the goals of policy, and the particular questions they require researchers to answer in order to clarify choices or enhance the likely effectiveness of any decisions they may take. The researcher, in other words, undertakes investigations at the behest of the policy-maker - in order to produce the relevant technical "facts" which the policy-maker then uses to guide decisions along those lines which (ideally) promise to provide the best marriage between ideological preference and proven efficiency. This (still perhaps most common) approach to managing the relationship between research and policy is reflected in a range of operational forms - from "in-house" research units, through systems of research sponsorship, to the customer-contractor principle.

In terms of the search for an effective way of integrating research and policy, a serious general defect of the discrete functions paradigm lies in the fact that, within it, research becomes something of a hostage to fortune. Since the presentation of data and the formulation of decisions remain separate under this approach, the way in which research is actually utilised in the policy-making process is ultimately unpredictable. Instead of being accorded a special weighting, or a protected (and not necessarily pre-eminent) position in the decision-making system, research in effect becomes an additional variable vying with others inside the decision-making arena; and as such, open to capricious or inconsistent usage to support or attack particular political positions, perhaps with inaccurate, biased or incomplete interpretations of the data themselves. The act of sponsoring research may of course itself also be used as a means of "buying" political time, in order to avoid rather than actively seek solutions to particular problems. The commitment to rationality which underlies this arrangement may therefore be weakened - and perhaps even undermined - by its practical enactment. As Habermas (1971), talking of a slightly different aspect of this issue, states:

> Rationality in the choice of means accompanies avowed irrationality in orientation to values, goals and needs.

The recent growth of specifically contracted research can probably in large part be attributed to dissatisfaction with the "soft" research-sponsorship model in which policy-makers give financial support to research projects whose aims and management responsibilities are essentially left in the hands of the researchers themselves, in the hope or expectation that the researcher's final report will contain usable findings or recommendations. The customer-contractor principle obviously attempts to ensure that research will be more specifically addressed to the concerns of policy-makers. The "customer" (the policy-maker or administrator) stipulates what he requires and the "contractor" (the reseacher) does it if he can.

The customer-contractor principle is of course long-established in North America; though it has been further reinforced by recent developments in social-science research funding (see, for example, Social Science and Humanities Research Council of Canada, 1981), and is now increasingly used by government at both federal and provincial levels in Canada. Under the (fairly typical) system operated by the Canadian Solicitor General's Office, for example, researchers have to submit tenders for undertaking investigations on questions stipulated by that Office as among their research requirements. Within this "entrepreneurial" system, researchers make no contribution to decisions concerning which questions or issues need examination. The customers specify the kind of information they wish, the date by which they require it, and usually also insist on retaining the sole ownership and control of the rights to publish any reports issued as a result of the research.[2]

A number of problems have arisen around these developments. Thus, it has frequently been complained that the questions posed by customers have been difficult to relate to the requirements of empirical investigation. Many of the comments around this issue have in fact echoed Booth's (1979) argument that policy-makers are rarely able to play the part of customers by specifying what they want from research, because (as pointed out in our earlier discussion) they seldom operate with any articulate or precisely-formulated notion of the goals they are pursuing; and because policy develops more as an ad hoc response to everyday pressures and difficulties, than through the single-minded pursuit of a rational and coordinated plan geared to the achievement of a stable objective. Since:

> ... policy tends to be continually re-interpreted in the light of experience and adjusted in response to the shifting balance of power between contending interests, the policy-maker is typically unable to say exactly where he is heading; (and is therefore) ill-placed to contract the reseacher to help him get there (Booth, 1979, p. 181).

Nor is the researcher any better able to play the role of contractor than the policy-maker is capable of playing the part of customer in an effective way. Booth suggests that where the researcher adopts the perspective of the policy-maker, research inevitably ends up confirming decisions that would already have been taken, or discounting options that were unlikely ever to have been chosen. Lompe (1968) has taken this argument further, in deploring the "fig-leaf function" served by some investigations, where certain researchers have on occasion received contracts because they can be relied on to produce data to support predetermined opinions.

Moreover certain customers, insisting on their rights of ownership of the research report, have refused to release final reports for wider publicity because they are considered to be too sensitive politically, or because they focus too much on "negative" aspects of the situations studied; and a number of contractors have had the experience of having to negotiate with customers over revisions (not all of them, of course, unreasonable) that have been required to be made in the final report.

The fact that, under these customer-contractor arrangements, problems of access are normally avoided would seem a relatively modest advantage to set against these other causes for concern. A growing number of Canadian Universities are refusing to accept such contracts, arguing that they are leading to an erosion of academic liberty. As a result, the trend has increasingly been for such research to be undertaken by independent research consultants or contactors, rather than by members of University staff; and this removal from an academic base may further undermine the independence of researchers and increase the danger, referred to above, of producing the findings that are "wanted" by the customers.

Recent Canadian experience has also led certain commentators to observe that investigations which are too specifically based on narrow policy or practice issues are unlikely to make for innovative work in this field. Again, this resonates with the criticisms made by Booth (1979), who argues that, if research is to play a creative part in helping the policy-maker understand the problems he is trying to resolve, researchers must challenge the questions asked of them, ask whether they are the most appropriate ones, and enquire whether there is not another way of looking at things which helps to make sense of them. He concludes that:

> The purpose of research ... is to stimulate new thinking and open up new ways of looking at things which help to introduce or foster a new emphasis and direction in the political debate about policy. Rather than being a handmaiden of policy, research is a source of new ideas which, when taken up and carried forward by political pressures, are the driving force of innovations in policy (p. 185).

In criticising Rothschild's crude distinction between "basic" and "applied" research, Donnison (1978) similarly suggests that the Dainton Committee's distinction between "practical", "strategic" and "basic" science is a more relevant one. He makes a plea for a "strategic" social-science contribution to policy matters, emphasising a:

> contribution grounded in analysis and theory, rather than over-simple presentation of 'the facts' (Bulmer, 1978, p. 19).

Policy, Practice and Research

The British implementation of the customer-contractor principle - inspired primarily by the recommendations of the Rothschild Report (Central Policy Review Staff, 1971) - would seem to have been rather less rigorous than has been the case in Canada. In chapter 2 of this book, for example, Stevenson discusses the operation of the research liaison groups within the DHSS, whose creation was intended to provide a more fruitful collaboration between researchers and administrators; but would appear to have been somewhat less successful than had originally been hoped in allowing the strict customer-contractor principle to be put into effect. In practice, these groups have tended to result in a "broad steer" for research, with researchers having learned how to adapt their proposals in a form which is broadly acceptable to both sides, but without the work necessarily being focused on problems in quite the way it was presumed the principle itself would encourage. In this respect, it perhaps operates somewhere between the "research sponsorship" and the "customer-contractor" models; although clearly the particular mix operating in the RLGs allows a greater degree of control over the focus chosen by researchers than would be the case under the research sponsorship approach tout court.

An alternative form of the discrete functions approach may be observed in the "in-house' research units which exist in central and local government departments. A large part of Booth's (1979) criticisms and conclusions, referred to above, are in fact specifically directed at research units in local-authority social services departments. His argument that the essential role of research is to help introduce new emphases and/or directions in debates about policy, adopting a partisan stance, rather than have researchers attempt to be morally-neutral technicians, undoubtedly carries some weight. There are, however, two basic criticisms which can be directed at it.

First, for in-service researchers to abandon their role as handmaidens to policy-makers and to adopt an independently critical stance would not seem the surest way of preserving their own credibility and legitimacy with administrators - and indeed their own jobs within the bureaucracy - particularly at a time of financial cutbacks. There are realistic constraints in their interpretation of their role. Secondly, Booth's conclusion would in any case seem unduly pessimistic and restrictive in its implications for the researcher's role. As indicated above, the traditional positivistic view of research perhaps still holds out some relevance for policy.

Thus, Rothman's (1980) study of the work of a sample of research units in the social services departments of a (small) number of London boroughs indicated that Social Services Directors saw a number of positive benefits emerging from such work. In particular, they valued receiving specific factual information which they felt to be useful to their decisions (though it seems likely, in all candour, that the basis of such information may on many occasions be rather shaky); saw research as providing some degree of "objectivity" in a complex operational environment; found research useful in correcting prevalent myths and false assumptions; and saw research as having a potential cumulative effect in influencing organisational decisions. They also saw special advantages in having researchers "on the spot", arguing that this meant they received timely information from a group to whom access was convenient, comprising colleagues with whom they had close working relationships and in whom they expressed confidence; and saw the researchers as culling and summarising information relevant to a problem, thus saving them time, and presenting it in a relevant way (Rothman, 1980, pp. 157-63).

It could of course, be argued that Rothman may have been rather fortunate in the units he studied, and that what he is describing are examples of unusually good practice. Moreover, some of the claimed advantages listed above do bring to mind Booth's strictures concerning the dangers of the researcher's identifying too closely with the perspectives of the policy-maker, and producing answers of the kind the Director wants to hear. The specific comment concerning the contributions of research in correcting prevalent false assumptions does, however, to some degree provide reassuring counterweight to this possibility. And Rothman's findings do indicate over all that research is valued and can be used in what are thought to be effective ways by directors. The general tenor of the comments elicited by Rothman also suggests that ressearch is seen as useful less in terms of providing "answers" to specific problems, than as a means of widening the perspective and considerations the policy-making group might adopt in considering the dimensions of and possible modes of dealing with any problem. This has obvious parallels with Weiss' (1977) argument about the "enlightment" functions of research; with Rein's (1976) and Donnison's (1978) respective pleas for a "value-critical" and a "strategic" approach; and with Booth's (1979) conclusion that the main purpose of research is to stimulate new thinking in ways which may foster "a new emphasis and direction in the debate about policy".

But does the contribution of research have to be confined to these "softer" and more indirect effects? Within all the variants of the discrete functions model, a basic problem does seem to centre on the fact that the researcher has no effective control over the way findings are used in the formulation of policy. Whilst this may ultimately be the politically correct and most appropriate solution, it is at least worth considering whether other models offer a more effective blend between rationality and democratic accountability. And in such a search, the literature normally points to two major alternative approaches to structuring the relationship between policy-makers and researchers, which we shall term the "technocratic" and the "critical interaction" ideals.

b) The technocratic approach. The technocratic model separates the decision-making roles of technical and political actors in a rather different way from that contained in the discrete functions paradigm. Under this approach, the politician's task (probably together with a small group of non-elected administrative advisors) is to identify the objectives that should govern the choice of solution to a problem. Following this, a comprehensive review of all of the alternative feasible modes of dealing with the problem, together with an evaluation of their (likely) consequences is undertaken by a set of technical "experts", with researchers of course playing a central role in this exercise. On this basis, a solution is chosen as a "master plan" for attaining the chosen goals, with the expert group being responsible for determining both the overall shape and the specific details of that strategy.

It seems hardly necessary to enter upon a detailed analysis of this model. Clearly, it ensures that the researcher has more direct control over the way in which technical knowledge is applied. But equally clearly, a number of additional difficulties would be created by the wholehearted application of such a model.

Foremost among these is the manifest threat presented to the principle of democratic accountability. Under the technocratic model, the elected member is reduced to the status of a cypher:

> the politician in the technical state is left with nothing but a fictitious decision-making power (Habermas, 1971, p. 64).

But behind this danger there also lie a number of less obvious difficulties which are inherent in the technocratic model.

First, in the search for a "rational" alternative to more politically-dominated systems of decision-making, it is important to note that the notion of "rationality" is itself problematical. As Berry (1974) has pointed out:

> Rationality is not a concept characterised by one value such as efficiency, but is characterised by multiple dimensions whose emphases vary by the planning situation (p.347).

The "rationalities" implied in technocratic approaches, according to Berry, are primarily technical (knowledge and beliefs concerning cause and effect) and economic (the optimal utilisation of scarce resources). To these two, it would seem necessary to add at least political rationality referring, in any competitive situation, to the actions of individuals as these are designed to take into account the relative power, etc. of other parties to the transaction and/or the values and objectives these same individuals may be pursuing (as is implied also in Littrell's discussion of "defeasibility", referred to earlier).

Moreover, the technocratic approach assumes that there is a "correct" - and largely technical - answer (or limited range of answers) to any particular problem. Given reliable knowledge, experts or committees holding widely differing views will always arrive at the same solution to a problem (see also Lompe, 1968). But the notion that research will enable one to identify the single "best" way of dealing with a problem assumes a) a greater degree of specificity in its answers than social science will probably ever be capable of furnishing; and (more importantly) b) a degree of consensus, which almost certainly does not exist, between different groups of individuals as to the essential nature of the "problems" they have to tackle, and of the most appropriate (or acceptable) ways of dealing with them. To quote again from Habermas (1971, p. 64):

> Within the framework of research operations that expand our points of technical control we can make no cogent statements about "value systems" ... either there are still other forms of decision than the theoretical-technical for the rational clarification of practical issues that cannot be completely answered by technologies and strategies, or no reasons can be given for decisions in such issues. In that case we would have to return to a (purely political) model.

To attempt to remove such elements from the political process not only denies the fact that democracy entails disagreement over ends as well as means; but also changes policy-making into at best a search for a rather dull consensus, and at worst a potentially authoritarian process.

The technocratic model can also be criticised at a rather more technical level in that it promulgates a synoptic view of decision-making; and this tends, for instance, to ignore the fact that human beings possess only limited problem-solving abilities (Etzioni, 1968) and that, in particular, their capacity for retaining, balancing and manipulating diffuse and complex sets of information is rather more modest than the technocratic model would require. Decisions must in any case perforce be made with inadequate information.

In summary, the technocratic approach ignores the limitations in human problem-solving abilities; fails to differentiate between different types of rationality; and takes the assumption that value questions can be at least sidestepped and, ideally, resolved by technical methods. With regard to the attempt to maximise the contribution of research to policy in the social services, it holds certain superficial attractions, but is naive (and perhaps even dangerous) in the assumptions it makes about the politics of decision-making; although as Berry (1974) suggests, it may well be appropriate for policy-making in fields like physical planning, where the planning environment is rather more stable, and where the elements which require to be borne in mind by the planner are perhaps more straightforward. The collapse of PPBS, and the relative failure of most other applications of research to the social services, underlines the error of assuming that the possession of knowledge will in itself transform policy-making in the social services into a purely technical, managerial exercise. The above analysis has perhaps also served to indicate that such a transformation would in any case be undesirable.

c) <u>Critical interaction</u>. Is it then possible to pick a course between the shallows of technology and the whirlpools of a more purely political context for the taking of decisions?

In general terms, attempts to apply knowledge to policy-making mean that the process of decision-making must itself be divided into three broad stages. In the first stage (value-determined) goals are specified. This is followed by a period of rational (<u>a priori</u>) analysis and the collection of relevant empirical material, with a view to devising an effective technical strategy (or set of strategies) for the attainment of these goals. In the third stage, policy-decisions are taken as to which of these strategies should be adopted. As indicated above, in both the discrete functions and the technocratic models, the functions of researcher and policy-maker are fairly rigidly separated, the researcher being involved solely at stage two in the discrete functions approach, and at the second and third stage under the latter model.

The critical-interaction approach attempts to replace this traditional separation of functions with opportunities for regular exchanges of views, perspectives and information between the two sets of parties at all points of the second and third stages. This may be seen partly as a question of devising an organisational form which will permit that interaction to take place; and partly also of coping with the problems created by the cognitive differences referred to above, in our discussion of the differing frames of reference of policy-makers and researchers.

Moynihan (1971), for example, without specifying how this is to be achieved, talks of the "responsibility" of social scientists to interpret their findings to policy-makers and practitioners. Caplan (1977) also identifies the need to bridge user and supplier perspectives as a priority; and proposes an indirect solution to the problem, involving the introduction of:

> a set of individuals representing
> different combinations of roles and skills
> located in an institutional arrangement
> that allows them to take into
> consideration the practical factors
> affecting both the production and use of
> knowledge (p. 196).

Caplan does, however, acknowledge that to create the combination of individual and insititutional characteristics needed for implementing his proposal would not be a trivial task. Sundquist (1978) makes a similar proposal concerning the use of research brokers, whose major responsibility would be to supervise and expedite the flow of knowledge into policy and practice.

Within the DHSS system, this basic function is intended to be covered at least in part by the liaison officers (working of course in collaboration with research liaison groups), whose responsibilities, according to Kogan et al. (1980, pp. 25–30), entail contact with research projects from the initiation stage; through the monitoring and evaluation of ongoing studies; to the final stage of bringing research findings to the attention of potential users. The material presented by Kogan et al. (1980, especially pp. 26–29) provides a rather equivocal picture of the effectiveness to date of this innovation. The liaison officers themselves put "committed time" into the evaluation and circulation of research findings within the Department. Internal documents also indicated that certain of the projects had been seen as producing useful results. Researchers, however, had little way of knowing whether their work had had any influence on policies, many feeling it had been ignored. Kogan has no direct evidence as to how much research actually influenced the policy-fields for which it was commissioned; but reports that research managers felt that the <u>policy divisions should be the prime movers in ensuring this</u> (our emphasis).

This experiment would therefore seem so far to have been only partially successful. Researchers, in particular, seem to have been left dissatisfied by their perceptions (or in several cases, ignorance) of how research was used. Whether this failure can be attributed to a (remediable) lack of communication between liaison officers and researchers; or to a more deep-seated misperception and distrust by researchers of users' approaches to and interest in research (see, for example, Rothman,

1979); or whether researchers were in fact accurate in their views of the extent to which research was utilised, is of course impossible to gauge at this point. And indeed, too little is known in specific terms about how the differing perceptions of the users and suppliers of research contribute to the level of utilisation of knowledge in decisions affecting both policy and practice. It also seems regrettable that the liaison officers do not involve themselves more directly in the translation of research findings into recommendations for policy. This does, however, perhaps again highlight the difficulty of bridging the gap between the two through the creation of an intemediary role.

Strictly speaking, the "critical interaction" model demands direct interchanges between policy-makers and researchers. The object is to enable each group to understand more of the perceptions, objectives and methods of, and constraints faced by the other, so that joint work may then fuse their differing contributions into a more effective product. Rich (1975), for example, argues for:

> continuous feedback between policy makers and the staff providing information to them. Both researchers and policy makers will be more sensitive to each other's needs and ways of communicating if this type of contact is established.

Ad hoc attempts have been made in certain Departments of the Scottish Office, for instance, to institute this principle through the medium of seminars on particular research projects, and their implications for policy. Effective application of the principle would, however, seem clearly to demand a rather more frequent, continuous and long-term set of interchanges than can take place in seminars alone, however useful these may be in specific cases.

These requirements would seem easier to satisfy in the context of "in-house" research, where there are obviously greater opportunities for more regular contact. Thus, in his study of research units in local government, Rothman (1980) concludes that the utilisation of research is facilitated by opportunities for "structured access" by researchers to applied personnel in both planning and service-delivery functions; and by the existence of various specific mechanisms within the organisations that link research with applied tasks and operational members of staff. Examples of such mechanisms were: development panels and working parties comprising a mixture of research, operational and planning staff; management teams, again with an appropriately mixed membership; research liaison groups; and seminars on research activities. In addition, the research unit:

> should be made up of personnel with combined competence in research ... and in application or operations (Rothman, 1980, p. 51).

Within such contexts, one could envisage researchers undertaking reviews of the research literature relevant to a particular policy-area, as well as conducting occasional data-gathering exercises of their own; and then discussing their conclusions in detail over a series of interchanges with those persons who have a more formal responsibility for policy-decisions within the organisation, in order to develop a workable set of recommendations and proposals. Something like the Nominal Group Technique (Delbecq et al., 1975; see also Delbecq and Van DeVen, 1971) might be a useful means of structuring and focusing interchanges within such meetings, in a way that would help to relate the discussion of research more effectively to particular policy issues.[3]

Such evidence as exists does therefore seem to indicate that the critical interaction model (or something very like it) can operate effectively and strengthen research's role in decision-making. Rothman's (1980) findings suggest in particular that commitment at a high administrative level within the organisation to the utilisation of research and a degree of familiarity among researchers with the kind of work carried out in the settings they are evaluating, as well as the existence of particular structural arrangements and characteristics such as those outlined above that facilitate communication between research users and producers, are important determinants of the extent to which organisations are able to implement research effectively.

Certain comments are, however, perhaps called for in respect of the above. First, such a model does seem more appropriate for decision-making units such as British local-government departments and (possibly) Canadian provincial-government ministries, where researcher and policy-maker, through physical proximity, more informal work-arrangements and relationships, and the generally smaller scale of the organisation, seem more likely to have opportunities for regular exchanges of views and information of the kind demanded by the critical interaction model. It is rather more difficult to envisage such interchanges taking place in the policy-making system described by Kogan et al. (op. cit.; see also, Henkel and Kogan, 1981), and by Stevenson in this book. Perhaps the introduction of a research "broker" or liaison officer is the nearest one can get to the critical interaction approach in large organisations. These questions would, however, repay further analysis.

Second, Ashford's (1981) analysis of the United Kingdom's system of government leads him to the conclusion that - basically because of the relative lack of opportunities for effective contact between politicians and unelected officials - the political contribution to policy-making is capricious and superficial. (The same basic observation would probably hold true of Canadian government, including the systems of provincial government.) Whilst a system such as that adumbrated above would seem unlikely to make this situation any worse; clearly neither could it be guaranteed to remedy it. The contacts described by Rothman (op. cit.) and those which would seem to be implied in our above outline would tend, not to exclude, but rather not to include elected representatives in the discussion and application of research. This is a particularly important problem for the critical interaction model since without proper involvement of politicians it is in danger either of reverting to one of, or of vacillating between, the two extremes of the discrete functions and technocratic approaches. A pointer towards a solution may be offered by such experiments as the system of officer-member groups which operate within the corporate management structure of Strathclyde Regional Council in the Scottish local-government system. Under this arrangement, permanent local-government officers, elected members and researchers form discussion groups around chosen policy areas with a view to exploring the nature and scope of the problems contained within those areas and, using research and administrative and practice experience, attempting to devise a set of proposals to deal with them. This difficulty may in large part relate to our earlier point about the size of the decision-making unit; although Strathclyde is a very large local-government area. Again, it would obviously be worth looking at alternative models and experiences of attempting to deal with this important problem.

Third, if it is true that the critical interaction approach works best within the context of an "in-house" research unit, one needs to take careful note of problems such as those pointed to by Willett in chapter 4, concerning the reduced independence of research in such units and of the need for policy research which is not specifically tied to the concerns of policy-makers. As has been stressed at several points in this paper, the knowledge coming from social-science research should be regarded as cumulative. Under the critical interaction model, researchers would probably need to spend a good deal of time reviewing existing research material and within that material, identifying relevant trends and conclusions for the development of policies within their own organisations. It is important that the need to develop the critical interaction approach within an "in-house" context should not diminish opportunities for research which questions existing procedures and points to alternatives.

Finally, and in relation to all of the above, whilst there may be certain direct indications from research as to how policies would need to develop, it seems much more likely that the main contribution of research will be that of "enlightenment" rather than the specific direction of policy. For research to expand into a role of more direct guidance (working, of course, in realistic conjunction with political objectives and constraints) requires the development of a larger and more systematic body of knowledge, both theoretical and empirical, which in turn demands the development of solutions to methodological and epistemological problems of the kinds referred to in earlier sections of this paper. This perhaps also underlines the suggestions made by Smith in chapter 9 that to argue that there can be a direct relationship between research and policy is to lose sight of the complex processes which are typical of the political pluralism of democratic Western systems of government.

RESEARCH, POLICY AND PRACTICE

The distinction between policy and practice is in certain ways a rather artificial one. But to the extent that policy-decisions are taken by certain (groups of) individuals, and the responsibility for operationalising and implementing those decisions is accorded to other individuals, that distinction is accepted as having some relevance. From the planner's point of view, the problem is that of ensuring that practitioners at the "front line" are given the freedom to interpret and act on what they see as the significant features of a case or situation whilst also ensuring that those interpretations and actions are consistent with what the policy or programme is attempting to achieve. Structural changes, in other words, are rather easier to bring about than those changes which relate to attitudes, behaviour, etc. within the organisation. Dorothy E. Smith (1965) refers to this as the phenomenon of "front line" organisation (see also Robertson, 1969). This basic idea also lies at the heart of the recent work on "street-level bureaucracy" (Lipsky, 1980; see also Hill, 1982), with Lipsky arguing that the various strategies devised by "street-level" bureaucrats to enable them to cope with the pressures and uncertainties of their work effectively become the policies they carry out. And arguing of course from rather different premises, Schon (1971) also insists that the formation of a policy cannot be separated from its implementation.

Many of the contributions to the present volume address this issue in one way or another. Thus, Willett argues that groups at relatively low levels in the prison hierarchy are able to resist policy changes in a way which undermines the intentions behind those policies. In demonstrating that different people construe "helping" in different ways and that help-givers do not necessarily think the same way about help as do their corresponding help-receivers, Shapiro suggests that there is no guarantee that "social structures will produce either the desired or the desirable impact upon our thinking"; and concludes that behind structural strategies, there lie more detailed strategies to do with the content and process of helping and the definitions of roles and settings related to it which must be recognised and attended to at the broadest level of policy and programme development. Dennis talks of the problems faced by environmental health officers when they have to deal with the pressures placed upon them by various different constituencies, and to make decisions which are seen as legitimate; and suggests among other things that the ambiguity of the knowledge with which these officials operate means that ostensibly objective judgments can be used to justify convenient bureaucratic ends. Smith criticises the assumption that policy is a "top down" process and suggests that the main impact of research may be upon the "implementers" rather than the "makers" of policy. And Asquith argues than only when the nature of the "ideologies" embraced by control agents, and the interests they serve, are identified will approaches to delinquency control be open to critical appraisal.

How, then, can "front line" behaviour be made consistent with policy; and what is more relevant to the purposes of the present volume, with what would appear to be indicated as desirable or more effective by the findings of research? In his useful analysis of the ways in which research may be used for developing practice in social work, Stewart Kirk (1979) suggests that analysts have tended to work with an oversimplified paradigm of the role of knowledge in professional practice. He argues that the use of knowledge is a complex phenomenon; and that researchers have been relatively oblivious to the processes through which knowledge is developed, disseminated and used (see also Resnick, 1973). Kirk makes a distinction between three basic approaches to the implementation of research, namely: a) the Research, Development and Diffusion model; b) the "Social Interaction" model; and c) the "Problem Solver" model.

The Research, Development and Diffusion (R.D. and D.) model is perhaps best exemplified by the work of Rothman (1979; 1980). This sees research implementation as a rational and linear process, which moves through a series of operational stages, from basic research (involving scans and summaries of relevant published research, and the development of propositions and generalisations from those summaries); through applied research, which attempts to translate existing knowledge into a set of principles for action, followed by further testing, development and refinement of "prototypes"; to mass production and packaging and (finally) dissemination of knowledge. The entire operation therefore assumes a planned and coordinated series of stages, with a clear division of labour and functions. It accordingly emphasises the role of research and the rational planning of efforts at diffusion; but pays little attention to the role of the "consumer" of research knowledge. As Kirk (1979, p. 5) notes:

In the R.D. and D. scheme consumers are a clearly defined and somewhat passive audience who will accept an innovation if it is delivered in the right way at the right time.

The Social Interaction paradigm, by contrast with the R.D. and D. approach, assumes the existence of a "diffusable" innovation, and is relatively indifferent to the technical features that have contributed to its discovery or development. Its concerns are much more with how the innovation is transmitted and adopted in practice; and how this process is influenced by social structure and relationships. In consequence, it is more sensitive than the R.D. and D. perspective to the way in which the process of diffusion is affected by the intricacies of human roles and relationships. A person's position in a social network, his interpersonal contacts, and the number and nature of his reference group identifications are all important variables in influencing the process of the diffusion of knowledge. This perspective therefore pays careful attention to the importance of social networks in analysing the way in which knowledge is transmitted and used within the social system of the user of research. This strength, however, gives rise to its own analytic weakness, since the Social Interaction model fails to give any consideration to or account of the links between the producers and the users of knowledge.

The "Problem Solver" model places the consumer of knowledge at the centre of its concerns. It is essentially a "user-oriented" paradigm of the process of dissemination and utilisation. It assumes that self-initiated change provides the firmest motivation for change, and the best chance of achieving lasting effects. This model therefore suggests that the problem-solving process should begin with consumers identifying the needs within their own practice, these needs then being diagnosed as problems to be solved. Research is then initated to identify those factors which contribute to the problem and attempts made to develp or adapt possible solutions to specific difficulties. These solutions are then used on a trial basis and evaluated in terms of the extent to which they reduce the needs they are designed to assist. If the solution does not work, the cycle begins again. This is therefore a primarily psychological model, which focuses attention on the psychological conditions under which new knowledge may be sought and used by consumers. Because of this emphasis, however, it perhaps over-emphasises the extent to which consumers are capable of generating their own solutions to problems.

Of these three approaches, the R.D. and D. model therefore concentrates most on producing technically valid recommendations; but is perhaps the weakest in the implementation phase, assuming as it seems to do that practitioners will be convinced by the evidence of effectiveness, etc. presented in research reports and thereby motivated to change their practice. Of the other two, the "Problem Solver" approach was contained in the recommendations of the CCETSW/PSSC (1980) report on "Research and Practice", which among other things recommended that more research should be undertaken by practitioners, in order to increase the amount of research done in social work and to relate it more effectively to issues which emerged as significant for practitioners themselves, so that results might be fed back into their practice. There is much to be said for this approach, which also corresponds to Schon's (1971) ideas concerning "social learning":

> The movement of learning is as much from periphery to periphery, or from periphery to centre, as from centre to periphery (Schon, 1971, p. 177).

This would, however, demand an increase in research skills on the part of practitioners far beyond the present rather low level of both competence and interest.

Other, more mundane, strategies are available. One of the primary traditional responses to the need to influence "front line" behaviour lies of course through the medium of professional training (see, for example, Thomlinson, 1981). But although this strategy has some definite advantages, in that it aims at affecting the attitudes, motivations and capacity for self-appraisal of the individual worker, it can also be objected that the training model is a) a rather long-term and piecemeal method of effecting change or consistency in behaviour; and b) in any case a somewhat unreliable method, in the light of such findings as those of Blau's (1955) classic study of welfare-agency staff and organisation, that the effects of training are fairly vulnerable to erosion by peer and work pressures, and the general ethos of the social group

within which one works. As against this, however, an
in-service training model, perhaps using the working
group as the focus of the educator's efforts towards
change, might provide a more robust basis for such a
programme, particularly if it could be linked to
research evaluation exercises carried out by
practitioners themselves.

Kirk (1979, pp. 12-13) suggests that his three
models of research utilisation might provide some
clues to the kinds of links that require to be
developed in order to ensure a more effective
relationship between research and practice. Thus,
the R.D. and D. model lays (a traditional
positivistic) stress on the importance of
development and testing of models of practice before
they are actually adopted. The Social Interaction
paradigm indicates that the dissemination of
research findings through academic journals is not
the most effective way of securing good
communication with practitioners; and that the
transmission of knowledge and ideas throughout a
profession is perhaps most effectively done through
individuals occupying key positions within the
practitioners' social networks. Thirdly, the
Problem-Solver approach suggests that, in order to
ensure effective integration with practice, the
issues studied by researchers should relate more
directly to the needs and concerns of practitioners.
He concludes that a research orientation should be
integrated with practice skills. "Only when there is
a spirit of enquiry and a readiness to innovate at
the level of the practitioner will external
information make a lasting impact on practice"
(ibid, p. 13).

There are perhaps two basic problems which
would need to be avoided if Kirk's conclusions were
to be accepted. First, an over-dependence on
practitioner-defined problems as a stimulus for
empirical work might incline towards the same
dangers of producing research which is
insufficiently critical or innovative in its
concerns and conclusions as were alluded to in our
earlier discussion of in-house research. Second, the
reliance on "key" practitioners suggested by the
Social Interaction model concentrates the power of
innovation in a relatively few hands. On the other
hand, research based on practitioners' concerns need
not exclude a continuing involvement of some
researchers in "strategic" (in Dainton's sense)
investigations; and the spectre of "passive"
practitioners waiting for advice on innovations from

their more informed or energetic colleagues might at
least partially be kept at bay by the development of
a special emphasis within the training of social
workers.

Rather than have teachers on training courses
interpret the relevance of research for practice,
then inculcate the special skills deemed necessary
to achieve what research may suggest to be
desirable, a more flexible and perhaps more
realistic way of relating empirical findings to
actual practice would be for training courses to
concentrate upon producing greater "research
awareness" among practitioners. This could be
attached to and reinforced by a system of in-service
training and development, in which practitioners
would be constantly encouraged to review their own
activities in the light of research evidence. To
this end, it would seem necessary that the content
of the courses of research training which the
CCETSW/PSSC (op. cit.) report "Research and
Practice" presents as one of its major
recommendations for improving the research
sophistication of social workers should be related
to practice, rather than being abstract
presentations of the formal features and techniques
of research. The emphasis, in other words, would be
less on producing skilled research technicians than
on training for the critical evaluation of practice.
Such a "front line learning" system might then allow
practitioners to respond more flexibly and in a more
informed way both to deficiencies in their own
practice or to changes in their working environment,
as these were highlighted by research findings.

An additional possible way of relating practice
to research (and, where appropriate, to agency
policy) lies in the use of guidelines. In its
implementation of the legislation for Community
Service by Offenders, for example, the Social Work
Services Group (1980) reviewed the research evidence
on the operation of similar schemes in other
jurisdictions, in order to draw up a set of
guidelines for what seemed the most appropriate
procedures for social workers to pursue, within the
Scottish legislation. Various of the Canadian
provincial applications of the "Diversion" principle
have similarly depended on the use of guidelines by
those personnel having the authority to divert
offenders out of the criminal justice system. The
main problem with guidelines is of course that
ultimately they are no more than statements of
guidance, possessing no legal force or status. Thus,

policemen in certain parts of Canada have complained that if "diversion" decisions based on guidelines subsequently prove unsuccessful, with offenders being found guilty of further offences, they tend to be criticised by superiors for contradicting normal procedures, rather than being praised for exercising their judgment within the guidelines. Practitioners at the front line in consequence tend to "play safe" with the result that practice tends to become rather conservative. That said, however, sets of guidelines (probably relating to specific practice areas) could obviously be a useful adjunct to the type of practitioner self-appraisal and development system described above, provided the operation of the guidelines themselves was open to regular review.

A final method for generating greater practitioner conformance with research and policy prescriptions would be to create a set of organisational incentives to foster behaviour of the desired type. Kirk (op. cit., p. 12) for example, suggests that:

> ... incentive systems should be designed to encourage practitioners to adapt to new knowledge. Why should they discard old practices? What are the consequences of not doing so?

Such systems need not be of the traditional bureaucratic "sticks and carrots" type, with prizes for the "social worker of the month" and penalties for departures from prescribed action. Indeed, the likelihood is that a reliance on sanctions in particular would simply alienate practitioners and produce consequences the reverse of those desired. Rather, the need would be for agency managements to construct a more "facilitative" environment, providing resources in the form of time and finance to enable staff to discuss and evaluate their own practice in the light of research and other evidence, and (where appropriate) to undertake investigations themselves (see, for example, Social Services Research Group, Scottish Branch, 1981).

CONCLUSIONS

Clearly, we are dealing with a complex and subtly inter-related set of issues. Effective integration of research into policy and practice would seem to be constrained not only by the type and quality of research that is undertaken, and more generally by the epistemological problems which confront attempts to work within a "scientific" framework in the study of human behaviour; but also by unrealistic and/or incompatible attitudes and expectations among the main parties to these relationships and the structures within which they must interact. Research and rational decision-making also imply change, and people tend to be resistant to change. Both policy and research need to tackle this resistance in a relevant way.

At an organisational level, if our analysis has been correct, the critical-interaction model would seem in principle to provide the most appropriate basis for a fruitful relationship between researchers and policy-makers; but a number of practical problems make this a difficult structure to implement -- at any rate in large organisations. Experimentation with variants might therefore be useful in pointing to ways of overcoming the difficulties highlighted by our analysis.

In terms of the uses of research, the conclusion must perhaps for the present be that the "enlightenment" or "value-critical" approaches are the most realistic ones. Research should be seen less in terms of identifying the "one best way" of solving a problem, than of illuminating important features of it which then must be solved through the exercise of judgment as well as knowledge. That said, both social scientists and policy-makers should, however, continue to attempt to find ways to achieve, where appropriate, a more direct impact of research upon decisions about policy and practice. To that end, we would suggest that it is necessary to examine this process of implementation in more detail; and to evaluate it with a view to determining the extent to which structural, cognitive and epistemological factors explain the present level of use (or non-use) of research. Existing research on the utilisation of knowledge has typically been based on participants' memory of events, or on the analysis of secondary data. In our view, proposals for increasing the utilisation of research are premature until we have a greater understanding of the roles of actors in generating knowledge that is judged useful for policy-deliberations, and those conditions that determine the balance between rational and non-rational factors in policy and practice decisions. In other words, investigations of research implementation have to date evaluated outcomes without building up a parallel understanding of the dynamics which produced those outcomes. An analogy might be drawn with research on casework and psychotherapy, where a considerable number of outcome evaluation studies have been undertaken, but with very little complementary research on the processes within the therapeutic relationship which produce those outcomes.

With regard to the concerns of this volume, researchers should accordingly undertake process evaluations designed to provide a systematic body of data on the range of uses of research and the factors associated with different patterns of use. This would seem to point to the need for a series of "process" case-studies. The kind of retrospective research which has been conducted in this area to date has given little understanding of the dynamics of the process; since it has typically sought to identify how far research is reflected in decisions taken, rather than answering the more fundamental questions of why and how those decisions were taken. There are undoubtedly important issues of power, status and control which would emerge from a critical analysis of process. Social scientists have the techniques and the ingenuity to undertake this task, which should provide data and insights that could be used to develop new approaches to linking knowledge with action of a kind that would ensure a more productive relationship between those using and those supplying research for both policy and practice. If these essays have provided some steps towards the attainment of that goal, they will have furnished a worthy memorial for the person to whom this volume is dedicated.

NOTES

1. See, for example, Lasswell, 1951, 1956; Freeman and Sherwood, 1970; Zurcher and Bonjean, 1970, Sections II and VI; Central Policy Review Staff, 1971; Foren and Brown, 1971, chapters 1 and 6; Tripodi, Fellin and Epstein, 1971; Cochrane, 1972; Rossi and Williams, 1972; Weiss, 1972; Abt, 1976; Falk and Lee, 1978, chapters 7-9; Datta and Perloff, 1979; CCETSW/PSSC, 1980; and House, 1980).
2. The fact that deadlines can now be set for the submission of research reports is seen as a particular advantage by many fund-giving agencies in Canada who complained that reports submitted under

more relaxed funding arrangements were frequently too late to be of much assistance to them.

3. Delbecq et al. (1975) suggest that the aims of the Nominal Group Technique (NGT) are to initiate and guarantee appropriate processes for what they see as the separate phases of creative problem-solving; to ensure balanced participation by and among members; and to incorporate mathematical voting techniques in the aggregation of any group judgment. A particular advantage claimed for NGT, which seems especially relevant to the present analysis, is that the structure it imposes on the processes of the group ensure increased participation by all members. This contrasts with the more conventional type of group discussion, which tends generally to be dominated by a few influential individuals whose status, personality, etc. make them and their ideas more prominent elements in the group's deliberations. NGT might therefore help to ensure that a more consistent and effective balance is maintained between technical and political contributions to policy discussions and decisions (see especially Delbecq et al., op. cit., pp. 3-10).

REFERENCES

Abt, C. C. (ed.) (1976) The Evaluation of Social Programs. Beverly Hills: Sage Publications.

Ashford, D. E. (1981) Policy and Politics in Britain: The Limits of Consensus. Oxford: Blackwell.

Berry, D. E. (1974) "The Transfer of Planning Theories to Health Planning Practice", Policy Sciences, 5, 343-361.

Blau, P. M. (1955) The Dynamics of Bureaucracy. Chicago: University of Chicago Press.

Booth, T. (1979) "Research and Policy Making in Local Authority Social Services", Public Administration, 57, 173-86.

Booth, T. (1981) "Some American Lessons for Social Services Researchers", Unpublished paper delivered to the Annual General Meeting of the Scottish Branch of the Social Services Research Group, Glasgow, 20 February.

Bucuvalas, M. and Weiss, C. (1972) "The Challenge of Social Research to Decision Making", in C. Weiss (ed.), Using Social Research in Public Policy Making. Lexington: D. C. Heath.

Bulmer, M. (1978) Social Policy Research. London: Macmillan.

Bulmer, M. (1978) "Social Science Research and Policy Making", in M. Bulmer, Social Policy Research. London: Macmillan.

Caplan, N. (1972) "A Minimum Set of Conditions Necessary for the Utilization of Social Science Knowledge in Policy Formulation at the National Level", in C. Weiss (ed.), Using Social Research in Public Policy Making. Lexington: D. C. Heath.

Caplan, N. (1977) "A Minimal Set of Conditions Necessary for the Utilisation of Social Science Knowledge in Policy Formulation at the National Level", in C. Weiss (ed.), Using Social Research in Public Policy Making. Lexington: D.C. Heath and Co.

Caplan, N., Morrison, A. and Stambaugh, R. (1975) The Use of Social Science Knowledge in Policy Decisions at the National Level: A Report to Respondents. Ann Arbor: University of Michigan Institute for Social Research.

Carleton University Centre for Social Welfare Studies (1977) Social Program Evaluations in Canada: An Inventory. Ottawa: Carleton University Centre for Social Welfare Studies.

CCETSW/PSSC (1980) Research and Practice. London: Central Council for Education and Training in Social Work.

Central Policy Review Staff (1971) The Organisation and Management of Government Research and Development (The Rothschild Report). Cmnd. 4814. London: HMSO.

Cherns, A. (1967) "The Use of Social Sciences", Inaugural Lecture delivered at Loughborough University of Technology, Loughborough, 24 June.

Cherns, A., Sinclair, R. and Jenkins, W. (1972) Social Science and Government Policies and Procedures. London: Tavistock.

Cochrane, A. (1972) Effectiveness and Efficacy: Random Reflections on Health Services. London: Nuffield Provincial Hospitals Trust.

Coleman, J. (1980) "The Structure of Society and the Nature of Social Research", Knowledge: Creation, Diffusion, Utilisation, 1, 333-350.

Cook, T. D., Cook, F. L. and Mark, M. M. (1977) Randomised and Quasi-Experimental Designs in Evaluation Research: An Introduction. Ottawa: Carleton University School of Social Work.

Datta, L. E. and Perloff, R. (eds.) (1979) Improving Evaluations. Beverly Hills: Sage Publications.

Davis, H. and Salasin, S. (1978) "Strengthening the Contribution of Social R and D to Policy Making", in L. Lynn (ed.), Knowledge and Policy: The Uncertain Connection. Washington: National Academy of Sciences.

Delbecq, A.L. and Van De Ven, A.H. (1971) "A Group Process Model for Problem Identification and Program Planning", Journal of Applied Behavioral Science, (July to August).

Delbecq, A.L., Van De Ven, A.H., Gustafson, D.H. (1975) Group Techniques for Program Planning: A Guide to Nominal Group and Delphi Processes. Glenview, Illinois: Scott, Foreman and Co.

Deniston, O. L., Rosenstock, I. M., Welch, W. and Getting, V. A. (1978) "Evaluation of Program Effectiveness and Program Efficiency", in F. J. Lyden and E. G. Miller (eds.), Public Budgetting: Program Planning and Evaluation. Chicago: Rand McNally (3rd edition).

Donnison, D. (1978) "Research for Policy", in M. Bulmer (ed.) Social Policy Research. London: Macmillan.

Eidell, T. and Kitchel, J. (1968) Knowledge Production and Utilization in Educational Administration. Columbus: University Council on Educational Administration.

Etzioni, A. (1968) The Active Society: A Theory of Societal and Political Processes. New York: The Free Press.

Falk, N. and Lee, J. (1978) Planning the Social Services. Farnborough, Hants: Saxon House.

Foren, R. and Brown, M. (1971) Planning for Service: An Examination of the Organisation and Administration of Local Authority Social Services Departments. London: Charles Knight.

Freeman, H. E. and Sherwood, C. C. (1970) Social Research and Social Policy. Englewood Cliffs, New Jersey: Prentice-Hall.

Gorham, W. (1967) "P.P.B.S.: Its Scope and Limitations (1) - Notes of a Practitioner", Public Interest, 8.

Habermas, J. (1971) Towards a Rational Society. London: Heinemann.

Haveman, R. H. (1970) "Public Expenditures and Policy Analysis: An Overview", in R. H. Haveman and J. Margolis (eds.), Public Expenditures and Policy Analysis. Chicago: Markham.

Heal, K., Sinclair, I. and Troop, J. (1973) "Development of a Social Climate Questionnaire for Use in Approved Schools and Community Homes", British Journal of Sociology, XXIV, 222-235.

Henkel, M. and Kogan, M. (1981) The DHSS Funded Research Units: The Process of Review. Uxbridge, Mx.: Brunel University, Dept of Government.

Hill, M. (1982) "Street Level Bureaucracy in Social Work and Social Services Departments", Research Highlights, 4: Social Work Departments as Organisations (ed. J. Lishman), 69-81. Aberdeen: University of Aberdeen Department of Social Work.

Holzner, B. and Marx, J. (1979) Knowledge Application - The Knowledge System in Society. Toronto: Allyn and Bacon.

House, E. R. (1980) Evaluating with Validity. Beverly Hills: Sage Publications.

Kirk, S. (1979) "Understanding Research Utilization in Social Work", in A. Rubin and A. Rosenblatt (eds.), Sourcebook on Research Utilization. New York: Council on Social Work Education.

Knorr, K. (1977) "Policymakers' Use of Social Science Knowledge: Symbolic or Instrumental", in C. Weiss (ed.), Using Social Research in Public Policy Making. Lexington: D. C. Heath.

Kogan, M., Korman, R. and Henkel, M. (1980) Government's Commissioning of Research: A Case Study. Uxbridge, Mx.: Brunel University Department of Government.

Lasswell, H. (1951) "The Policy Orientation", in D. Lerner and H. Lasswell (eds.), The Policy Sciences: Recent Developments in Scope and Methods. Stanford: Stanford University Press.

Lasswell, H. (1956) The Decision Process. College Park: University of Maryland Press.

Lazarsfeld, P. and Reitz, J. (1975) An Introduction to Applied Sociology. New York: Elsevier.

Lindblom, C. and Cohen, D. (1979) Usable Knowledge - Social Science and Social Problem Solving. New Haven: Yale University Press.

Lipsky, M. (1980) Street Level Bureaucracy. New York: Russell Sage.

Littrell, W.B. (1976) "Editor's Introduction", in W.B. Littrell and G. Sjoberg (eds.), Current Issues in Social Policy. Beverly Hills: Sage Publications.

Lompe, K. (1968) "The Role of the Social Scientist in the Processes of Policy-Making", Social Science Information, 7(6), 159-175.

Lynn, L. (ed.) (1978) Knowledge and Policy: The Uncertain Connection. Washington: National Academy of Sciences.

Mayntz, R. (1977) "Sociology, Value Freedom and the Problems of Political Counselling", in C. Weiss (ed.), Using Social Research in Public Policy Making. Lexington: D. C. Heath.

Moos, R. H. (1974) Evaluating Treatment Environments: A Social Ecological Approach. New York: Wiley.

Moynihan, D. (1971) "The Role of the Social Scientist in Action Research", SSRC Newsletter, 10, 2-5.

National Council of Welfare (1976) One in a World of Twos - A Report by the National Council of Welfare on One-Parent Families in Canada. Ottawa: National Council of Welfare.

National Council of Welfare (1979) Women and Poverty. Ottawa: National Council of Welfare.

Prewitt, K. (1980) "Social Science Utilities", Society, 17, 6-8.

Rein, M. (1976) Social Science and Public Policy. Harmondsworth: Penguin.

Rein, M. and Schon, D. (1977) "Problem Setting in Policy Research", in C. Weiss (ed.), Using Social Research in Public Policy Making. Lexington: D. C. Heath.

Rein, M. and Tannenbaum, S. (1979) "Social Science Knowledge and Social Work Practice", in A. Rubin and A. Rosenblatt (eds.) Sourcebook on Research Utilization. New York: Council on Social Work Education.

Research Highlights, 1 (1981a) "Decision Making in Child Care" (ed. E. Reinach). Aberdeen: University of Aberdeen Department of Social Work.

-----, 2 (1981b) "Normalisation" (ed. J. Lishman). Aberdeen: University of Aberdeen Department of Social Work.

-----, 3 (1982a) "Developing Services for the Elderly" (ed. J. Lishman). Aberdeen: University of Aberdeen Department of Social Work.

-----, 4 (1982b) "Social Work Departments as Organisations" (ed. J. Lishman). Aberdeen: University of Aberdeen Department of Social Work.

Resnick, H. (1973) "Accountability - The Social Welfare Researcher as Scientist/Politician", in Social Work in the New Age of Accountability. Seattle: University of Washington School of Social Work.

Rich, R. (1977) "Uses of Social Science Information by Federal Bureaucrats: Knowledge for Action Versus Knowledge for Understanding", in C.

Weiss (ed.), Using Social Science Research in Public Policy Making. Lexington: D. C. Heath.

Richardson, E. (1972) National Journal, 29 January, quoted in H. Glennerster, Social Services Budgets and Social Policy. London: Allen and Unwin.

Rivlin, A. (1970) "The Planning, Programming and Budgeting System in the Department of Health, Education and Welfare: Some Lessons from Experience", in R. H. Haveman and J. Margolis (eds.), Public Expenditures and Policy Analysis. Chicago: Markham.

Robertson, A. (1969) "Organisational Control in Remedial Institutions", British Journal of Social Psychiatry, 3, 202-214.

Rose, R. (1977) "Disciplined Research and Undisciplined Problems", in C. Weiss (ed.), Using Social Research in Public Policy Making. Lexington: D. C. Heath.

Rosenblatt, A. (1968) "The Practitioner's Use and Evaluation of Research", Social Work, 13, 53-59.

Rossi, P. H. (1979) "Past, Present and Future Prospects of Evaluation Research", in L. E. Datta and R. Perloff (eds.), Improving Evaluations. Beverly Hills: Sage Publications.

Rossi, P. H. and Williams, W. (eds.) (1973) Evaluating Social Programs: Theory, Practice and Politics. New York: Seminar Press.

Rothman, J. (1979) "Gaps and Linkages in Research: Enhancing Utilization Through a Research and Development Approach", in A. Rubin and A. Rosenblatt (eds.), Sourcebook on Research Utilization. New York: Council on Social Work Education.

Rothman, J. (1980) Using Research in Organisations. A Guide to Successful Application. Beverly Hills: Sage Library of Social Research.

Rubin, A. and Rosenblatt, A. (eds.) (1979) Sourcebook on Research Utilization. New York: Council on Social Work Education.

Rule, J. (1978) Insight and Social Betterment: A Preface to Applied Social Science. New York: Oxford University Press.

Rutman, L. (1977a) Formative Research and Program Evaluability. Ottawa: Carleton University School of Social Work.

Rutman, L. (1977b) Planning an Evaluation Study. Ottawa: Carleton University School of Social Work.

Rutman, L. and DeJong, D. (1977) Federal Level

Evaluation. Ottawa: Carleton University School of Social Work.

Schon, D.A. (1971) Beyond the Stable State. London: Temple Smith.

Scott, R. and Shore, A. (1979) Why Sociology Does Not Apply: A Study of the Use of Sociology in Public Policy. New York: Elsevier.

Seidman, D. R. (1978) "PPB in HEW: Some Management Issues", in F. J. Lyden and E. R. Miller (eds.), Public Budgetting: Program Planning and Evaluation. Chicago: Rand McNally (3rd edition).

Sharpe, L. (1977) "The Social Scientist and Policy Making: Some Cautionary Thoughts and Transatlantic Reflections", in C. Weiss (ed.), Using Social Research in Public Policy Making. Lexington: D. C. Heath.

Simey, T. (1968) Social Science and Social Purpose. London: Constable.

Simpson, R. (1979) "Understanding the Utilization of Research in Social Work and Other Applied Professions", in A. Rubin and A. Rosenblatt (eds.), Sourcebook on Research Utilization. New York: Council on Social Work Education.

Sinclair, I. (1971) Hostels for Probationers: Study of the Aims, Working and Variations in the Effectiveness of Male Probation Hostels with Special Reference to the Influence of the Environment on Delinquency. Home Office Research Study 11 340106 X. London: HMSO.

Smith, D.E. (1965) "Front-Line Organisation of the State Mental Hospital", Administrative Science Quarterly, 10, 381-399.

Social Sciences and Humanities Research Council of Canada (1981) Strategic Grants Program Guidelines: The Family and Socialisation of Children; The Human Context of Technology. Ottawa: Social Sciences and Humanities Research Council of Canada.

Social Services Research Group, Scottish Branch Committee (1981) Response to "Research and Practice" Report by CCETSW and PSSC. Dundee: Social Services Research Group, Scottish Branch Bi-Annual Report. September.

Social Work Services Group (1980) Guidelines for Local Authority Social Work Departments on Introduction and Operating of Schemes for Community Service by Offenders. Edinburgh: Social Work Services Group of the Scottish Education Department.

Sundquist, J. (1978) "Research Brokerage: The Weak

Link", in L. Lynn (ed.) Knowledge and Policy: The Uncertain Connection. Washington: National Academy of Sciences.

Thomlinson, R.J. (1981) "Outcome Effectiveness Research and Its Implications for Social Work Educators", Canadian Journal of Social Work Education, 7, 55-91.

Thompson, M. S. (1975) Evaluation for Decision in Social Programmes. Farnborough, Hants: Saxon House/Lexington.

Thompson, V. A. (1969) Bureaucracy and Innovation. Birmingham: University of Alabama Press.

Thompson, V. A. (1976) Bureaucracy and the Modern World. Morristown, New Jersey: General Learning Press.

Town, S. (1978) "Action Research and Social Policy: Some Recent British Experience", in M. Bulmer (ed.), Social Policy Research. London: Macmillan.

Townsend, P. (1962) The Last Refuge: A Survey of Residential Institutions and Homes for the Aged in England and Wales. London: Routledge and Kegan Paul.

Tripodi, T. Fellin, P. and Epstein, I. (1971) Social Program Evaluation: Guidelines for Health, Education and Welfare Administrators. Itasca, Ill.: F. E. Peacock.

Warren, M. (1969) "The Case for Differential Treatment of Delinquents", Annals of the American Academy of Political and Social Science, 381, 47-59.

Weiss, C. (ed.) (1977a) Using Social Research in Policy Making. Lexington: D. C. Heath.

----- (1977b) "Research for Policy's Sake: The Enlightenment Function", Policy Analysis, 6, 532-545.

----- (1978) "Improving the Link Between Social Research and Public Policy", in L. Lynn (ed.), Knowledge and Policy: The Uncertain Connection. Washington: National Academy of Sciences.

----- (1980) "Knowledge Creep and Decision Accretion", Knowledge: Creation, Diffusion, Utilization, 1, 381-404.

White, M. J. (1978) "The Impact of Management Science on Political Decision-Making", in F. J. Lyden and E. G. Miller (eds.), Public Budgetting: Program Planning and Evaluation. Chicago: Rand McNally.

Wildavsky, A. (1968) "Budgeting as a Political Process." International Encyclopaedia of Social Science.

Wildavsky, A. (1970) "Rescuing Policy Analysis from PPBS", in R. Haveman and J. Margolis (eds.), Public Expenditures and Policy Analysis. Chicago: Markham.

Williams, W. (1971) Social Policy Research and Analysis: The Experience in the Federal Social Agencies. New York: Elsevier.

Williams, W. and Evans, J. W. (1969) "The Politics of Evaluation: The Case of Headstart", Annals of the American Academy of Political and Social Science, 385, 118-132.

Wilson, J. (1978) "Social Science and Public Policy", in L. Lynn (ed.), Knowledge and Policy: The Uncertain Connection. Washington: National Academy of Sciences.

Zurcher, L. A., Jr. and Bonjean, C. M. (eds.) (1970) Planned Social Interventions: An Interdisciplinary Anthology. Scranton: Chandler Publishing Co.

THE CONTRIBUTORS

Dr. Stewart Asquith - Lecturer, Department of Social Administration, University of Edinburgh.

Dr. Jack Byles - Senior Research Fellow, Department of Psychiatry, McMaster University.

Mr. Norman Dennis - Reader, Department of Social Studies, University of Newcastle-upon-Tyne.

Dr. John Gandy - Professor, Faculty of Social Work, University of Toronto.

Dr. Hans Mohr - Professor, Osgoode Hall Law School and Department of Sociology, York University, Toronto.

Roy Parker - Professor of Social Administration, University of Bristol.

Dr. Alex Robertson - Senior Lecturer, Department of Social Administration, University of Edinburgh.

Dr. Ben Shapiro - Associate Professor, Faculty of Social Work, University of Toronto.

Mrs. Susan Sinclair - Senior Lecturer, Department of Social Administration, University of Edinburgh.

Gilbert Smith - Professor of Social Administration, University of Hull.

Olive Stevenson - Professor of Social Policy and Social Work, University of Liverpool.

Dr. Terence Willett - Professor, Department of Sociology, Queen's University, Kingston, Ontario.